Lives of the Modern Poets

LIVES
of the Modern Poets

WILLIAM H. PRITCHARD

Faber and Faber
London • Boston

First published in the United States of America by Oxford University Press, 1980

First published in Great Britain in 1980 by Faber and Faber Limited
3 Queen Square London WC1N 3AU
Printed in the United States of America
All rights reserved
© William Pritchard 1980
ISBN 0 571 11618 3

Since this page cannot legibly accommodate all the copyright notices,
the following page constitutes an extension of the copyright page.

Acknowledgment is made for permission to quote from the following works:

To my Mother

Acknowledgments

I am grateful to the following for reading and commenting on the manuscript, in part or entire: Warner Berthoff, Thomas R. Edwards, Richard Poirier, and Roger Sale. Marietta Pritchard has been, as in the past, the intelligent unspecialist I try to write for. Cheryl Westfall helps convince me that somebody out there reads my prose. And Julian Symons again insisted that I finish the book and not take too long about it.

James Raimes, of Oxford University Press, originally encouraged and has subsequently supported my attempt to write about these modern poets. Stephanie Golden of Oxford made many helpful suggestions and necessary corrections, for which I am extremely grateful.

I should like also to acknowledge Theodore Baird, whose life as a reader and questioner of literary works I have been continuingly enriched by.

Chapters from this book appeared, in slightly altered form, in the *American Scholar,* the *Hudson Review,* and the *Southern Review.*

Amherst, Mass.   W. H. P.
July 1979

Contents

Lives of the Modern Poets

Introduction

Lives of the Modern Poets: the title cannot be accused of being over-modest, since allusion to Samuel Johnson's *Lives of the English Poets* is in itself an act of pretension. But I make it anyway, in the belief that juxtaposing my endeavor with the massive accomplishment of a great critic helps me put my own aim more clearly: to provide introductions to, and revaluations of, the nine most interesting and important poets writing in English in the first part of this century. In claiming to "introduce" them, I have in mind a reader who is literate, at ease with a complicated novel, less so with poetry perhaps; but who in any case is curious about, if relatively unfamiliar with, at least some of the figures treated here. As for the revaluation, I am convinced that something fresh and valuable can be said about these individual poets when they are juxtaposed and compared with one another from the perspective of some decades later. Why do we keep reading them? To begin with, I want to justify my title: to suggest the sense in which I am writing "Lives" of these poets; after that to consider and defend "modern" as a term of classification. Along the way I should like also to distinguish my kind of critical procedure from certain tendencies in contemporary literary study.

3

The particular circumstances of Johnson's *Lives* were that a group of booksellers wanted biographical and critical prefaces to various English poets from the previous hundred or so years, the poets anthologized to be chosen by the booksellers—although Johnson was allowed to add a few of his own choosing. But as Paul Fussell points out in his useful discussion of the *Lives*, we should not think of the book as a series of biographies. Its original title was "Prefaces" rather, and Fussell suggests that the purely biographical elements didn't interest Johnson greatly: "When engaged in mere biographical narration, he is quite willing to cut corners, to borrow from others, to rest content with vagueness or with minor error." By contrast, Johnson's interest is most strongly felt in passages where is is sketching a "character" for his poet—describing Swift hosting Gay and Pope at dinner, or etching in unforgettable strokes the latter's physical bearing ("The person of Pope is well known not to have been formed by the nicest model"). Or when, through quotation and apt comment, he makes the judgments and discriminations among individual poems with which his "common reader" is presumed to concur. As appreciative criticism, both informal and elegant, the *Lives* has no peer.

In suggesting that this great collection of fifty-two prefaces possesses "a coherence as well as an amplitude which no other English criticism can claim," T. S. Eliot once asked why there had been no later criticism of the same kind, and answered himself by judging that it was because nineteenth-century criticism had "become something less purely *literary*." In Coleridge, in Arnold, in Pater, literary criticism merged with rather different concerns—philosophy or aesthetics or ethics; while in the modern world there was the "very noticeable" influence of psychology and sociology upon criticism:

> On the one hand, these influences . . . have enlarged the field of the critic, and have affirmed in a world which otherwise is inclined to depreciate the importance of literature, the relations of literature to life. But from another point of view

> this enrichment has also been an impoverishment, for the
> purely literary values, the appreciation of good writing for its
> own sake, have become submerged when literature is judged
> in the light of other considerations. . . . It is simply that the
> conditions under which literature is judged simply and natu-
> rally as literature and not another thing, no longer prevail.

Eliot made the statement in 1944, and even with the New Critics'
example there is at present little to suggest that judging literature
as what it is and not another thing is any more likely to prevail, or
even to be practiced with much enthusiasm; never has the notion
of "purely literary values" been more conspicuously called into
question than at present.

Over the past decade a number of critics have taken to task the
ways of speaking and writing about literature which, presumably
until just lately, we naïvely employed. Among these ways are the
assumption that a poem has an identifiable author whose life is
not the same as the words he has arranged on a page, but whose
life these words somehow draw interest from and succeed in illuminating. Or the belief that although different readers will dis-
agree about how, in particular cases, these words are to be understood or interpreted, some opinions are demonstrably better than
others; that certain appeals to "words on the page" are possible,
or at least had better be made. Or the belief that the individual
reader, for all his subjective quirks and his historical and cultural
situation, must attempt what Matthew Arnold called a "real estimate" of the work in question; must attempt to see the object
"as in itself it really is," and should not apologize for so doing.

As against these and many other presumed misconceptions—the
misguided simplicities of what once passed for common sense—a
number of American and Continental academicians (some English
ones too, thought not nearly so many) offer alternative procedures, characterized this way by a contemporary critic, Warner
Berthoff:

> It is a warp into the negative, a stress on literary and imagi-
> native *making* as also in some decisive way, perhaps preemi-

nently, an *unmaking;* an activity less renewing than blighting in its full effect, less an augmentation of general well-being than a fundamental deprivation. . . . Thus, "creation," that Romantic and modernist talisman, becomes simultaneously "decreation." The making of new forms, art's definitive task, must coincidentally be a "deformation" of (presumably) forms already existing. Or it is a "deconstruction" either of previous imaginative constructions or of the very "reality" which provided the artist his creative opening.

One neglects these "new analysts" only at one's peril. Denis Donoghue, reviewing a book by David Kalstone on some contemporary American poets, found it bothersome not that Kalstone used "traditional" vocabulary in dealing with the relation between a writer's life and his work, but that he hadn't taken the time to defend this vocabulary against a new analyst like Roland Barthes, who attacked such a "personal" terminology of "self," "individuality," "tone," and "voice" as a capitalist trick: "the image of literature to be found in ordinary culture is tyrannically centered on the author, his person, his life, his tastes, his passions," says Barthes. While sympathizing with Kalstone's use of these terms, Donoghue claimed that "We are in trouble if such words as self, person, subject, author, voice and tone have to be justified before they can be used, but we cannot take their validity for granted, we must earn it."

I would agree we are in trouble, but I see no way to "earn" the validity for such a terminology except by practical demonstration that, in the case of particular authors and their works, the terms take us further into the literary experience—that they make the work of art and the artist more available to us. So that a book like the one Donoghue was reviewing, and most surely the present one, stands or falls by how interesting is its writing about the individual poet, not by its ability to argue successfully on theoretic grounds with the masters of that terrain—Barthes or Derrida or Geoffrey Hartman. I know of no better answer to make to them than the one F. R. Leavis gave when asked years ago by René Wellek to state the principles out of which his (Leavis's) own criticism proceeded. Leavis replied that any statement he could make of those principles would be so much cruder than his actual critical practice that he must decline Wellek's invitation.

If these paragraphs take us away from Johnson and the notion of writing "lives" or prefaces to individual poets, consider one of the most famous anecdotes Boswell tells about him:

> After we came out of the church, we stood talking for some time together of Bishop Berkeley's ingenious sophistry to prove the non-existence of matter, and that everything in the universe is merely ideal. I observed, that though we are satisfied his doctrine is not true, it is impossible to refute it. I never shall forget the alacrity with which Johnson answered, striking his foot with mighty force against a large stone, till he rebounded from it, "I refute it *thus.*"

The anecdote has been quoted all too often and Boswell's characterization of Berkeley's philosophy is dubious; but Johnson's response to Berkeley, and Leavis's to Wellek, are analogous in their refusal to believe that statements of principles, no matter how subtle, are more important than experience of the world's body. Leavis believed that the world's body of literature was tough enough to withstand any verbal attempts to cast doubt upon its givenness, to pretend it was something other than the "thing" it is. My own enterprise presumes that there are poets who have written poems which in one way or another have something to do with their own life and with the common life; and that we need these poems because, as Wallace Stevens believed, somehow the sound of their words helps us to live our lives.

A stone-kicking simplicity of approach doesn't mean that complex ideas about what an "author" is are beyond my imagination. When Michel Foucault tells us that the "aspects of an individual we designate as an author . . . are projections, in terms always more or less psychological, of our way of handling texts: in the comparisons we make, the traits we extract as pertinent, the continuities we assign, or the exclusions we practice"—I agree; with the confidence that the traits I extract, the continuities I assign, the exclusions I practice, are generally valuable rather than the reverse. Of course, Johnson didn't worry about "projecting" and didn't put quotation marks around his terms. He proceeded instead "not dogmatically but deliberately" to set forth the facts and judgments of each preface, employing a tripartite structure consisting of a biography, a character sketch of his subject, and finally a criticism of the works in chronological order.

I have not attempted to imitate this procedure, since we no longer see the facts of a man's life, his character, and his works as existing in separate compartments. And for most of the poets considered here there exist biographical studies which are authoritative and painstaking, if not "definitive" or complete: in the main they are factually dependable. Therefore I have contented myself with extracting the merest skeleton of a series of events important to the "life." When, as in the case of the later, poetry-writing Hardy, or with E. A. Robinson or Stevens, that life is almost wholly a life of writing (Stevens's activities at the insurance company effectively resist probing commentary!) then those events will be relatively few. Yeats and Pound on the other hand present public careers of great activity and interest, although in Yeats's case the career is so fully dramatized in the poems, is so much their main subject, that biographical treatment over and above them feels oddly a bit superfluous. At any rate I have mentioned ("extracted") the happenings which seemed most important to me, and they are presented mainly to provide a reader, uninstructed in the particular poet, with some footholds and with the briefest mention of matters that may enter later into the critical discussion.

New analysts like to talk about the "disappearance of the author," as if, like God presumably, he has absconded from the words on the page we thought he put there. This puzzling notion does not square with my own reading of lyric poems which, at least in the practices of the poets considered here, seem to me replete with presence, with personality. When I remark about some lines that they are unmistakably Hardy's or Crane's, I mean that we can recognize and identify, indeed we can *hear*, the distinctive way these words are arranged in lines and stanzas. But I mean also, as Robert Lowell said about Crane's poetry, that "the push of the whole man is there," and that poems reveal or conceal a temperament, a presence, a Wordsworthian man speaking to men. Or so my myth of reading has it. Thus I have tried to weave my discussion of "character" into the business of describing and judging the poetry: passages from letters, revealing anecdotes, bits of gossip, remarks made by one poet about another—these are interesting in themselves and also for the way they confirm our sense of the poet in his poems. I have made liberal use of such character-revealers, especially some less familiar examples of them.

As a rule I have not been concerned with providing "readings" for various poems, since there are in most cases more than enough of these already. Temperamentally I am less interested in the practice—too often a grim one—of interpretation by an extended prose exegesis, than in suggesting what the experience is like of reading a poet on the basis of his best or most typical poems. Here my classroom bias is apparent, since the wonderful thing about a classroom (and there are things not wonderful) is that one can and must spend time in reading poems aloud, pausing to catch an inflection here, a drop in the voice there. Anyone who had tried to convey these effects in writing knows how difficult it is to succeed at.

Finally, these "Lives" are filled with other critics, my American and English predecessors who, in relation to most of the poems considered here, have contributed to a rich, supremely interesting achievement. When Johnson wrote about Pope he had Dennis, Warburton, the Wartons, and a few others to consider; writing about Pound or Yeats or Eliot in this late age of our century one is grateful for and burdened by an overwhelming amount of commentary, much of it excellent. We have lived through an age of criticism. So if I seem to fuss too much with previous critics—particularly in the Pound and Eliot chapters—it is because they are in my way; because their responses when memorable and brilliant, sometimes when extravagant or wrong-headed, are part of the atmosphere in which the poem or poet now lives. It is possible, I suppose, to write a book and pretend that one's self is the source of all the insights and perceptions expressed about these writers. But not possible for me, who am usually aware that somebody has been there first; best then to try and go on from there, having acknowledged the fact.

If this description suggests the sort of lives of modern poets to be constructed here, the next questions are, of course, which modern poets and which "modern." Writing this late in our century, it would seem that some more adequate term must be found to distinguish the poetry written in its earlier part; while "contemporary" is an odd word to designate post–World War II work by Lowell or Richard Wilbur that is nearly forty years old. Does our reliance on the term "modern" indicate an unfortunate sloppiness in the way we speak of poets from the early twentieth century? Here, as is often the case, Matthew Arnold brings comfort. His essays on the Romantic poets—on Wordsworth, Keats, Byron, and Shelley—were composed in the 1870's and 80's, but in his famous 1864 essay "The Function of Criticism in Our Time" he made his most influential, general pronouncement about them: "life and the world being in modern times very complex things, the creation of a modern poet, to be worth much, implies a great critical effort behind it; else it must be a comparatively poor, barren, and short-lived affair." Arnold went on to compare Byron unfavorably to Goethe on this score, then asserted that "the burst of creative activity in our literature through the first quarter of the century had about it something premature":

> . . . from this cause its productions are doomed, most of
> them, in spite of the sanguine hopes which accompanied and
> do still accompany them, to prove hardly more lasting than

the productions of far less splendid epochs. And this prematureness comes from its having proceeded without having its proper data, without sufficient materials to work with. In other words, the English poetry of the first quarter of this century, with plenty of energy, plenty of creative force, did not know enough.

And he concludes the paragraph with a lament that Wordsworth, for all his profundity, had not read more.

Arnold's tone may be provoking here, and there are plenty of ways to quarrel with him about what "know enough" means, but my interest is rather in the similarities between his admittedly incomplete revaluations of Wordsworth, Byron, Shelley (he never wrote the essay on Shelley's poetry which he planned to), and Keats (considered in the letters only), and my own efforts in this book. Arnold didn't write about the "Romantic Poets" but spoke instead of a "modern poet" needing a "great critical effort" behind him, an effort he found lacking in the English poetry of the first quarter of the nineteenth century. My assumption is that, whether or not one agrees with Arnold, Anglo-American poetry in the first quarter of this century did have a great critical effort behind it: it is to be found in Pound's and Eliot's essays and reviews; in Frost's letters; in Yeats's prose; in the letters of Crane, Stevens, and Williams. With the names of Hardy and Robinson added to this group, one may choose to follow Harold Bloom in designating many of these poets as the true heirs of the Romantics, English and Emersonian; my own effort is quite different, consisting rather in unapologetically using "modern" as a literary historical label to designate nine figures who seem to me the most distinguished poets writing in English in this period.

Virginia Woolf proposed that somewhere around 1910 human character changed. There is every reason to say as much about Anglo-American poetry, which in the second decade of this century became certifiably modern. The crucial time is "somewhere around" 1914, the year when Yeats (who was, I am aware, Irish) published *Responsibilities* with its proud declarations and dedications of new purposes in a style which Pound, reviewing the volume, praised for its "hardness." Pound himself was to bring forth *Cathay* in the next year with its significant experiments devoted, among other things, to breaking what he later called the "heave" of pentameter. Frost's *North of Boston* was published in 1914 and also reviewed by Pound, who praised it for presenting "life" honestly. Hardy's *Satires of Circumstance,* dated 1914, contains the great "Poems of 1912–13" sequence, and is, at least in retrospect, a major poetic event. D. H. Lawrence's first book of verse, *Love Poems and Others,* appeared in 1913; E. A. Robinson's best one, *The Man Against the Sky,* in 1916. Eliot published "Prufrock" and Stevens "Sunday Morning" in 1915. Williams was beginning to write some of the poems for which he is remembered, and with *Al Que Quiere!* (1917) he burst into sudden blaze; while Crane in 1914 was six years away from his entry into mature composition.

Each of these books, as well as the individual poems by Eliot and Stevens, was not only markedly distinct from what Frost called in 1913 the "Tennysonian-Swinburnian" elaborately textured poetry of sound, but also from the school of "sincere" self-display, whether decadent as in Dowson or Symons, or uplifting as in Alfred Austin, William Watson, or Bliss Carman. More interestingly, each was clearly an advance on or a significant development from the previous work the poet had published. Each poet, including Eliot, had moved beyond his early romance with what Leavis has disparagingly termed "the poetical": Yeats's early poems; Hardy's labored profundities in some of his earlier ones; Frost's dreaminess in parts of *A Boy's Will;* Eliot's and Stevens's juvenilia and early Harvard preciosities.

Operating at a high enough level of abstraction, a critic with sufficient ingenuity could probably take these nine poets and show that they hold certain principles and practices in common; but I am not this critic nor do I have the intention of arguing that the nine really do belong together in ways more profound than is indicated by the chronological continuity of work that converges around 1914. It is worth pointing out that the two most vigorous attempts by recent critics to deal with poetry in this era and assert the priority of a tradition or of a central group of writers have had to make some exclusions and downgradings. In *The Pound Era,* and in his other valuable books, Hugh Kenner has allowed Eliot almost top billing with the era's chieftain, assigned Williams and Marianne Moore to meritorious roles, and dealt with Yeats as an essentially older, differently oriented poet. For Kenner, Stevens is more or less a sport; Frost and Crane have no place in the Pound tradition; Robinson and Hardy are in a different world. By contrast, Harold Bloom's books on Yeats and Stevens and his essays on Robinson and Crane insist that the great modern tradition is post-Romantic, a continuation of the genius of Blake, Wordsworth, Shelley, and Emerson. Bloom's hostility to Pound and Eliot is well known, and he seems to have little regard for Williams.

Both Kenner and Bloom are, in the latter's term, "strong" critics of modern poetry, with a view of the period very much committed to canonizing certain writers at the expense of others. In this respect, though it sounds a poor thing to be, I choose to be a "weak" critic, since for years I have read each of these nine poets with admiration and affection, as well as with frequent irritation—the effects of which irritation may show up in my treatment of Yeats and Stevens. But they are powerful enough to survive any complaints, and in general I think that major poets benefit by having the worst said against them that can be said. Only by putting a possible case against a style, at least expressing some reservations about it, can the necessary discriminations and evaluations be made. At any rate, it is a little more interesting that way. Hardy, Yeats, Robinson, Frost, Pound, Eliot, Stevens, Crane, and Williams: taken together they represent an achievement comparable to any poetic age in English poetry, and insofar as the Americans are considered, to represent *the* great age of our poetry. A dangerous way to talk, and perhaps Arnold was wiser in remphasizing his doubts about the achievement of the modern poets from the first quarter of his century. But I do not think so, and have written these prefaces in hopes of suggesting in what ways the modern poets are alive for us today.

1

THOMAS HARDY
Circumstantial Satirist

In 1926 Virginia Woolf visited Thomas Hardy at his Max Gate home in Dorchester, and recorded the following impressions in her diary:

> He seemed perfectly aware of everything; in no doubt or hesitation; having made up his mind; and being delivered of all his work, so that he was in no doubt about that either. . . .
> The whole thing—literature, novels, etc., all seemed to him an amusement, far away too, scarcely to be taken seriously. Yet he had sympathy and pity for those still engaged in it. But what his secret interests and activities are—to what occupation he trotted off when we left him—I do not know.

Although Hardy was eighty-six at the time, the younger writer's observation strikes me less as an insight into the poet at an advanced stage of his life, than as a permanent truth about the extraordinary character of a man for whom "the whole thing"—literature, other people, the great world—seemed far away. But a very likely occupation for him to have trotted off to after Virginia Woolf left would have been the writing of another poem.

At that time, Hardy had written no novels for thirty years, had written instead an astonishing number of poems; in the long line of English and American poet-novelists—Scott, Emily Brontë, Melville, Meredith, D. H. Lawrence—he assumes a commanding position. But these poems, presented in a single volume, are forbidding. James Gibson's 1976 edition of them runs to 930 pages exclusive of miscellaneous material, and contains 919 individual poems, of which the 117th—located just two places before "The Darkling Thrush"—has, like many others, been overlooked. "Winter in Durnover Field" carries a scenic epigraph which serves to introduce us to a conversation between some inhabitants of that field:

> SCENE.—*A wide stretch of fallow ground recently sown with wheat, and frozen to iron hardness. Three large birds walking about thereon, and wistfully eyeing the surface. Wind keen from north-east; sky a dull grey.*
>
> (*Triolet*)
>
> *Rook.*—Throughout the field I find no grain;
>   The cruel frost encrusts the cornland!
> *Starling.*—Aye: patient pecking now is vain
>   Throughout the field, I find . . .
> *Rook.*—   No grain!
> *Pigeon.*—Nor will be, comrade, till it rain,
>   Or genial thawings loose the lorn land
>   Throughout the field.
> *Rook.*—   I find no grain:
>   The cruel frost encrusts the cornland!

It may be noted that although Starling and Pigeon are at no loss for words to express this deplorable situation, are eager to be agreeable or hopeful about the future, and are pleasant conversationalists to boot, it is Rook who has the first and the last words, as well as an interpolation in the middle of the poem—"No grain!" Rook doesn't rationalize or understand his predicament; he exclaims, and his emphasis is negative, on what he *doesn't* find. Nor does he feel the need to be social or thoughtful, ruminative or complex: like Hardy in Virginia Woolf's portrait, he is in no doubt or hesitation, having made up his mind.

Why should any poet write such a poem and how are we to understand the kind of sensibility from which it could spring? How do we take "Winter in Durnover Field"? As yet another illustration of Hardy's pessimism? As a winter bagatelle, barely worth pausing over? Perhaps both, though hardly interesting on such counts. It is at least curious and worth remarking how much attention, of a special sort, Hardy has lavished on his little creation. He informs us that it is a triolet, and its lines are prefaced by careful stage directions, even down to the flat information that the field has "large birds walking about thereon." When we try to visualize the scene it turns into an animated cartoon, though not in color; and it is surely hard to devote much energy to teasing out a deeper or thematic significance—one doesn't want to push those large birds out of the way so as to get at some presumed "meaning."

In his slyly composed *The Later Years of Thomas Hardy,* ostensibly written by his second wife, Florence, but in fact written by Hardy himself, he makes in a chapter dealing with his return to writing poetry in his fifties an extended statement or defense of his poetic practice. There is an often-quoted plea for the importance of "cunning irregularity" in poetry, as well as in architecture, the profession of his young manhood. Hardy insists that what critics might mistake for unwitting awkwardness in his poems was in fact contrived and practiced exploitation of the irregular in rhythm. Further evidence is produced to show that he was no mere "apprentice," that he had accumulated many notes on rhythm and meter and carried out many experiments. He then goes on to emphasize "lastly" what readers have taken to heart even less than the image of him as a craftsman: that he had a "born sense of humour, even a too keen sense occasionally," and that "reviewers deficient in that quality" were thus at a loss to know how to proceed. He defines this humor as Swiftian rather than Dickensian: "verses of a satirical, dry, caustic, or farcical cast" were the sort he often produced.

Hardy's reputation as an ironist (a collection of his stories is titled *Life's Little Ironies*) adheres mainly to his earlier novel-writing self; while the poetry is praised for possessing a quite opposite effect of deep, if sometimes stumbling and awkward, sincerity. As Donald Davie has pointed out, this is really a way of condescending to him. If Yeats and Eliot and Pound were subtle, allusive, complex, and weighty, Hardy was, well . . . sincere. Anyone who studied poetry in American universities after World War II, in the age of the New Criticism, probably remembers an exciting first encounter with "Sailing to Byzantium" or "Gerontion" or even perhaps with *Mauberley*. By contrast, acquaintance with Hardy's poems, if it occurred at all (he was often just omitted from courses, being neither quite Victorian nor quite Modern) was through the more familiarly "poetic" voice of the "The Darkling Thrush," a poem few found too difficult or remote. Certainly no one owned a copy of *Complete Poems,* the volume which any reader of Hardy must learn to live in even though he may never familiarize himself with all of its individual parts. Prolonged immersion in it reveals how persistently interesting and compelling is Hardy's presence.

My way of evoking that presence is to direct attention where it should always be directed when lyric poetry is the subject—to matters of what I call, if confusingly at times, *voice*. When the poet is Yeats one can hardly ignore the voice, or the changing voices, through which his poems speak to us, often speak very loudly to us. With Hardy, voice is dangerously easy to ignore, to the advantage of neither poem nor reader. We should emphasize further the cunning irregularity of his mind, and the "born sense of humour, even a too keen sense occasionally" which the voice displays or expresses. When, in a word I believe was first used about Hardy's poems by R. P. Blackmur, that voice is anonymous its effect is no less powerful, though harder to specify. There is a nice paragraph of characterization in *The Later Years,* devoted to contesting the notion that Hardy was "simple." No, says the biographer, "he had the formal subtlety peculiar to his own generation; there was something deliberately 'ordinary' in his demeanour which was a concealment of extraordinary fires." These fires burn throughout the poetry.

Hardy's official career as a publishing poet stretches from *Wessex Poems* (1898) to *Winter Words,* which appeared in 1928, the year of his death. In *The Later Years* we are told that because of the "misrepresentations" he had suffered from being the author of *Tess of the D'Urbervilles* and *Jude the Obscure,* he determined, in 1896, to write no more novels, only poetry. But, he says, these misrepresentations

> turned out ultimately to be the best thing that could have happened; for they well-nigh compelled him, in his own judgement at any rate, if he wished to retain any shadow of self-respect, to abandon at once a form of literary art he had long intended to abandon at some indefinite time, and resume openly that form of it which had always been more instinctive with him, and which he had just been able to keep alive from his early years, half in secrecy, under the pressure of magazine writing.

His recent biographer, Robert Gittings, suggests that in addition to whatever frustrations Hardy felt about the public reception of *Jude,* or his wife's distaste for the novel's doctrine as she understood it, he was coming to find the writing of novels a physical burden in their sheer weight of words. Gittings also suggests that the "highly personal themes of his secret youth" could express themselves more judiciously in poems than in novels. Hardy had written a number of poems in the 1860's of which the most impressive was "Neutral Tones"; now, writing seriously again, he began to reap what Ezra Pound called "the harvest of having written 20 novels first," and continued to do so for the last thirty-odd years of his life.

Of these years in which Hardy became an ever more honored literary giant, so that by the time Virginia Woolf visited him in 1926 it must have been like going to meet a mythical figure, the most significant event—for our purposes here the sole significant event of his later life—was the sudden death in 1912 of his wife Emma, from whom he had been seriously estranged since the 1890's. Although Hardy enjoyed going up to London, staying at the Athenaeum, attending plays and social gatherings, and although he engaged in a number of romantic affiliations with younger women, one of whom was to be his second wife (these affiliations are described by Mr. Gittings with meticulous care and tact), his life became identified with his poetry to an extent only matched among the modern poets by Wallace Stevens. With Yeats or Eliot or Pound, life and poems seem almost equally interesting; with Hardy, particularly with later Hardy, the poet of our concern here, one is interested in the life of the poems.

His career as poet may be divided into three parts, of which the first comprises the work from his first three volumes (*Poems of the Past and Present*, 1901, and *Time's Laughingstocks*, 1909, followed *Wessex Poems*). Some of these poems bear dates from the 1860's and the London addresses where Hardy lived at that time. One group of them flowers out of a visit to Italy and the Continent in the late 1880's; another group, dated 1899, was stimulated by the Boer War; another, larger group is made up of narratives and ballad-like anecdotes in which eternal traits of character are displayed. I pass over these groups without further comment, though they contain many lively and capable performances. But Hardy's most characteristic and finest voice is found in the following shorter poems from these volumes, in order of their appearance in *Complete Poems:* "Neutral Tones," "The Impercipient," "At an Inn," "I Look Into My Glass," 'Drummer Hodge," "The Souls of the Slain," "Rome: At the Pyramid of Cestius near the

Graves of Shelley and Keats," "A Broken Appointment," "Wives in the Sere," "The Last Chrysanthemum," "The Darkling Thrush," "The Self-Unseeing," "The Rejected Member's Wife," "The Farm-Woman's Winter," "Shut Out That Moon," and "On the Departure Platform."

The last of these illustrates Hardy's deepest, most pervasive qualities and also points up the peculiar kind of difficulty there is in writing about his art. It is one of his lesser-known poems, presumably written about the woman who was to become his second wife, though such information is of no help in understanding what makes the poem distinctive:

> We kissed at the barrier; and passing through
> She left me, and moment by moment got
> Smaller and smaller, until to my view
>   She was but a spot;
>
> A wee white spot of muslin fluff
> That down the diminishing platform bore
> Through hustling crowds of gentle and rough
>   To the carriage door.
>
> Under the lamplight's fitful glowers,
> Behind dark groups from far and near,
> Whose interests were apart from ours,
>   She would disappear,
>
> Then show again, till I ceased to see
> That flexible form, that nebulous white;
> And she who was more than my life to me
>   Had vanished quite. . . .

These first four stanzas of the poem tell us what happened, enacting with considerable skill a voice in process of saying how it was that day; and we follow along, participating in the man's "diminishing" perspective, moving from one stanza to the next as "She would disappear, // Then show again. . . ."

The best tribute ever paid to Hardy's poetry was Ezra Pound's in *Guide to Kulchur* (1938), where he made two essential points:

first that "No man can read Hardy's poems collected but that his own life, and forgotten moments of it, will come back to him, a flash here and an hour there. Have you a better test for true poetry?" Whether for "man" here we can read "man or woman" I am not sure, since the perspective of most, though not all, of the poems is a male one. But what clearly animates this particular one is the poet's bringing back to himself a hitherto forgotten moment which he proceeds to rehearse in most delicately careful detail. The final two stanzas ruminate about the experience:

> We have penned new plans since that fair fond day,
> And in season she will appear again—
> Perhaps in the same soft white array—
>   But never as then!
>
> —"And why, young man, must eternally fly
> A joy you'll repeat, if you love her well?"
> —O friend, nought happens twice thus; why,
>   I cannot tell!

Hardy may not have found the perfect way to end this lyric—the interpolated question by a "friend" creaks more than a bit—but what comes through most clearly are the exclamatory negatives, particularly the four words "But never as then!" When, in Pound's phrase, a forgotten moment comes back to the speaker in a Hardy poem, his truest response to it is to insist upon its uniqueness and the impossibility of repeating it. The exclamation mark is a wonderfully expressive device with which to make this insistence, since along with the regret, the pang of loss when the past moment is viewed in memory's landscape, there is also a present exhilaration of not merely recalling the moment but of asserting its forever-lostness: "nought happens twice thus," and so "never as then."

There is an analogy between this exhilaration and the sort which animated Rook (in "Winter in Durnover Field") as he kept announcing that throughout the field he found no grain. Or there is "The Rejected Member's Wife," a poem about a woman whose husband has been defeated in the parliamentary election; thus she will never again stand smiling in her pain, at his side, waving to the crowd that has rejected him. Other people will come along and go through the same delights of triumph and agonies of defeat:

> But she will no more stand
>   In the sunshine there,
> With that wave of her white-gloved hand,
>   And that chestnut hair.

The poem is secure enough to end with just that much said and no more. Donald Davie speaks of Hardy's "playful and mournful serenity"; something like that quality is felt in these reiterated pledges that things will not come back, not ever again be the way they once were.

Pound's other significant point in his tribute to Hardy succinctly locates the difficulty anybody experiences in writing about the poems: "When a writer's matter is stated with such entirety and with such clarity there is no place left for the explaining critic." This remark has particular application to Hardy and is not merely a matter of poet kicking critic out of the way of another poet. Certainly Pound is making use here of terms central to his own way of thinking about what poems should do: they should *present* or state "matter," not write about or describe or strike attitudes toward it. (I am speaking at least of Pound the Imagist, circa 1913.) Yet because of its allusive weight, its diction, the elaborations of its verse structure, there is usually some room or need for the critic of Pound's poetry to do a bit of explaining, even when the poem's "matter" is rather slender. But consider how "The Darkling Thrush" states everything with such clarity as to silence commentary or render it superfluous:

> The land's sharp features seemed to be
>   The Century's corpse outleant,
> His crypt the cloudy canopy,
>   The wind his death-lament.
> The ancient pulse of germ and birth
>   Was shrunken hard and dry,
> And every spirit upon earth
>   Seemed fervourless as I.

It is difficult to believe in the fervorlessness of a central presence here, since the poet goes about his task of charting the landscape, then announcing the thrush's song, always with such unerring confidence and accuracy. In other words the poem's "I" is a relatively conventional one, lacking the rich dramatic interest built up around the first person in a poem by Robert Frost, say, or Robert Lowell. Neither the poem's formal properties nor its display of a speaking "I" seems to demand much in the way of explanatory analysis.

On occasion the "explaining critic" inserts himself into the plot of one of Hardy's poems, as in a little-known gem tucked between "The Darkling Thrush" and "Winter in Durnover Field." For five stanzas "The Last Chrysanthemum" sings with elegance about deprivation:

> Why should this flower delay so long
>   To show its tremulous plumes?
> Now is the time of plaintive robin-song
>   When flowers are in their tombs.
>
> Through the slow summer, when the sun
>   Called to each frond and whorl
> That all he could for flowers was being done,
>   Why did it not uncurl?
>
> It must have felt that fervid call
>   Although it took no heed,
> Waking but now, when leaves like corpses fall,
>   And saps all retrocede.
>
> Too late its beauty, lonely thing,
>   The season's shine is spent,
> Nothing remains for it but shivering
>   In tempests turbulent.
>
> Had it a reason for delay,
>   Dreaming in witlessness
> That for a bloom delicately gay
>   Winter should stay its stress?

Wordsworth's "The Lesser Celandine" is behind this someplace; and it is not surprising that when Hardy chose to write about a flower he would find one that came too late, had no business being there at all, and was in for a hard season of shivering. This is the flower he can love, just as he can welcome the thrush if it is on its last legs ("Aged," "frail, gaunt and small"), and admire a grainless rook or a rejected member's wife. Yet never does he command a language more "delicately gay" than in this poem's fifth stanza; nor is the question asked a real question. Hardy has stated his matter with such entirety and clarity, has made up the best that can be said for this lonely, lovely chrysanthemum, that anything more is superfluous. So the final stanza of the poem comes as an embarassing bit of gaucherie:

> —I talk as if the thing were born
>   With sense to work its mind;
> Yet it is but one mask of many worn
>   By the Great Face behind.

Here Pound's explaining critic has intruded, reminding us that he's committed the pathetic fallacy, and saluting—under one of its many names—the Great Face (in other poems it is the Immanent Will or Purblind Doomster). But in truth the poem has already completed itself; its "matter"—the plight of belatedness—has been stated wholly. Nothing Hardy wrote over the ten years following "The Darkling Thrush" requires us to give a radically different account of it; so it is not surprising that critics found more to work on as they observed Yeat's changing style in the new century's first decade, or at the end of it encountered the earliest work of Pound. Hardy, who had turned seventy in 1910, could hardly be expected to provide any further surprises.

With various stirrings of new life visible in volumes of poetry published in and around the year 1914, one might understandably have overlooked the appearance of yet another by Hardy—his fourth book of poems, *Satires of Circumstance: Lyrics and Reveries with Miscellaneous Pieces,* published in November of that year, after England had entered the Great War. We learn from J. O. Bailey's useful handbook on the poetry that the title was supplied by Hardy's publisher (Macmillan), who took it from his title for the last group of poems in the book, "Satires of Circumstance in Fifteen Glimpses." These short poems had been published in a magazine in 1911 and struck ironic attitudes toward various human foibles and affectations. Hardy was uneasy about the thus-titled volume since, as he says in *The Later Years,* the fifteen earlier "satires" were "caustically humorous productions which had been issued with a light heart before the war":

> So much shadow, domestic and public, had passed over his head since he had written the satires that he was in no mood now to publish humour or irony, and hence he would readily have suppressed them if they had not already gained such currency from magazine publication that he could not do it.

As if to atone, he assures us that the "Lyrics and Reveries" section of the new volume "contained some of the tenderest and least satirical verse that ever came from his pen."

The domestic shadow which had passed over Hardy's head was the death of his wife in late November of 1912. During the next few months he wrote the remarkable "Poems of 1912–13," a group of eighteen lyrics (three more were added later) in response to that death. Although these are placed after the "Lyrics and Reveries" section of *Satires of Circumstance,* we can safely assume that he thought of them as prime examples of his "tenderest and least satirical verse," and that he worried about how his reputation as professional pessimist and "bitter" portrayer of life's little ironies might deform responses to what were very personal poems. Yet Macmillan's title was really the right one for the volume, and the 1912–13 lyrics are of great interest partly because they are not just tender, do not forego the strengths of his best satirical poetry.

But before taking up these poems and their biographical genesis, two of the most rightly anthologized of Hardy's works deserve attention as fine examples of the public poet's satiric strengths. "Channel Firing" and "The Convergence of the Twain" are the second and third poems in the "Lyrics and Reveries" section, but this heading fails to suggest the fabulous quality of each poem and the ambiguous way each reveals Hardy's presence. "Channel Firing" begins quietly and firmly with the voice of a dead man speaking from his coffin in rather four-square fashion:

> That night your great guns, unawares,
> Shook all our coffins as we lay,
> And broke the chancel window-squares,
> We thought it was the Judgment-day
>
> And sat upright. . . .

The man proceeds to relate how God had to reassure these dead people that it was not in fact the Judgment-day but merely the nations preparing for another war (Hardy dates the poem April, 1914), and that since the world was still mad they were not to get their hopes up. At this news the dead subside, one of them, Parson Thirdly, opining that instead of preaching he should have "stuck to pipes and beer." So far it looks to be a satire of circumstance in a familiar Hardyan vein, an exercise turned out with perhaps too much facility. But the final stanza tolls its message:

> Again the guns disturbed the hour,
> Roaring their readiness to avenge,
> As far inland as Stourton Tower,
> And Camelot, and starlit Stonehenge.

One of Hardy's very best critics, John Crowe Ransom, has nicely pointed out how the meter makes us stress the "henge" in "Stonehenge." Ransom paraphrases the end of the poem this way: "Our expectations have been defeated, but we still insist on our moral universe; the roar of the guns prevail, but now it assaults the shrines without effect"; and he concludes that "The thing heard upon the air is evil, but the thing seen is the religious monument hung and illuminated beneath the stars."

There is nothing in the poem that forbids this elegantly humanistic way of understanding it; but suppose instead one chose to emphasize, for the sake of discussion, how *far* the roaring of the guns penetrated. As far as Camelot and Stonehenge, a long way back in history and myth; thus one might read the conclusion in a less affirmative way than Ransom does, and might say instead, "Look how far back war goes, learn how it will ever be with us, realize how little there is you can do about it." Different emphases are possible since all the poem's voice does is to declare, with rapt attentiveness and rhythmic power, what the guns are doing. But what everyone can agree about, I should think, is the sense of elevation—mainly through its use of romantic names, places, and monuments—achieved by the final stanza, and perhaps felt by Hardy as he composed it. It may be that no statements about Man and War and History are as true as the juxtapositions and repetitions which occur in "Channel Firing." Somehow the roaring of the guns ends up feeling dignified; and the reader may find himself entertaining some ennobling thoughts about war, rather than musing regretfully on the folly of mankind.

There is a similarly odd deflection from humanistic attitudes in his famous poem about the *Titanic* disaster. Much has been written in admiration of the marmoreal stanzas in which the great sunken ship is described—

> Over the mirrors meant
> To glass the opulent
> The sea-worm crawls — grotesque, slimed, dumb, indifferent

—and through which Hardy, in explaining what happened, carefully prepares the coming together of the ship and its mate:

> And as the smart ship grew
> In stature, grace, and hue,
> In shadowy silent distance grew the Iceberg too.

The ending of the poem in which they meet, in which "consummation comes, and jars two hemispheres," is at the least a memorable one. But when we inquire about the reader's cumulative response, I think few would describe it as a sagely grave nodding at the ironical consequence of overwhelming pride and vanity. The

"Convergence" is just too much fun to read for such responses seriously to exist; in fact it is but a slight overstatement to compare this poem with another utterance about the *Titanic,* a song whose chorus ends with the ringing declaration "It was sad when that great ship went down" ("Husbands and wives / Little children lost their lives," etc.), to be boomed out with enthusiasm by communal singers who have drunk deep.

By designedly avoiding a personal, thoughtfully elaborated response to War or Disaster; by giving us instead such intricate constructions as "Channel Firing" or "Convergence of the Twain," Hardy appears as an ingenious, highly inventive entertainer, enlivened by the very examples of human folly which in life saddened or horrified him, as when he lost two acquaintances in the *Titanic* sinking. It comes as no surprise then to hear his second wife announce in a letter that her husband is upstairs, "writing an intensely dismal poem with great spirits." These facts may be borne in mind when confronting the expressive sadness of "Poems of 1912–13."

In those poems, more than at any other place in his work, we see Hardy writing out of his experience of loss and guilt, to make more dramatic and more "open" utterances than the entertaining and impressively crafted ones observed thus far. Yet crafted and entertaining they still are. Robert Gittings tells us that in 1891 Emma Hardy had begun the diary which may or may not have been titled "What I Think of My Husband." We shall never know for sure, since upon reading it after her death Hardy committed it to the flames. In 1899 Emma wrote to a woman who had asked her for marital advice that at age fifty (Hardy was nearly sixty) a married man gets restless: "Eastern ideas of matrimony secretly pervade his thoughts and he wearies of the most perfect and suitable wife chosen in his earlier life"—a sentence both touching and comic in its pretense at disinterested worldly wisdom. Whatever

Eastern ideas came and went in his head, Hardy formed a number of relationships with other women, and in 1907 met Florence Dugdale, a young Dorset-born girl who was to be his love and his mate after Emma's death.

What we know of Hardy's marriage to Emma in its later years is depressing. Though they lived together at Max Gate, the Dorchester house where Hardy spent the remainder of his life, they saw each other only at dinner and even then, Gittings says, did not speak. Hardy's stays in London were increasingly made on his own. When the Robert Louis Stevensons visited at Max Gate, Mrs. Stevenson afterward wrote patronizingly of "A pale gentle, frightened little man, that one felt an instinctive tenderness for, with a wife—ugly is no word for it—who said 'Whatever shall we do?' I had never heard a human being say it before." More significantly, it appears that Emma's death might not or need not have been quite so unforeseen as her husband's poems after the event were to claim. She had been visibly suffering from impacted gallstones, but Hardy managed rather successfully to shut his eyes to her condition. Thus the claim made at the end of "The Going," first of the 1912–13 poems, that "O you could not know / That such swift fleeing / No soul foreseeing— / Not even I—would undo me so" becomes a trifle more problematic if we try to match up the "I" with Hardy the man.

Yet neither embarrassment nor cynical knowingness are helpful attitudes to carry into our reading of these poems; and there is no reason not to affirm, even if it is a difficult and uneasy affirmation, Eliot's separation between the man who suffers and the mind that creates—between the life and the art. One might also note that Emma left behind her another personal manuscript which Hardy also read but did not burn, and which was eventually published— what J. O. Bailey describes as a "childlike but appealing record of Emma's girlhood and youth up to the time of her marriage." The editors of this published manuscript say that reading it "threw Hardy back to that joyful enchanted time, forty years earlier, when they had met and become engaged." Thus the poems originated as much in loving memory as in guilt and bad conscience. At any rate they have been handsomely admired by a number of critics beginning with Middleton Murry in 1921. F. R. Leavis saw them (at least saw "The Voice" and "After a Journey") as standing at the very center of Hardy's distinction as a poet, and called them "a triumph of character." More recent accounts by Douglas Brown and Irving Howe have hailed their imaginative integrity, richness of design, and vocal authenticity. In Brown's words, Hardy succeeds in remaining "most naturally himself when most deeply distressed." If these poems have been praised at the expense of others which don't spring so directly from Hardy's life, they will now—if we accept his biographer's account of that life— have to pay their own way, create their integrity and authenticity wholly by means of their internal shape and gestures, rather than by their correspondence to external fact. And in these terms they most assuredly succeed.

"The Going," first in the sequence and one of the best, begins gently and with sad playfulness, by reproaching the woman for not letting her husband know she was going to die:

> Why did you give no hint that night
> That quickly after the morrow's dawn,
> And calmly, as if indifferent quite,
> You would close your term here, up and be gone
> > Where I could not follow
> > With wing of swallow
> To gain one glimpse of you ever anon!

Now she teases him by seeming to appear "At the end of an alley of bending boughs," and is remembered as the heroine of romance from forty years ago:

> You were she who abode
> By those red-veined rocks far West,
> You were the swan-necked one who rode
> Along the beetling Beeny Crest. . . .

The closing stanzas of "The Going" point up most clearly Hardy's distinctive procedure in these poems:

> Why, then, latterly did we not speak,
> Did we not think of those days long dead,
> And ere your vanishing strive to seek
> That time's renewal? We might have said,
>   "In this bright spring weather
>   We'll visit together
> Those places that once we visited."
>
>   Well, well! All's past amend,
>   Unchangeable. It must go.
> I seem but a dead man held on end
> To sink down soon. . . . O you could not know
>   That such swift fleeing
>   No soul foreseeing—
> Not even I—would undo me so!

Rhythmically speaking, we note how what they "might have said"—the lines in quotation marks from the penultimate stanza—take on a lilting simplicity which the unsonglike pace of the final verse movingly opposes. Douglas Brown finds the distinction of this, as well as the other elegies, to lie in "*dramatic* vitality" and goes on to make the following interesting remarks:

> . . . the peculiar excellence lies in the disengagement of the self. There may be an "I," named or speaking, for this loss has happened; but the grief does not turn inward upon "I, Thomas Hardy" nor ask attention for him.

And he notes that a number of poems in the sequence break off just at the moment when grief threatens to become self-regarding, resulting in an effect that is both human and impersonal, "dramatic" and poised.

I agree that "The Going" is an absolutely distinctive Hardy poem, its first-person presence ("while I / Saw morning harden upon the wall") felt in more vividly particular ways than that of "The Darkling Thrush" or "On the Departure Platform," where the focus is importantly somewhere else. But more can be said in explanation of its dramatic life. The poem is dated December 1912, and either the writing of it helped Hardy clarify his feelings

about Emma's death, or they had already been clarified in this letter to Florence Henniker on the nineteenth of that same December:

> In spite of the differences between us, which it would be af-
> fectation to deny, and certain painful delusions she suffered
> from at times, my life is intensely sad to me now without her.
> The saddest moments of all are when I go into the garden
> and to that long straight walk at the top that you know,
> where she used to walk every evening just before dusk, the
> cat trotting faithfully behind her and at times when I almost
> expect to see her as usual coming in from the flower-beds
> with a little trowel in her hand.

This is admirably direct and fully expressed; it also points up, by
contrast, the indirection and strangeness of Hardy even at his presumably most "sincere," as in "The Going." There his impulse
toward the dramatic propels the voice into putting questions
which are not put in the letter to Mrs. Henniker. The letter-writer
expects her to understand what "delusions" Emma suffered from,
and knows it would be "affectation" to deny the differences which
had separated the Hardys; nonetheless, his life is now "intensely
sad" without her.

But "The Going" looks back and questions the relationship in
its less than glorious aspect: "Why, then, latterly did we not
speak, / Did we not think of those days long dead," as the syntax continues into the next line. But within the first line itself,
merely "did not speak," an enormous and unanswerable question
compared to the what-might-have-been-saids that follow. The "I"
is thus precipitated into the bleakness of the last stanza: "Well,
well!"—an exclamatory gesture that can be heard in various ways
and refuses to be pinned down to any one of them; "All's past
amend," and "It must go"—two desperate gestures at saying eternal commonplaces, the saying of which gives little help; the ellipsis
after "soon," words having failed him . . . ; and the final exclamation, passionately negative as so often in Hardy: "Oh you
could not know . . . No soul foreseeing— / Not even I—." In an

important way the poem is a satire of circumstance after all, as Hardy's letter is not. To paraphrase: "It's not your fault that you didn't say goodbye to me when you died, though it does seem rather thoughtless of you to have left the world quite so abruptly. I wonder why your illusion suddenly appears before my eyes, deceiving me into thinking you're alive? After all, you *were* the girl of high romance I courted years ago; why, when neither of us was speaking much to each other, didn't we recall those days?" No wonder the throttled reflections of the last stanza seem the only appropriate way to conclude. One has been instructed in the way this tragic event is also an instance of life's rather large ironies: the irony, the joke, is on the man who's left behind to experience them.

Perhaps the most pleasurable and satisfying effect of reading these poems in sequence is the way they lead up to the great affirmation of "At Castle Boterel." Early in the sequence stands "Rain on a Grave" ("Clouds spout upon her / Their waters amain / In ruthless disdain,—") and "I Found Her Out There" ("I found her out there / On a slope few see / That falls westwardly")—vigorously expert poems of the fancy which aspire to protect the dead woman from the elements, or somehow spirit her away from Dorset to the Cornwall of her true home. This geographical distinction forms the basis for Donald Davie's fine account of what he terms the poems' "Dantesque focus"

> by which "every natural site has the ethical rank of the rational beings who dwell in it"—[precluding] not just the psychological analysis so brilliant in Meredith's *Modern Love,* but also any moral discrimination, and apportioning of blame between the two partners to a marriage that had gone disastrously wrong. Max Gate is simply the landscape of treason; thereabouts he will betray her, she will betray him. North Cornwall is the landscape of loyalty; thereabout he will be true to her, she will be true to him. The use of landscape is as starkly emblematic as that.

And he goes on to argue, perhaps with some overstatement, that "remorse" and "reproach" are thus excluded from the poems.

As I understand Hardy's temperament the "Dantesque focus" of these poems is indeed crucial, since his poetry does not typically display the complexities either of psychological analysis or of moral discrimination. Once again, in Pound's terms, to be a poet who states his material with "entirety and clarity" precludes the sorts of tentativeness and qualification necessary—at least as our modern understanding has it—for certain kinds of complexity. One might add that Hardy's strongly rhymed (not always felicitously so) lines and tight formal stanzas are also difficult to exploit in ways that half-state or insinuate or suggest in "psychological" terms. For example, in the eighth poem of the sequence, "The Haunter," the dead woman speaks for the first time, confiding in us about the man whom she's hovering near but whose words she can't answer. She lets us know, however, that when she was alive, when she *could* answer, he didn't much want to talk:

> When I could let him know
> How I would like to join in his journeys
> Seldom he wished to go.

And eventually she asks us to "Tell him a faithful one is doing / All that love can do / Still that his path may be worth pursuing, / And to bring peace thereto." It sounds noble; but reread and juxtaposed with "The Voice," which follows, it appears that circumstances have their satirical side; since her pledge of faithfulness ("If he but sigh since my loss befell him / Straight to his side I go") is also a pledge not to let him alone.

"The Voice" ("Woman much missed . . .") has been widely admired, is one of Leavis's "great" Hardy poems, yet I doubt that a convincing account can be given of why it is clearly superior to a good many others. Here the man fancies that the woman is calling to him; he can't believe his ears, calls back her "Cornwall" self for inspection once more, then doubts the whole business:

> Or is it only the breeze, in its listlessness
> Travelling across the wet mead to me here,
> You being ever dissolved to wan wistlessness,
> Heard no more again far or near?

and sums up:

> Thus I; faltering forward,
> Leaves around me falling,
> Wind oozing thin through the thorn from norward,
> And the woman calling.

Yes, it is you that I hear; no, it is only the breeze: the final stanza
in refusing to choose one over the other (the wind keeps "oozing
thin" and the woman "calling") calls a halt to further dramatic
development, looks back at itself, and names once more the "faltering" hero's situation. It is less a poetry of argued, progressive
statement than a talismanic charm which fascinates and enchants
by a line such as "Wind oozing thin through the thorn from nor-
ward," which is nothing less or more than a tour de force of
expression. "The Voice" is not notable for moral or psychological
discriminations; its circumstantial satire is of more elemental concern and is felt mainly through the element of sound.

But the two masterpieces from the sequence are "After a Journey" and "At Castle Boterel," poems which register most fully,
humanly and particularly, the man's recovery of himself in his saying of the most that can be said about his relationship with the
dead woman. No longer "faltering forward," there is a leisured
amplitude in both poems into which the reader is led, as her spirit
leads the man:

> Yes: I have re-entered your olden haunts at last;
>   Through the years, through the dead scenes I have tracked
>   you. . . .

In "After a Journey" the pursuer's voice is released into speaking
with a range of tones, and it can address the "Voiceless ghost" of
its first line with a lovely mixture of supplication, teasing reproof,
and tender vouchsafing:

> What have you now found to say of our past—
>   Scanned across the dark space wherein I have lacked you?
> Summer gave us sweets, but autumn wrought division?

> Things were not lastly as firstly well
>   With us twain, you tell?
> But all's closed now, despite Time's derision.
>
> I see what you are doing: you are leading me on
>   To the spots we knew when we haunted here together,
> The waterfall, above which the mist-bow shone
>   At the then fair hour in the then fair weather,
> And the cave just under, with a voice still so hollow
>   That it seems to call out to me from forty years ago,
>   When you were all aglow,
> And not the thin ghost that I now fraily follow!

The truths about how summer was sweet, autumn not so; of how their relationship didn't maintain its glorious beginning—are true but somehow irrelevant. "All's closed now" has no particular referent but is an absolute gesture of conclusion. Yet the next stanza opens up with a great recovery of powers to the wonderful point where, suddenly, the cave calls out as if from forty years ago (that almost monosyllabic line is itself a wonder!) and where the clichés of romance ("When you were all aglow") now feel fresh and alive. It is the life and power of the poetic imagination to call up and call back the past, which "After a Journey" testifies to especially in its last four lines:

> Trust me, I mind not, though Life lours,
>   The bringing me here; nay, bring me here again!
>   I am just the same as when
> Our days were a joy, and our paths through flowers.

Leavis rightly thinks these lines moving and the poem a "triumph of character." One might add though that the assertion of sameness—"I am just the same as when / Our days were a joy ..."—is also a loyal simplification of the man's character: we have seen the sense in which he isn't the same, in which "Time's derision" has taken its toll. In this poem, being "just the same" is less a condition than a hard-won assertion. We remind ourselves that Hardy was a poet back then, just as he is now in 1913; that forty-five years previously he had written a poem about love gone wrong called "Neutral Tones." The imagination persists, despite time's derision.

"At Castle Boterel" is the companion poem which, though less appreciated than "After a Journey," strikes me as even deeper in its commitment to the imagination's persistence and dominion over Nature. What makes the particular expression so interesting here is the way Hardy's voice manages to discover rather than merely assert a truth—a discovery which happens before our eyes and before his too. In a drizzle the man looks behind him at a "fading byway" and it is suddenly replaced by a forty-years-ago scene of "Myself and a girlish form benighted / In dry March weather." Having climbed the road the couple alight to ease the pony's load, then "it" happens:

> It filled but a minute. But was there ever
>   A time of such quality, since or before,
> In that hill's story? To one mind never,
>   Though it has been climbed, foot-swift, foot-sore,
>   By thousands more.
>
> Primaeval rocks form the road's steep border,
>   And much have they faced there, first and last,
> Of the transitory in Earth's long order;
>   But what they record in colour and cast
>   Is—that we two passed.

There is perhaps no more expressive dash in lyric poetry than the one in that last line, as the voice moves all the way from acknowledging, in grandly spacious ways, how much the rocks have "faced" of transitory Nature "(Earth's long order") to another kind of "facing," as the man looks to see what they have to tell him—which is "that we two passed." As human a moment as can be found in Hardy's poems, the concluding stanzas give it further poignancy:

> And to me, though Time's unflinching rigour,
>   In mindless rote, has ruled from sight
> The substance now, one phantom figure

Remains on the slope, as when that night
   Saw us alight.

I look and see it there, shrinking, shrinking,
   I look back at it amid the rain
For the very last time; for my sand is sinking,
   And I shall traverse old love's domain
      Never again.

No longer, as in "After a Journey," does he cry out, "Nay, bring me here again!" The imaginative expenditure has been such as to render further expeditions unwise or unnecessary, certainly anticlimactic. But for the most unillusioned of modern poets to have said this much, to have recorded as a great fact "that we too passed," is Hardy's triumph over his own penchant for the anonymous, also a fine moment in the poetry of our century.

Next day she found that her lover,
   Though asked, had gone elsewhere
And that she had possessed him in absence
   More than if there.
                    From "In the Marquee"

In his useful and incisive book on the poetry, Samuel Hynes observes that it is easier to characterize Hardy's style by saying what it is *not* than what it is—not lyrical, not melodious, nor spare, nor austere. The "Poems of 1912–13" are his most eloquent efforts in the direction of a strongly individual style; "After a Journey" and "At Castle Boterel" prime examples of vigorous and intense dramatic performances. At the end of the latter poem the voice records a shrinking of a "phantom figure" and vows to "traverse old love's domain / Never again." The real Hardy lived to write many more poems, some about his relationship with Emma, but never, in respect to the dead woman, with the fullness of "traversing" seen in the 1912–13 group. Perhaps the crowning irony with regard to those poems is that Florence Dugdale, living at Max

Gate though as yet unmarried to Hardy, was deeply distressed by the flood of poems Emma's death had occasioned. While at the same time, the guilt and remorse which so spurred Hardy's creative and elegiac energies were partly in consequence of the attention he had paid Florence over the last five years, at the cost of ignoring—even to her death—his own wife.

Age seventy-two when he wrote those poems, Hardy was to publish four further volumes which contain some of his finest efforts, as for example "During Wind and Rain," "In Time of the Breaking of Nations," "Midnight on the Great Western," "And There Was a Great Calm . . ." "The Fallow Deer at the Lonely House"—and a number of others. He continued to indulge his inclination to say no, not, nor, and other negative affirmations. An oddly humorous moment occurs late in *Complete Poems* when #918 announces itself as "We Are Getting to the End," a poem about the end of "dreams" and unreal expectations about the world, but also (we may feel) about our heroic struggle to read through the previous 917 poems. Poem 919, "He Resolves to Say No More," contains four stanzas whose last lines reveal the following progression: "Yea, none shall gather what I hide!"; "What I discern I will not say"; "What I have learnt no man shall know"; "And show to no man what I see." In other words, any talk about grimness or pessimism of thought in these two final poems must contend with the quite unmistakable current of wry playfulness and verbal aggressiveness which informs them and strikes us more interestingly than do the grim thoughts themselves—hardly a new thing for Hardy to be thinking.

"Why should not old men be mad?" Yeats asked in the title of one of his own last poems. Hardy's late volumes in their sanity answer that question, though never of course by entertaining it directly. Occupied with his second wife in writing the two-volume autobiography, living on at Max Gate as a famous personage, he kept as always his own company. Robert Gittings provides an amusing instance of this in the form of an anecdote Florence told about accusing her husband of not having spoken to anyone outside the house for twelve days. "I have spoken to someone," said Hardy triumphantly. "The man who drove the manure cart." Much impressed, Florence asked what he said to the man: "Good morning," was Hardy's reply. There exists also a document titled "The Domestic Life of Thomas Hardy," purportedly written by a "Miss E.E.T." who was his parlormaid near the end of his life. From her reminiscences one takes away gossip like the following: "Hardy was, in a sense, a negative character whom, one gathers, the staff neither liked nor disliked." We learn that he always spoke "quietly and softly," that he never showed anger, that he sought solitude, played no games, collected nothing. "I think of him as always writing," says "Miss E.E.T."

He was writing mainly about the effects of time as observed and felt in his own life and in the natural world he became, if anything, increasingly sensitive to and observant of. Yet the real distinction of poems ensuing from this observation lies not in matters of apt imagery or "wise" reflections about life, but in the unearthly detachment with which a voice speaks. Reading through the four volumes from the last ten years of his life, beginning with *Moments of Vision* in 1917, we are struck by the predominance of this toneless voice somewhere from underwater or from beyond the grave, speaking to nobody in particular—though we are permitted to listen—with complete, assured, and impartial authority. Frequently the situation is generalized, pointed even more toward allegory and fable than were the earlier poems. In the concluding words of "Going and Staying," a charming poem published in *Late Lyrics and Earlier* (1922), the lovers look close at Time

> And saw his ghostly arms revolving
> To sweep off woeful things with prime,
> Things sinister with things sublime
>   Alike dissolving.

It is this impartiality of change and equality of dissolution, despite season or age, that most grips his imagination. In "The Missed Train" (from *Human Shows, Far Phantasies,* 1925), the man thinks back to the time when he traveled home after visiting his lover, missed the train, and had to spend the night in a small inn where all night he dreamed about her, feeling both lonely and consoled by her spirit. The poem concludes

> Thus onetime to me . . .
> Dim wastes of dead years bar away
> Then from now. But such happenings to-day
> Fall to lovers, may be!
>
> Years, years as shoaled seas,
> Truly, stretch now between! Less and less
> Shrink the visions then vast in me.—Yes,
> Then in me: Now in these.

To use language as "dead" as this, and make the result very much the opposite, is an achievement. How much it is necessary and how much we are invited to fill in the blank spaces, the ellipsis, the dash, with inexpressible and unsayable yearnings and musings—one cannot specify. But the familiar words are able to assert, simultaneously, how far behind him is his own past, momentarily recovered in a poem, and how this is not just his but "maybe" anyone's past: how it's all different, but always the same in the anonymous community of ultimate things. The last line is perfectly, finally balanced, as in an epitaph, since these are surely the last words.

The late Nature poems show another, related kind of anonymity. *Human Shows, Far Phantasies* is filled, not surprisingly, with winter scenes, and "A Light Snow-Fall After Frost," one of Hardy's least-known, most delightful poems, has three stanzas presenting, with great subtlety and particularity, the appearance on a country road of two men seen in succession against the backdrop of a snowfall. What is concluded from these unextraordinary events?

> The snow-feathers so gently swoop that though
>   But half an hour ago
> The road was brown, and now is starkly white,

> A watcher would have failed defining quite
>   When it transformed it so.

Not even the observer-poet, but just "a watcher" who "would have failed" if he had tried to do what nobody in fact has tried to do. To praise a line like the concluding one, with its single "it" doing the work of transformation—whenever it happened—on another "it," is to recognize Hardy's strange distinction as a poet. There is no one who writes in quite this way, nor is less likely to be eagerly imitated.

Even when the poem's "I" bears affiliations with the eighty-some-year-old man who wrote it, the presence is disengaged, almost spectral. Consider a poem from *Human Shows* with the promising Hardyan title "Nobody Comes":

> Tree-leaves labour up and down
>   And through them the fainting light
>   Succumbs to the crawl of night.
> Outside in the road the telegraph wire
>   To the town from the darkening land
> Intones to travellers like a spectral lyre
>   Swept by a spectral hand.
>
> A car comes up, with lamps full-glare,
>   That flash upon a tree:
>   It has nothing to do with me,
> And whangs along in a world of its own,
>   Leaving a blacker air;
> And mute by the gate I stand again alone,
>   And nobody pulls up there.

We might remark that if somebody had pulled up there Hardy wouldn't have written a poem about it. Here is "The Darkling Thrush" twenty-four years later, without even the consolations a man might feel in at least imagining a thrush to be aware of some "blessed hope" he himself is not. In this late poem everything is de-poetized: even the heightening at the end of the first stanza consequent upon the repetition of "spectral," and the anapestic lilt, give way to the passing car, so remote an intruder it may as well be characterized with a word Hardy uses only once in the *Complete Poems*—"whangs." In his handbook Bailey softens the poem by suggesting that the man must be feeling "expectation, disappointment, and loneliness" after the car passes. But who is to say? Who can penetrate that "blacker air" or dare to ascribe a tone (sadness? wistful regret? stoic fortitude?) to "And nobody pulls up there"? "A watcher would have failed defining quite / When it transformed it so," and so must the watcher as reader fail to define quite—in the sense of an understanding, sympathetic comprehension—the feelings (if they can be said to be feelings) of this man alone. In "The Darkling Thrush" he was "unaware"; he is now "mute." It is hard to resist summoning up once more the voice of Rook: "Throughout the field I find no grain."

Hardy had hoped to publish his last volume on his eighty-eighth birthday but fell some months short of it, dying peacefully in January of 1928. In his introduction to *Winter Words* he tells us that it is probably his "last appearance on the literary stage" and that it would be "idle" to pretend he is excited about publishing these poems; still "the pieces themselves have been prepared with reasonable care, if not quite with the zest of a young man new to print." This lively tone also holds us at arm's length, lest we should be too zestful in applying fierce standards of excellence to the volume. Although Harold Bloom has claimed that it shows a sudden and dramatic recovery of Hardy's poetic powers, a look at the volume or volumes published prior to it reveals to me no heightening or diminishment of poetic quality in the final one.

When the poems in *Winter Words* deal most directly with other people they tend to be sensationally morbid in Hardy's blackly humorous way. In the dialogue "Her Second Husband Hears Her Story," a wife relates how she sewed up her drunken first husband in bed, so as to be safe from any possibly amorous offerings. The

husband consequently dies of a stroke, though whether that too
was in her intent she will not say. " 'Well, it's a cool queer tale!' "
says second husband gamely, perhaps taking thought for his own
future. In "Henley Regatta" a young woman is first presented
weeping that she will be unable to go to the Regatta because it is
raining; years later, and another Regatta Day, she is "a Regatta
quite her own":

> Inanely
> She laughs in the asylum as she floats
> Within a water-tub, which she calls "Henley,"
> Her little paper boats.

And "The Mongrel" is a quite unbearable piece about how a man
betrays his dog by tossing him to his death in the harbor so as to
avoid paying the dog tax. There are no complications of feelings
in these poems; they are strikingly effective, cruel exercises in
"pessimism," and they mock their author's prose attempts to
show that he was always above such things.

At the other extreme, but issuing from the same sensibility, are
the "elemental" poems Hardy wrote all his life but never with
quite the simplicity of statement he managed in old age. "Throw-
ing a Tree," once thought to have been the last poem he wrote,
does no more than lay down, in alternately rhymed anapests, the
cutting down of a tree in the New Forest, concluding this way:

> . . . Reached the end of its long staying power
> The tree crashes downward; it shakes all its neighbours throughout,
> And two hundred years' steady growth has been ended in less than two
> hours.

And what do you think of that? the poem seems to be content
with saying. There is no statement, no "wisdom" into which the
reader can move comfortably; nor does the poem's surface attempt to charm or engage us. That is part of what Hardy's final
simplicity entails.

At his best in these last poems he does without self-con-
sciousness what the young Hemingway was making his career out

of doing at the same time (*A Farewell to Arms* and *Winter Words* were published but a year apart!). "An Unkindly May" is by any standards a slight poem; yet another thing Hardy's late work does is make us think twice about what is "slight" and how we can tell for sure. It is merely a poem of a few lines about bad weather in May—pigeons, rooks, vultures, flowers, and sheep all getting soaked. But it is framed, at beginning and end, by a couplet about a shepherd: beginning, "A shepherd stands by a gate in a white smock-frock: / He holds the gate ajar, intently counting his flock," and ending "That shepherd still stands in that white smock-frock, / Unnoting all things save the counting his flock." The wording, which could so easily have been cute, charming, or clever, resolutely refuses to be any of them, and the shepherd remains.

Let us end where we began, with birds, and with the poet at his most impersonal, most elemental in his concerns:

> The thrushes sing as the sun is going,
> And the finches whistle in ones and pairs,
> And as it gets dark loud nightingales
>   In bushes
> Pipe, as they can when April wears,
>   As if all Time were theirs.
>
> These are brand-new birds of twelve-months' growing,
> Which a year ago, or less than twain,
> No finches were, nor nightingales,
>   Nor thrushes,
> But only particles of grain,
>   And earth, and air, and rain.

Here one notices the artful, subtle rhyme-pattern and appreciates how entire was Hardy's commitment to rhyme; yet we read the poems scarcely noticing the rhyming cement that holds them together in a central way. And as the "as if" moment of the first stanza is trumped once more by the deeply stressed negatives of the second, ending up with an "only"—"only particles"—that leaves us to do what we will with the miracle of life and its evanescence, we can echo and extend Pound's comment on Hardy's poetry: "Now *there* is a clarity. There is the harvest of having written 20 novels first." "Proud Songsters," poem #816 in the *Complete Poems*, is the harvest of having written roughly 815 poems first.

2

W. B. YEATS
Theatrical Nobility

"I fear, I greatly fear, that I have just seen the greatest actor in the world." This remark (supposedly made by Sarah Bernhardt about Nijinsky) is quoted by Randall Jarrell to suggest what William Butler Yeats might have said about Robert Frost. Yet it could as well be uttered by any reader of Yeats's poetry. For his gravestone, that actor wrote the following epitaph:

> *Cast a cold eye*
> *On life, on death.*
> *Horseman, pass by!*

These lines, the last ones from "Under Ben Bulben," the last poem in Yeats's last volume, are highly quotable. They raise the epitaph writer above mundane concerns and emotional turbulences, and ask the passing horseman to imitate what we assume Yeats cultivated in his own character—the pride of heroic demeanor.

Let us now become fanciful about the scene this epitaph projects, imagining the horseman to approach Yeats's stone whereon the lines are carved. How intrigued he will find himself, and how unlikely that he will proceed, obediently, merely to "pass by." He

49

will speculate instead on what a distinctive note is sounded by the directive; or on what sort of character once composed it and now lies under the sod. Whatever he says to himself, it is certain that his eye will have become more heated, more passionately active than it was before he read the message; and if, like Yeats, he should try casting a cold eye on anything, it will be in dramatical, histrionic, warmly stagy ways. Our horseman has now been turned into a reader, trying out the lines on himself or on some imagined other in various tones of voice, with varying degrees of pause and inflection. He is participating in what Yeats's readers find an especially irresistible activity: the attempt to imagine a speaking voice and embody in that voice a human being with certain purposes and values. The horseman has become involved in a dramatic engagement made lively by the energy of posture Yeats's lines demand.

The injunction to *"Cast a cold eye"* is a late instance of a recurring moment in Yeats's poetry when he instructs himself or others in how to be unillusioned or "cold" about life and death, love and the writing of poems. In "All Things Can Tempt Me" he would have his verse be "Colder and dumber and deafer than a fish"; or, looking back in 1914 on his youthful mythological poetry unfortunately misused by "the fools," he cries scornfully, "Song, let them take it, / For there's more enterprise / In walking naked" ("The Coat"). Or he promises to write, for his imagined Fisherman, "one / Poem maybe as cold / And passionate as the dawn." Or, most dramatically in "The Circus Animals' Desertion," he would cease to pursue "masterful images" but lie down instead "where all the ladders start, / In the foul rag-and-bone shop of the heart." My concern is not with the shades of meaning and implication these pronouncements take in particular poems; rather with a similarity in the gesture of their making. In each case something "warm," adorned and embroidered, brilliantly created by the brilliantly endowed poet, is turned on, put by, or rejected in favor of something less word-driven, more in touch with unarticulated "basic" life. And in each case these moments of rejection are presented to us as memorable, poem-stopping gestures which we warm to and may later walk about quoting in vigorous and heartening ways.

Yeats's poetry is so filled with the people and places he cared about, the beliefs and issues he debated as an active publicist and partisan of many causes, that the events of his life seem somehow inevitable, as we find ourselves accepting unreflectively one striking happening after another. He was born in 1865, his father (John Butler Yeats) an indefatigable painter and greatly perceptive reader of literature, some of whose matchless remarks are fortunately available to us in the letters he wrote home during the latter part of his life in New York City. The younger Yeats was born in Dublin and moved back and forth between there and London in his childhood, with frequent visits to his grandparents in the west of Ireland. His first lyrics were composed when he was in his teens and published when he was twenty, by which time his interest in the occult had manifested itself in his founding, with others, the Dublin Hermetic Society. Moved back to London, he abandoned his art studies in favor of becoming a professional writer, published his first poems in English magazines, and became a member of Madame Blavatsky's Theosophical Society. These interests in psychical and supernatural experience found expression in his co-editing a three-volume edition of William Blake's works. Yeats also helped to start a literary society, the Rhymers' Club, which he celebrated in his own poems and which was the focus of his association with Dowson, Lionel Johnson, and other English and Irish poets of the fin de siècle. His first volumes of poetry were published in the nineties, as were his first plays, some collections of Irish fairy tales and stories, and a novel with a strong basis in Irish lore.

During the first ten or so years of the twentieth century Yeats was deeply involved in the Irish National Theatre, along with his great friend and patron Lady Augusta Gregory—at whose Coole Park home he spent many summers—and with the playwright John Synge. He participated in stormy controversies about which he then wrote with both disdain and bitterness; meanwhile he made a number of American tours, reading his poetry and lecturing to appreciative audiences across the country. Yeats was a good businessman and shrewdly made of these tours a financial success. In 1908 he presided over a sumptuous eight-volume edition of his poems, plays, and stories, the poems in particular showing the effects of the continuing and serious revision he made of his early work.

Throughout his career Yeats enjoyed the company and affections, to one degree or another, of many remarkable women, of whom the most intellectually distinguished was Olivia Shakespear, mother of the woman Ezra Pound was to marry. But the most important woman in his life, the major influence on the sorts of poems he wrote, was Maud Gonne, the patriot and revolutionary whom he met in 1889, fell in love with, proposed marriage to and was rejected by more than once. After Maud's husband was killed in the Easter Rising of 1916, about which Yeats wrote one of his best poems, he proposed to her for a last time, and then—upon her refusal—to her daughter, Iseult. Again refused, undeterred, he married Georgie Hyde-Lees in 1917, who almost immediately (on their honeymoon, supposedly) began the automatic writing which was to flower into the elaborate system of correspondences and historical analogies Yeats eventually titled *A Vision*.

He had purchased an old partially ruined tower in Ballylee, near Lady Gregory's estate, and proceeded to restore it so that he and his wife could live there for at least part of the year. Mrs. Yeats bore him a daughter and a son. By 1922 he had published the marvelous second section of his *Autobiography, The Trembling of the Veil,* and had also been elected to membership in the Irish Senate. His crowning public honor was to come the next year when he received the Nobel Prize for poetry and journeyed to Stockholm to accept the honor. In 1927, the year before his most difficult and impressive book of poems, *The Tower,* was published, Yeats suffered a collapse brought on by lung congestion and influenza. He remained in poor health for some years, spent winters in Italy, and rejoined his old friend Pound at Rapallo where he wrote "A Packet for Ezra Pound," the prologue to *A Vision.* He continued to produce some of his best and most personal poetry. In 1934 he underwent the Steinach rejuvenation operation, which he was convinced enhanced his sexual as well as his poetic powers. Commissioned by Oxford University Press to edit the *Oxford Book of Modern Verse,* he wrote an introductory preface of great interest for its revelations of his taste in poetry, and for his frankly expressed opinions of the merits of poets such as Eliot and Pound. In 1938 he moved to the south of France, where he died the next year; his body was returned to Ireland and he was buried in Drumcliff Churchyard, Sligo, with the inscription on his stone as in "Under Ben Bulben." His *Last Poems* was posthumously published and he never lived to make a final revision of his collected poems.

Criticism of Yeats might be said to have done itself in, by so thoroughly explicating the poems within inches of their lives that no one has a very good idea of where to go next. Reviewing some recent studies of Yeats, Denis Donoghue—at one point Yeats's official biographer—reminds us that that biography is not yet written, that the complete letters won't be published for some time, and that Yeats's stature as a modern poet is not clearly established. He refers to the beginning of "The Choice," a late short poem:

> The intellect of man is forced to choose
> Perfection of the life, or of the work,
> And if it take the second must refuse
> A heavenly mansion, raging in the dark.

Donoghue thinks that Yeats chose perfection of the life, chose to fulfill himself in many public and private ways, and did not rage enough in that dark which is necessary to bring forth poetic masterpieces (Donoghue is not inclined to argue with F. R. Leavis's assertion that there are only three "great" Yeats poems). At any rate he suggests that criticism of the poet should make itself more critical, and that the way to accomplish this is to "look at the language."

This seems a curious directive. Where else, except at the language, would one look? Yet it is true that much of the writing about Yeats is not about his language, but about his use of the folklore and legends, or the political and social features, of Ireland's history; or about his use of archetypical materials—theosophical, Rosicrucian, the gyres and moon-phases of his own system. More interestingly, it may also be that there is good reason, even granted the many articles directed at individual poems like "Sailing to Byzantium," "The Second Coming," and "Among School Children," why Donoghue should ask that more attention be paid to the language. In an important sense Yeats's poems do not encourage this kind of attention, at least not the early ones.

Consider the chorus to "The Stolen Child," from his first volume, published in 1889:

> *Come away, O human child!*
> *To the waters and the wild*
> *With a faery, hand in hand,*
> *For the world's more full of weeping than you can understand.*

Recently a friend of mine quoted these lines aloud and remarked—"Now *that's* the Yeats I like—when he's really being outrageous!" I knew what he meant, and knew also that appreciating the poet in this way—a valid and important way—has precious little to do with "looking at the language." Or take the opening lines of another early poem, from *The Wind Among the Reeds* (1899):

> I have drunk ale from the Country of the Young
> And weep because I know all things now:
> I have been a hazel-tree, and they hung

> The Pilot Star and the Crooked Plough
> Among my leaves in times out of mind. . . .

This might be thought more difficult because of those odd, capitalized items, and indeed it is hard to take seriously a voice which announces that it previously existed as a hazel-tree; but such difficulties are not ones to be pondered and worried about by closer attention to the language—an explanatory footnote or two would be more to the point. The most enthusiastic admirer of the early poems is probably Harold Bloom, but he looks at their language merely in order to demonstrate correspondences with and "swervings away" from Blake and Shelley; or to praise the "universal" language of "The Stolen Child" or the universal aspect of "popular poetry" like "The Song of Wandering Aengus":

> Though I am old with wandering
> Through hollow lands and hilly lands,
> I will find out where she has gone,
> And kiss her lips and take her hands;
> And walk among long dappled grass,
> And pluck till time and times are done
> The silver apples of the moon,
> The golden apples of the sun.

This is lovely, simple, mythic, and entrancing if we let ourselves be entranced; but close scrutiny of its language is not what it needs.

To put it another and more extreme way: one can go on studying the images and themes of Yeats's early poems just so long as one doesn't assume the existence of a reader with reasonably mature interests and demands. Doubtless this sounds intolerably stuffy, and too reminiscent of Leavis's half-a-century-old strictures on Yeats's early disabling commitment to a dream-world. But what does one say about such a fine exhibit of these poems as the well-lacquered one which begins

> When my arms wrap you round I press
> My heart upon the loveliness
> That has long faded from the world . . . ,

then proceeds with instances of this loveliness such as jeweled crowns, tapestries, roses, and

> The dew-cold lilies ladies bore
> Through many a sacred corridor
> Where such grey clouds of incense rose
> That only God's eyes did not close:
> For that pale breast and lingering hand
> Come from a more dream-heavy land,
> A more dream-heavy hour than this;
> And when you sigh from kiss to kiss
> I hear white Beauty sighing, too. . . .

"He Remembers Forgotten Beauty," one of the poems Bloom admires from *The Wind Among the Reeds,* is also the one Stephen Dedalus plays with in Joyce's *Portrait of the Artist,* when he yearns instead to press into being the loveliness that has not yet come into the world. It is surely the sort of poem young Stephen would be attached to (as he is to "Who Goes with Fergus," another Early Yeats) and would quote while lying on his bed, dreaming his heavy dreams.

It is not so clear though just how our imagined "mature" reader is to behave with respect to the stage-props, the langorous atmosphere, or the easy movement from "you" (sighing from kiss to kiss) to "white Beauty" (a rather grand phenomenon): perhaps we are specially privileged to listen in on such a dreamy musing and must be careful not to disturb the dreamer. Of course we would never tolerate such stuff in prose; the poetry supposedly makes the difference—supposedly, because I don't think that it does in fact. The facility with which Yeats runs on here, the absence of an interesting mind engaged in something other than naming, fondling, or lamenting the fading of all things, are everywhere felt. Furthermore, as has been pointed out by everyone including Yeats himself, somewhere around the turn of the century he became dissatisfied with his early poems. The reviewers had enthused about poems like "He Remembers Forgotten Beauty," or "The Stolen Child," or "Song of Wandering Aengus," or the Fergus ones, or most famously "The Lake Isle of Innisfree," by saying that their beauty was "incommunicable," their metaphors "irresistible" and "inexhaustible," their spirit "insubstantial and uncapturable as a gust of the night," their rhythms "incalculable." Robert Louis Stevenson sought words "in vain" to express his inexpressible feelings about "Innisfree." By 1900 Yeats may have gotten bored by all this inarticulate gush; at any rate, as he said much later on, "suddenly everybody got down off his stilts . . . nobody went mad; nobody committed suicide." In 1903 he was already consigning "period" values to his early work: "The close of the last century was full of a strange desire to get out of form, to get to some kind of disembodied beauty . . ."; or telling John Quinn that a just-published collection of his early essays was "too lyrical, too full of aspirations after remote things, too full of desires," and promising to become more "defiant." Meanwhile he would continue to reprint and revise the early lyrics.

Yeats's poetry through *The Wind Among the Reeds* is an artful achievement, but has to be read with less than a fully sympathetic response. Its recommended attitudes are too simple, its rhythms too cultivatedly going about their business of pretending to assuage desire, when they really mean to stir it up. The fact that readers have found and perhaps still do find something in themselves that answers to the opening of "Innisfree"—"I will arise and go now, and go to Innisfree"—may well be a matter of our ability to flatter ourselves that we are really quite deep souls, with a whole set of inexpressible yearnings, beyond words and momentarily stirred to life by a poem. "I hear it in the deep heart's core," concludes "The Lake Isle"; we may fancy that we too hear an "it," even something as rich as "lake water lapping with low sounds by the shore." But there is no reason to be specially tender about this part of ourselves, or to respect unduly or exempt from ironical contemplation poems which minister to it.

The question of whether poets "develop," whether some do and some don't, or whether "development" is clearly a good thing to be able to manifest (Oscar Wilde said that only mediocrities develop) should be raised in connection with Yeats, since T. S. Eliot has already done so. Eliot began his Abbey Theatre lecture, delivered in 1940 after Yeats's death, by attesting to the "extraordinary development" he perceived in Yeats's poetic career. Unlike Shakespeare's, the development was not from the excellence of early works to the excellence of later ones, but from the production of accomplished but insufficiently personal "anthology pieces" found in early volumes, to the "beginning to speak for a particular man" which Eliot saw in poems like "Adam's Curse" and "The Folly of Being Comforted" (from *In the Seven Woods,* 1904) and which bursts into full blaze in the dedicatory epistle to *Responsibilities* (1914)—"Pardon that for a barren passion's sake, / Although I have come close on forty-nine. . . ." In beginning to speak for himself, Eliot said, Yeats began to speak for humankind as well.

Eliot's account has naturally been extremely influential, to the extent of overshadowing his earlier, deprecating comments (never reprinted) deploring Yeats's "remoteness" and calling him egoistical and Irish, a writer of poems whose effect was, like Swinburne's, that of "repeated doses of gin and water." In the 1940 lecture Eliot revised this emphasis, stressing instead how Yeats wrote himself into the twentieth century by cultivating "defiance" through the strong rhythms of an individual voice. A recent history of modern poetry by David Perkins remains satisfied with this way of talking:

> By 1910 he had learned how to write poetry that sounded like "the actual thoughts of a man at a passionate moment of life" and compelled himself to speak directly from his personal self, writing of the actual women in the actual world and in his own life.

As example, the historian quotes from "No Second Troy":

> Why should I blame her that she filled
> My days with misery, or that she would of late

> Have taught to ignorant men most violent ways,
> Or hurled the little streets upon the great,
> Had they but courage equal to desire?

Yeats's poem is praised because it is about "the actual woman in the actual world and in his own life"; and other critics have felt strongly that Maud Gonne's presence, the fact that so many poems are "about" her, is something to be taken serious account of in estimating Yeats's achievement. Yet how on earth can one take it into account? Unsurprisingly, there is little to say beyond naming and gesturing at the "actual woman" we presume the poem to have been written about. So Norman Jeffares, in his commentary on the *Collected Poems,* simply plugs in Maud's name and qualities to this or that line in the poem—

> What could have made her peaceful with a mind
> That nobleness made simple as a fire,
> With beauty like a tightened bow, a kind
> That is not natural in an age like this,
> Being high and solitary and most stern?

—as if we could now see the lines more truly for thinking of her. One might of course look backward to an earlier poem like "The Rose of the World" ("Who dreamed that beauty passes like a dream"), where "Troy passed away in one high funeral gleam," and find it to be "about" Maud Gonne in a more languidly pale manner. But such a development in style must be demonstrated from the words on the page, rather than by any reference to the "actual woman."

Unquestionably, "No Second Troy" invites us to hold up "defiantly" the good, proud words—"nobleness," "high," "solitary," and "most stern"—against the rabble, "the age" that was unable to appreciate this Helen:

> Why, what could she have done, being what she is?
> Was there another Troy for her to burn?

No, sings out the reader who thrills to the dismissive rhetorical questions. Yeats, speaking for himself, is also beginning—in

Eliot's phrase—to "speak for man." Or so the account would run that takes Yeats, as Eliot seems to have taken him in the posthumous tribute, in Yeats's own terms. I would claim that the only way to get outside these terms, thus attain a criticism and appreciation wider and more interesting than Yeats's reflexive one, is to ask about the nature of our response to this "actual man" speaking. Does he also speak for us, does he speak for "man"? Recall Hardy's "On the Departure Platform," written about the same time as "No Second Troy." Admittedly the circumstances are dissimilar: there is no brawling public world Hardy must feel superior to and defend his love from; and perhaps therefore he has the time, even the leisure, to become surprised and touched by the remembered vision of the woman vanishing down the departure platform to the train, no doubt to reappear, but "never as then." Hardy's invitation is for us to exercise a wonder or puzzlement at life's ways; we are all, in the title of the volume where the poem appeared, Time's Laughingstocks, and contemplating ourselves in this light may be good for the spirit, since it is the light of truth. In this sense Hardy speaks for "man" even though the man's voice in the poem is not as distinctly individual as it will be in the "Poems of 1912–13" to come, or as is the one in "No Second Troy."

Yeats's voice in that poem is distinctly individual because it presents the passionate speech of a man who has something particular on his mind, and because its syntax artfully moves that voice over and beyond the formal limits of the quatrains, as if at the pressure of strong feeling. The defense and justification of what "she" has done—even done to him—is made lucidly, simply, and with economy. It might be argued that the voice's attitude is not as simple as I have made it out to be; that just so far as "her" actions are true to her heroic nature, they are also absurd and wasteful "in an age like this." Yet the poem still seems to me a less engaging utterance than Hardy's, less able to provide new sustenance and satisfactions when we return to it. "No Second Troy" is all there on the surface, its attitudes fully "struck," its dramatic posture loud and clear. It works by excluding, by simply not

bringing up for consideration, anything which might work against
the brilliantly contrived sequence of impossible questions it pre-
tends to entertain. Until about midway through his thirties,
Yeats's poetry consists of a number of bittersweet lyrics and ballads which try to ease the pain of living by "rewording in melodious guile" ("Song of the Happy Shepherd") the sorrows of love,
and which also in the rewording look to stir up new depths of
feeling in the listener. Then at a certain point, around the turn of
the century, the poems banish this pale lamenting and cultivate
defiance in a style of bitter rectitude which shades off into self-
righteousness. Neither of these styles can accommodate much
humor, nor do they allow the reader much play in responding to
them. The signals are all there to follow, the attitudes broadly
and clearly laid out in song or in clipped speech by a voice that
finds it difficult to imagine another voice in response.

Nothing in the biographies or the letters suggests that these
poems were anything other than direct expressions of the man
who wrote them. There are few moments (some of them occur in
his essays) when the younger Yeats chooses, or is able, to place
himself in a humorous or even in an especially sympathetic light:
reserved, dignified, and polite, his letters also say remarkably little
of interest (compared with Frost's or Pound's) about poetry. One
is more than usually amused to read accounts of those who visited
him at one of his "evenings" in Woburn Buildings in London,
such as the following rendition by Douglas Goldring of an evening
dominated by Pound, whom Yeats had met in 1908 and who for a
time acted as his secretary:

> My own emotions on this particular evening, since I did not
> possess Ezra's transatlantic *brio,* were an equal blend of rev-
> erence and the desire to giggle. I was sitting next to Yeats on
> a settle when a young Indian woman in a *sari* came and
> squatted at his feet and asked him to sing "Innisfree," saying
> she was certain he had composed it to an Irish air. Yeats was
> so anxious to comply with her request, unfortunately, like so
> many poets, was completely unmusical, indeed almost tone-
> deaf. He compromised by a sort of dirge-like incantation,

> calculated to send any unhappy giggler into hysterics. I bore
> it as long as I could, but at last the back of the settle began to
> shake and I received the impact of one of the poet's nasty
> glances from behind his pince-nez. Mercifully, I recovered
> but it was an awful experience.

Granted, Douglas Goldring had a yen for mischief-making; yet it
is hard to resist the temptation to imagine with less than reverence
(if with more than a giggle) this middle-aged poet "nobly" striving
to render his famous poem. Occasionally Yeats could command
the ironically humorous style, as when, in his Madame Blavatsky
days, he writes to Kathleen Tynan (in 1888) that "A sad accident
happened at Madame Blavatsky's lately, I hear. A big materialist
sat on the astral double of a poor young Indian. It was sitting on
the sofa and he was too material to be able to see it. Certainly a
sad accident!" But only occasionally. He is probably the modern
poet most vulnerable to affectations which are not inevitably
amusing; and this weakness in style of life carries over into his poetry.

In an epigraph to his volume of poems *Responsibilities* (1914),
Yeats announced that "In dreams begins responsibility," dedicat-
ing the volume with the epistle which begins "Pardon, old fathers,
if you still remain / Somewhat in ear-shot for the story's end" and
concludes with an address to his uncle, William Pollexfen, "silent
and fierce old man":

> Pardon that for a barren passion's sake,
> Although I have come close on forty-nine,
> I have no child, I have nothing but a book,
> Nothing but that to prove your blood and mine.

The "barren passion's sake" must be understood as a comment on
his lengthy preoccupation with Maud Gonne, as well as fore-
shadowing the little poem about how man is forced to choose
"perfection of the life or of the work." But to Yeats at this mo-

ment in his career both life and work were anything but perfect, despite his achieved eminence ("He is the big man here in poetry of course," Frost wrote home in 1913). When Pound reviewed *Responsibilities* in May of 1914, he praised it for its "hardness" and for the "curious nobility" he found central to Yeats; this noble tone he admired was a continuation of the one previously encountered in "No Second Troy." But though as a propagandist for Imagism, Pound had a great deal invested in "hardness," it was a dangerous, perhaps an impossible quality for Yeats to command successfully. The poet-as-dreamer had grown accustomed to taking himself solemnly, and it was unlikely that simply by deciding to become "hard" instead of soft he could change his spots; more likely he would substitute one sort of histrionics for another.

At any rate, "In dreams begins responsibility" should not be taken to mean that the younger dreamer has now assumed more public burdens; there may rather be an implied "only" before "In dreams" which makes those dreams all the more essential for any kind of right action or awareness. It is a teasing statement, worthy of Yeats at his deepest and best, and predictive of things to come. In the most impressive poem from *Responsibilities*, "The Cold Heaven," Yeats's "barren passion" for Maud Gonne flowers into a dramatic rendering of what responsibility might mean:

> Suddenly I saw the cold and rook-delighting heaven
> That seemed as though ice burned and was but the more ice,
> And thereupon imagination and heart were driven
> So wild that every casual thought of that and this
> Vanished, and left but memories, that should be out of season
> With the hot blood of youth, of love crossed long ago. . . .

The poem's first half is a dream, out of which something is incurred—a visionary moment we come to expect in more Yeats poems than not. Upon inspection the language reveals a Yeatsianism ("rook-delighting") and his recurrent trick of eliminating possessives (before "imagination" and "heart") so as to make the experience more universal and irresistible. And there is the favorite word "wild," employed as an assurance that strong feelings are involved. Yeats is not averse to using it as a "good" word in other poems, admiring "The Wild Old Wicked Man" or, in "Among School Children," imagining how Maud Gonne must have looked in her childhood ("And thereupon my heart is driven wild").

But there is nothing in "The Cold Heaven's" diction, imagery, or even its tone of voice which inspires awe, is compelling and interesting; awe and interest are created wholly by the masterful movement of the verse, a movement Yeats over the past ten years had grown extremely practiced at effecting by enjambing his lines and breaking them in subtle ways. The key effect can be located in the unpunctuated clause beginning "And thereupon" and coming down abruptly on "Vanished" at the beginning of a line, followed by the comma-break. Movement is also the salient feature of the poem's second half:

> And I took all the blame out of all sense and reason,
> Until I cried and trembled and rocked to and fro,
> Riddled with light. Ah! when the ghost begins to quicken,
> Confusion of the death-bed over, is it sent
> Out naked on the roads, as the books say, and stricken
> By the injustice of the skies for punishment?

"The problem in reading Yeats is to preserve one's own mind and voice in his presence," says Denis Donoghue. I preserve my mind and voice in the presence of "The Cold Heaven" by not myself becoming riddled with light; by being less moved at the presumed man's moving experience here than I am by the poet's ventriloquism, his creation of two sentences—a statement and a question—strung out over twelve lines. When one calls this poem "rhetorical," or speaks of ventriloquism and implies that the puppet-speaker is hollow, Yeats does not therefore stand condemned. But it may be that the very brilliance of his voice makes it not one we can enter into with sympathetic understanding, even though the predicament it articulates bids to be wider than an individual one. In that sense the voice is a little too much for us.

In "The Cold Heaven," and in some of the best poems Yeats wrote in the years following *Responsibilities,* he does not suggest that dreams are to be rejected in favor of reality (as the dream of Maud Gonne would be replaced by the reality of Georgie Hyde-Lees) but that it is necessary to ask harder, less rhetorical questions about the self which spins out the dream. "The Cold Heaven" shows him in strong command of a passionate syntax: "the actual thoughts of a man at a passionate moment in life," as he put it in *Reveries Over Childhood and Youth,* the first section of his autobiography, also published in 1914. But a year later, as preface to a short book (*Per Amica Silentia Luna*) in which he developed his notion of the anti-self, Yeats wrote "Ego Dominus Tuus," a poem which is something stranger than "the actual thoughts of a man." For all its esoteric paraphernalia, it remains a poem to be appreciated for itself and for the way it complicates and strengthens the dialectic of dream versus reality. And it provides central dramatic locations for Yeats's poetry from his fiftieth year until the end of his life.

The dialogue form of "Ego Dominus Tuus" loads the dice in favor of the spokesman named "Ille" ("Willie," quipped Pound) who instructs "Hic" in the necessarily "tragic war" with life which the true artist must wage. "Hic" believes one can love life and make poetry out of that love, as did "impulsive men that look for happiness / And sing when they have found it." But "Ille" contradicts him:

> No, not sing,
> For those that love the world serve it in action,
> Grow rich, popular and full of influence,
> And should they paint or write, still it is action:
> The struggle of the fly in marmalade.
> The rhetorician would deceive his neighbours,
> The sentimentalist himself; while art
> Is but a vision of reality.

And Ille puts in most extreme terms the inevitable alienation of artist from world:

> What portion in the world can the artist have
> Who has awakened from the common dream
> But dissipation and despair?

Ille's vocabulary features the language of Early Yeats—"dream," "vision," "sing," "world"—seasoned with tougher words those early poems couldn't accommodate—"marmalade," "rhetorician," "sentimentalist," "dissipation." Their interplay here signals a widening of Yeats's ambitions, an increase in risk-taking over both his earlier languorousness and his later sarcastic tautness. Quite simply, the quoted lines are challenging for what they assert to be the relation of art to "reality": the former "is but" a vision of the latter, a very sad or promising situation depending on how you look at it. Yeats's Rhymers' Club friends, particularly Ernest Dowson and Lionel Johnson, were overwhelmed by the world, fell into "dissipation and despair," were—in the words of a famous *New Yorker* cartoon—sick little poets. In "Ego Dominus Tuus" Yeats writes a prolegomenon to the future healthy poetry he will produce.

But the lines suggest also how far he has moved from the "hardness" Pound praised in *Responsibilities.* In 1915, while living with Pound in Sussex, he read Wordsworth's *Excursion,* also *The Prelude;* and the blank verse of "Ego Dominus Tuus" shows a more exploratory sensibility at work than can be observed in Yeats's previous work. Fifty years old, unmarried, "perfection of the life" a long way from realization, he doubtless found his earlier art less than perfect. Perhaps the loneliest moment in his poetry occurs in "The Wild Swans at Coole" (1917), when he observes the swans and thinks back nineteen years to the time he first saw them and heard their "clamorous wings":

> I have looked upon those brilliant creatures,
> And now my heart is sore.
> All's changed since I, hearing at twilight,
> The first time on this shore,
> The bell-beat of their wings above my head,
> Trod with a lighter tread.

They are "unwearied still," but he is old and caught in the great Romantic poetic cliché—my human awareness, which no swan is burdened with or blessed with, makes me feel very sad. That Yeats managed not merely to go on lamenting in this way, that *The Wild Swans at Coole* volume of 1917 (augmented in 1919) was not, as Middleton Murry predicted it would be in a review, a "swan-song"—is the invigorating story of his subsequent career.

Referring to a volume of Yeats's essays (*The Cutting of an Agate*) in 1919, T. S. Eliot spoke of his subject as "a Foreign Mind": in his prose as well as his verse, Yeats showed himself to be not "of this world." Perhaps, Eliot speculated, it was a matter of his Irishness; but "The difference between his world and ours is so complete as to seem almost a physiological variety, different nerves and senses." Yeats's Paterian prose in these essays was "seductive"; yet his personality remained remote:

> His remoteness is not an escape from the world, for he is innocent of any world to escape from; his procedure is blameless, but he does not start where we do. His mind is, in fact, extreme in egoism, and, as often with egoism, remains a little crude. . . .

On the positive side, Eliot adds that in Yeats's poetry the egoism is given a "positive, individual and permanent quality."

Our first response is that this must be an elegant Eliotic put-down, insufferably snobbish (what is "our world" anyway?) and perhaps not innocent of envy. Or at any rate (we might reply), this criticism is only applicable to the disciple of Pater, the Celtic Twilight dreamer who by the middle of the 1910's had passed from the stage to be replaced by a more attractively human customer. And, getting Eliot off the hook, we could point to his later, more generous tributes to Yeats, especially the Abbey Theatre one mentioned previously. Instead of doing any of this however, let us take Eliot at his word and consider his criticism in the light of three poems Yeats wrote between 1916 and 1919, by common consent three of his best. Revealing him at his most accessible, they are the least "remote" examples of his work that can be found: "Easter 1916," "In Memory of Major Robert Gregory," and "A Prayer for My Daughter." Each focuses intently on some person or event outside the lyric speaker's mind—an unhappy mind, dried up, distracted, or in despair—which under the influence of its subject is touched into new life. The "common dream" from which, in "Ego Dominus Tuus," the true artist must awaken is in these three poems replaced by a more intense, more subjective "vision of reality," and the poems end in one or another kind of quiet exultation: "A terrible beauty is born."

My concern with these poems—which have received ample and intelligent commentary—is, as with Yeats generally, not to interpret or admire, but to make clearer the dimensions of "the Yeats problem." "Looking at the language," as Donoghue would have us do, won't solve this problem, though it is of course the only place to look. Consider first the Robert Gregory elegy which Frank Kermode in *Romantic Image* treats as a central poem in his argument about the "image," as well as the poem where Yeats for the first time puts it all together—"perhaps the first [poem] in which we hear the full range of the poet's voice," "the first full statement of . . . a complex and tragic situation: the position of artists and contemplatives in a world built for action." And Kermode sums it up this way: "After it, for twenty years, Yeats's poems, whenever he is using his whole range, are identifiable as the work of the master of the Gregory elegy."

Since *Romantic Image* is a formidable book, let us remember that at about the time Kermode was etching this praise of the Robert Gregory elegy as a Yeatsian touchstone, Yvor Winters was saying this about it: "It is commonly described as one of the greatest poems in our language; I confess that I think it is a very bad poem." In defense of his judgment Winters proceeds through the poem, finding awkward details, verbosity, an overuse of the demonstrative adjective ("that enquiring man John Synge") as a mechanical device for conferring emphasis, dull diction, padding, and exorbitant praise given to the dead Gregory as Renaissance man. About his fabled horsemanship Winters remarks, "He may have been a great horseman, but so is many a jockey," and concludes his attack on the poem as follows:

> We have familiar stereotypes in the last stanza: cold rock and
> thorn, stern colour, delicate line, secret discipline, none of
> them really described or defined; we have the facile com-
> monplaces of the final lines of stanzas eight and nine and the
> somewhat comical example of misplaced particularity in the
> final line of stanza eleven ["What made us dream that he
> could comb grey hair?"]. In the twelfth and final stanza,
> Yeats tells us that he had hoped in this poem to comment on
> everyone whom he had ever loved or admired but that
> Gregory's death took all his heart for speech. He had man-
> aged to write twelve stanzas of eight lines each, however,
> before he stopped. . . .

I see this as not merely amusing but also trenchant criticism
(F. W. Bateson is rumored to have asked, with regard to Yeats's line
about Gregory combing grey hair, "What was he, a barber?"); yet
can it be that only Winters and a few others have seen through
Yeats and are able to understand as "a truly bad poem" what
most readers have, like Kermode, taken to be a masterly, moving
elegy?

By contrast, such a situation does not arise with respect to one
of Hardy's elegies written after Emma's death. Hardy's postures
are more shifting, his declarations never quite ringing out as declarations, therefore difficult to criticize, to take issue with. Yeats,
here and as on so many earlier and later occasions, is the heroic
lyricist who will put before us everything that is on his mind:

> I had thought, seeing how bitter is that wind
> That shakes the shutter, to have brought to mind
> All those that manhood tried, or childhood loved
> Or boyish intellect approved,
> With some appropriate commentary on each;
> Until imagination brought
> A fitter welcome; but a thought
> Of that late death took all my heart for speech.

Thus the door is opened for a Winters to retort that at least he
managed to write ninety-six lines before he was overcome. But

Yeats would have seen nothing odd in that fact. He directs no irony at the self in his poems except in the most romantic and "bitter" of ways, as in the "sixty-year-old smiling public man" jibe in "Among School Children." "His mind is, in fact, extreme in egoism": Eliot's remark is just even if directed at the closing moments of the Gregory elegy, where it is hard to avoid feeling that we are being invited to admire the grieving poet for his wise and handsome subordination of words to inexpressible grief.

In a similar manner we are invited to admire the worried father of "A Prayer for my Daughter" who, as the wind from the Gregory elegy continues to roar, has "walked and prayed for this young child an hour." He hopes that she will not be blessed with too much beauty, since that beauty may exist at the expense of "natural kindness" or "the heart-revealing intimacy / That chooses right," and since he himself has seen

> . . . the loveliest woman born
> Out of the mouth of plenty's horn,
> Because of her opinionated mind
> Barter that horn and every good
> By quiet natures understood
> For an old bellows full of angry wind[.]

We remember that Maud Gonne was a passionate political orator. And Yeats's daughter must also avoid her father's fate:

> My mind, because the minds that I have loved,
> The sort of beauty that I have approved,
> Prosper but little, has dried up of late,
> Yet knows that to be choked with hate
> May well be of all evil chances chief.

On the other hand, a mind without hatred, without the "arrogance" which the poem also speaks against, will be like a tree:

> May she become a flourishing hidden tree
> That all her thoughts may like the linnet be,
> And have no business but dispensing round
> Their magnanimities of sound,
> Nor but in merriment begin a chase,

> Nor but in merriment a quarrel.
> O may she live like some green laurel
> Rooted in one dear perpetual place.

What kind of assent or respect does this lovely stanza elicit? One needn't be a feminist to feel uneasy about the vision of a flourishing daughter, skipping here and quarreling there but always out of "merriment," living "rooted" in the radically innocent way father imagines for her, thinking thoughts that are really only "thoughts" or (in the fine Marvellian line) "magnanimities of sound." Of course there are ways to get round any such embarrassment; one may gloss the poem with Yeats's prose statements in praise of that Unity of Being which modern life no more possesses; or take seriously the iconography (as Kermode does in his chapter "The Tree") and assimilate the daughter into a symbolic tradition. My own preference is otherwise, since for me this poem, like all Yeats's poems, depends for its charm on the speaker's winning readiness and humility (so he would hope) to confess his own inadequacies and faults, and upon the magnanimities of sound which occur in its artfully rambling stanzas. Not so much in order to make a coherent argument, as to convince us we are in the presence of a rich and complex human being.

In the poem's penultimate stanza Yeats, as he does in the Gregory elegy, rises to a generalizing style that is powerful and impressive:

> Considering that, all hatred driven hence,
> The soul recovers radical innocence
> And learns at last that it is self-delighting,
> Self-appeasing, self-affrighting,
> And that its own sweet will is Heaven's will. . . .

These are wonderful lines to declaim, in a classroom or driving along the highway; is it unfair to ask about the kind of assent we give them? *When* does the soul recover "radical innocence"? When is "at last"? When are the soul's will and Heaven's identical? Surely this "when" is not some point in time, or some imagined future in which things will be different; rather it exists in the poem, at the moment of eloquence when Yeats puts it into words. It is indeed a "romantic" image that tells us not much about daughters or about fathers either, but a great deal about W. B. Yeats. "Words alone are certain good" runs a crucial line from the first exhibit in the *Collected Poems,* in which a Happy Shepherd advises us to tell our sad story into the lips of a seashell:

> And they thy comforters will be
> Rewording in melodious guile
> Thy fretful words a little while.

The voice which puts words and sentences together in "A Prayer for my Daughter" is a much more flexible one than any commanded by Early Yeats; all the better to guilefully charm the daughter and ourselves as readers into believing something we know not quite what, except that it sounds marvelous.

These two eloquent and ambitious poems—the elegy for Gregory and the prayer for his daughter—should be taken as absolutely central to an understanding of Yeats's mature poetry, but should not be taken as further contributions to English's poetry's classic humanism, in the line of Ben Jonson, Dryden, Pope, Samuel Johnson, Wordsworth, and Keats. Nor are they imagistic efforts of the "hard" sort admired by Pound in the *Responsibilities* volume, or of the "romantic" sort exfoliated by Kermode and other interpreters. In reading them it is essential to keep attention focused on the speaking voice which so annoys Yvor Winters (who calls it the "bardic tone") and has so delighted admirers of Yeats. "Easter 1916," to which even Winters allows merit although he faults its romantic doctrine, can be admired largely for the suppleness with which the voice weaves itself over the trimeter, always keeping us a bit off balance as syntax and speech-emphasis are played off against the rigidities of meter:

> Hearts with one purpose alone
> Through summer and winter seem
> Enchanted to a stone
> To trouble the living stream.

> The horse that comes from the road
> The rider, the birds that range
> From cloud to tumbling cloud,
> Minute by minute they change. . . .

Efforts to paraphrase this poem's third section, from which these lines are taken, are doomed to failure. By their participation in the Easter uprising, the revolutionaries have been "changed, changed utterly" from the lovely or hateful individuals they were previously. "The stone's in the midst of all," and it may be, as Yeats fears in the poem's final section, that "Too long a sacrifice / Can make a stone of the heart." But as, in the third section, the horse plashes in the stream, the long-legged moor-hens dive, the birds and clouds range and tumble, we find ourselves enchanted by events rendered in a language beyond ordinary discourse. And we wake from this enchantment only to confront the painful questions with which the poem ends, most especially "And what if excess of love / Bewildered them till they died?"

My conviction is that "Easter 1916" and the later "Among School Children" stand at the summit of Yeats's poetry because they manage to combine large vocal "enchantings" with a more unresolved and open questioning, with enlarging explorations of the possibilities in an event: a sixty-year-old man in a schoolroom; a poet celebrating his activist friends and fellow Irishry. Even though "Easter 1916" ends with the writing out of the revolutionaries' names, "MacDonough and MacBride / And Connolly and Pearse" before the refrain announces that a terrible beauty is born, the poem has previously reached such a pitch of disillusioned interrogation—"What if . . ."—that no solutions or resolutions are possible except by fiat of naming, or by the repetition of a song-like motto. Concurrently there is an appropriate subordination of the "I"—"the bardic voice"—into a figure who sees around his words even as he uses them. In dreams begins responsibility: "Easter 1916" turns out to be a muted and impersonal poem whose "responsibility" involves no clear course of action but rather an uneasy and fitful seeing-around of all action.

Yet in expressing admiration for this poem it may be that I am doing little more than revealing once again my reservations about the major Yeatsian mode of heroic self-dramatization. As Harold Bloom says rightly, "Easter 1916" is an "exception" in the Yeatsian canon, "a model of sanity and proportion . . . genuinely Yeats's eighteenth-century poem." And he therefore finds very little to say about it, concerned as he is with tracing the "visionary" Yeats's relationships to Romantic poets. But there are other poems which are also models of sanity and proportion, and a number of them written, perhaps significantly, during the years 1912–22: the years of the Easter uprising; of Yeats's final proposal to Maud Gonne; of his subsequent marriage and settling into the tower; his children's birth; the juxtaposition of his esoteric studies and the Irish Civil War. "An Irish Airman Foresees His Death," "On a Political Prisoner," "The Leaders of the Crowd," many parts of the always challenging "Meditations in Time of Civil War" (particularly I, V, and VI), "1919": the sanity of these poems lies in their skeptical attempt to effect balances between the ego's demands and a public world unresponsive to those demands; their proportion is a matter of crispness, pointed economy of statement, a relatively pure diction largely untainted by occultisms or Irishisms. Neither "crude" nor "extreme in egoism," they are the poems of Yeats which provide the clearest refutation of Eliot's charge.

It is also worth noting that they have been less "explicated" than the usual run of Yeats's work, perhaps because their language is so finely articulated, their syntax so exemplary, their tone firm and strong:

> I know that I shall meet my fate
> Somewhere among the clouds above;
> Those that I fight I do not hate,
> Those that I guard I do not love. . . .
> ("An Irish Airman . . .")

Did she in touching that lone wing
Recall the years before her mind
Became a bitter, an abstract thing,
Her thought some popular enmity:
Blind and leader of the blind
Drinking the foul ditch where they lie?
                    ("On a Political Prisoner")

We are closed in, and the key is turned
On our uncertainty; somewhere
A man is killed, or a house burned,
Yet no clear fact to be discerned. . .

We had fed the heart on fantasies,
The heart's grown brutal from the fare;
More substance in our enmities
Than in our love. . . .
        ("Meditations in Time of Civil War," VI)

It may be too that I admire these poems because they are less or not at all dependent upon Yeats's system, contain less of what Blackmur called the "magic," and are to that degree sanely proportioned. For rather than accepting Yeats's esoterica and assuming that by understanding the formulations of *A Vision* we will be able to read the later poems with success, we should rather cast a cold eye on any language or concepts encountered which are comprehensible only through external reference. To give but one example of such reference: when in the opening poem from *Last Poems*, "The Gyres," the following lines occur in the climactic stanza, where "those that Rocky Face holds dear shall"

From marble of a broken sepulchre,
Or dark betwixt the polecat and the owl,
Or any rich, dark nothing disinter
The workman, noble and saint, and all things run
On that unfashionable gyre again,

we are witnessing not a triumph but a betrayal of the language—even though any good Yeatsian knows how to explicate the passage.

I will be all too brief about the rich and richly criticized achievement of Yeats's later work. The fact is that for all the virtues of the non-system poems, Yeats published his most difficult and dazzling ones while very much committed to that system, to phases of the moon, gyres, "workman, noble and saint." It was *The Tower* (1928) and *The Winding Stair* (1933) that established once and perhaps for all his reputation as a great lyric poet: "Sailing to Byzantium," "The Tower," "Leda and the Swan," "Among School Children," "A Dialogue of Self and Soul," "Byzantium," "Vacillation"—these poems bore a weight of interpretation and commentary in the 1940's and beyond which no other modern poems except *The Waste Land* have had to bear. Much of this commentary was made with an eye to demonstrating the relationship of poem to system, and perhaps because of such commentary we now find it possible to read these poems—or most of them, most of the time—by largely forgetting about the conceptual structure around which they are organized.

But it is not only a matter of familiarity, of achieving the ease with a poem like "Sailing to Byzantium" that comes with repeated readings and from its having been subjected to countless analyses. For compared to "Easter 1916," the Byzantium poems of ten years and more later seem both visionary and single-minded in their purposes. Relatively uninterested in cultivating shade and nuance, they are more at home in extremes and less concerned than some of their predecessors with posing unanswerable questions to themselves. These "visionary" performance poems take imperious or dismissive or brilliantly exploitative attitudes toward experience. They invite the reader to recite, declaim, and gesture his way through lines whose outcome seems somehow made up in advance, rather than being the result of an unfolding dramatic struggle within the poet's mind. It is as if, in fact, the whole thing had been staged—marvelously staged, but staged nonetheless:

> Once out of nature I shall never take
> My bodily form from any natural thing,
> But such a form as Grecian goldsmiths make
> Of hammered gold and gold enamelling
> To keep a drowsy Emperor awake;
> Or set upon a golden bough to sing
> To lords and ladies of Byzantium
> Of what is past, or passing, or to come.

These lines from "Sailing to Byzantium" are a supreme instance of what Yeats practices in many poems: a display rather than an exploration of himself. I say this not to wish that it were otherwise, but to suggest that poems in this style deepen less upon fuller acquaintance through rereading than the more dramatic, "ambiguous" ones which remain open, even uncertain, in their bearing. It is to the latter poems that a reader can bring something of himself; changed, if not utterly, at least not merely theatrically.

The more "open" poems continue to entertain questions even at their end, as in the last stanza from this late one:

> All his happier dreams came true—
> A small old house, wife, daughter, son,
> Grounds where plum and cabbage grew,
> Poets and Wits about him drew;
> *"What then?" sang Plato's ghost. "What then?"*

The self-portrait in "What Then?" is of Yeats's last decade, in which something approaching "perfection of the life" as well as the work seemed within his grasp: the happier dreams of marriage and family; of the radical rootedness of Thoor Ballylee (the Tower, both a physical and a symbolic fact); of the Nobel Prize and his increasing pre-eminence as *the* master poet (Hardy had died in 1928). Yet the "sixty-year-old smiling public man" whom the school children stare at "in momentary wonder" knows that he is really but an old scarecrow; accordingly the poetry of *The Tower* and the poems which followed rose, Yeats himself believed, to heights of bitterness which surprised even him.

In by far the best examination of how language is used in *The Tower* and beyond, John Holloway has carefully noted how far Yeats's style is from the ordinary language of conversation, from the colloquial. Objects are called up by fiat rather; the poems create a new language and a newly made world comprising "not simply the objects which he promulgates, but also and along with them the acts of thought by which these are promulgated and manipulated." This sort of creation occurs early in "Coole Park and Ballylee" (1929), a poem Mr. Holloway does not quote:

> Upon the border of that lake's a wood
> Now all dry sticks under a wintry sun,
> And in a copse of beeches there I stood,
> For Nature's pulled her tragic buskin on
> And all the rant's a mirror of my mood. . . .

Immediately he hears the "sudden thunder" of a swan ascending and exclaims, "Another emblem there!" This calling up as by fiat, making a new language apart from the "ordinary" one, declaring and declaiming in that imperious manner he was so attracted to, is of course no new story for Yeats. There is a wonderful, probably apocryphal anecdote describing his response to someone who pointed out, with reference to one of his early poems, in which "the peahens dance on a smooth lawn," that in fact peahens don't dance. Yeats replied, with what degree of injured merit or sly humor we can't say, "With the poultry yards I have no concern." Highly amusing as this attitude is, it is at least potentially distasteful, particularly when fleshed out with the bitterness and rant ("And all the rant's a mirror of my mood") to which he was prone.

What makes the best poems of late Yeats something more than "bitter" exclamatory ranting is the co-presence of whatever it is in the poet's self that can hear the question sung by Plato's ghost— "What then?" Conscience, the "troubled heart" of "The Tower," the remorseful, retrospective experiencer of what Eliot in "Little Gidding" called "the rending pain of re-enactment"—these qualities humanize the poetry and redeem Yeats, if just barely, from the louder and hollow declarations he also commits. *Not* to triumph too quickly and too imperiously: this is the deepest poetic problem he faced, and to my eyes faced most movingly in "The Tower" and "Among School Children." Both poems have old age as their ostensible subject, but both also confront, as they develop, the "issue" raised by these lines from the penultimate stanza of "Among School Children":

> Both nuns and mothers worship images,
> But those the candles light are not as those
> That animate a mother's reveries,
> But keep a marble or a bronze repose.
> And yet they too break hearts. . . .

After which the "Presences" are invoked who, since they "all heavenly glory symbolize," are therefore "self-born mockers of man's enterprise." These heartbreakers and mockers live in the "where" of the final stanza:

> Labour is blossoming or dancing where
> The body is not bruised to pleasure soul,
> Nor beauty born out of its own despair,
> Nor blear-eyed wisdom out of midnight oil.

And the poem ends with the famous gesture of ecstatic yearning directed at the indivisible "great-rooted" chestnut tree and at the dancer unable to be known or understood in separation from the dance's performance.

In this poem Yeats speaks from *here,* not *there* "where the body is not bruised" and all earthly defects don't apply. He makes no strained affirmations of the rightness of life (as at the end of "Dialogue Between Self and Soul"—"Everything we look upon is blessed") nor arrogantly complacent rejections of it in favor of another world, the "there." He refuses to transcend the "here," as he likewise refuses to do at a superb moment in "The Tower," when in the act of boasting about how he's going to study techniques of transcendence, he does not transcend:

> Now shall I make my soul,
> Compelling it to study
> In a learned school
> Till the wreck of body,
> Slow decay of blood,
> Testy delirium
> Or dull decrepitude,
> Or what worse evil come—
> The death of friends, or death
> Of every brilliant eye
> That made a catch in the breath—
> Seem but the clouds of the sky
> When the horizon fades;
> Or a bird's sleepy cry
> Among the deepening shades.

As the long, beautifully drawn sentence winds itself out, it becomes anything but exultant or complacent in its spurning of the world, and leaves us instead with the sad facts of decay and death in nature. If "The Tower" comes close to rant when invoking Ireland's heroic past ("The people of Burke and of Grattan") or when calling up "young upstanding men" who know how to fish and are thus fit to inherit Yeats's "pride," we see at the end that those outbursts are excessive and momentary gestures at kinds of certainty and clarity he never possessed for very long.

In the course of one of the strongest attacks on Yeats's work, the English critic D. S. Savage scoffed at his famed "development" as really no more than development in a vacuum. Savage found a "central hollowness" at the center of the poet's writing, found that Yeats never developed "wide and deep insights" into life, that his last poems though sometimes possessing "barbaric beauty and splendor" could also, at a moment, descend into loud and vulgar flourishings (as in "Under Ben Bulben") about "the indomitable Irishry." At one point in his essay Savage says—speaking about "The Tower," but it could as well be about many other poems—

that it is "only held together by the poet's rhythmical and rhetorical skill." Savage assumes he has made a telling and damaging point here about Yeats's limitations; but he fails to imagine just how big an "only" that is—like Forster's "Only connect," or Eliot's "There is only the dance." Yeats's rhythmical and rhetorical skill was employed, up until the very end of his life, in the service of saying things no other modern poet would try to get away with saying, as in these lines from "The Municipal Gallery Revisited" where he confronts the portraits of Lady Gregory, John Synge, and other Irish friends and compatriots:

> Heart-smitten with emotion I sink down,
> My heart recovering with covered eyes;
> Wherever I had looked I had looked upon
> My permanent or impermanent images. . . .

Succumbing to a reverent posture, he bends his "medieval knees" and eventually addresses us, asking that we look at these pictures "And say my glory was I had such friends." If it were possible to read this poem with a mixture of respect, affection, and a raised eyebrow at Yeats's presumption on us, on those friends who live now merely—or did they always so live?—as his "images," his glory, then we would be paying fit tribute to this poet of temperament and extravagance. At any rate a mixed response saves us from on the one hand too primly or severely dismissing the bulk of the poems because the man speaking in them is not "good" enough; or, on the other—and perhaps more insidiously because it is so much more common—remaining wholly caught up and mastered by, wholly at the mercy of, the dramatizing heroicizing voice.

When in his preface to the *Oxford Book of Modern Verse* (1936) Yeats came to discuss Pound, he found in him "more deliberate nobility and the means to convey it than in any contemporary poet known to me." Yeats may or may not have forgotten that twenty-two years before, in reviewing *Responsibilities,* Pound had found nobility "the very core of Mr. Yeats's production, a constant element in his writing." Fair enough, and it is these two

noblemen who of all modern poets present us with the most challenges to our moral and human sense of what is fitting, of how far
to go, of what claims it is legitimate or admirable for the self to
make. The final lines from Yeats's very late poem "The Circus
Animals' Desertion" are often quoted as evidence that here, at
last, the poet sees through his own enchantment with dreams and
images, and after a long career of pursuing them now turns in a
radically new direction—inwards, to a more humanly gritty response to the world:

> Those masterful images because complete
> Grew in pure mind, but out of what began?
> A mound of refuse or the sweepings of a street,
> Old kettles, old bottles, and a broken can,
> Old iron, old bones, old rags, that raving slut
> Who keeps the till. Now that my ladder's gone,
> I must lie down where all the ladders start,
> In the foul rag-and-bone-shop of the heart.

But has there ever been a more sensational promise to lie down?
We all have hearts, presumably, but only Yeats can call up a "foul
rag-and-bone shop" of one at the very instant when he claims to
be bidding farewell to "masterful images." It was a fitting way to
end his career of not lying down.

3

E. A. ROBINSON
The Prince of Heartachers

Edwin Arlington Robinson's stock does not stand very high at present and is not likely to rise. His situation is embodied in my own copy of his *Collected Poems* of 1930, an edition published before his death and not containing the final long poems; yet even without them the book runs to 1007 pages. I purchased it in 1963 for two dollars at a secondhand bookstore in Northampton, Massachusetts. The plain dust jacket and the pages are agreeably yellowing; the print—like the old Macmillan *Collected* Hardy—is not the most attractive nor even particularly legible. Inside someone has attached a clipped-out picture of Robinson's cottage at the MacDowell Colony. The someone was probably Mrs. William Millar Cochran to whom, on July 8, 1932, the book was presented by the "Executive Board, Northampton Women's Club." In other words, it is undeniably the sort of book that belongs firmly on one's shelf, on no occasion to be taken down and read. As Robinson himself wrote in an early poem about George Crabbe, "Give him the darkest inch your shelf allows."

Although the long poems which make up over half the volume are often blamed for putting readers off, it is not evident that—

apart from a few anthology standbys, inevitably "Richard Cory" and "Miniver Cheevy"—Robinson's shorter poems now fare much better. And although he has his accorded moment in the American literature survey course (one or perhaps two classes discussing his relationship to naturalism, or his treatment of character), it is of the sort dutifully given to another American writer, to the author of *The Rise of Silas Lapham*. This treatment is of course an unfortunate mistake. Robinson, like William Dean Howells, is a wonderful artist, and as we have hardly begun to appreciate the pleasures of Howells's novels and memoirs, so have we hardly begun to find our way around Robinson's poems. But Robinson was an odder man and artist than Howells, and if it is difficult enough to talk interestingly about how Howells's "middleness" affects his narratives and the kinds of resolutions they do and don't provide, it is even harder to make relevant sense about Robinson's poems. Thus the survey course finds it expedient to consider them as more or less adequate vehicles for big ideas about destiny and mortality, which big ideas, when abstracted from the poems in which supposedly they figure, are pretty tedious fare. Unlike "modernist" work such as Eliot's, Pound's, or Hart Crane's (I use the term simply to designate a dense verbal surface that frequently feels obscure at first reading and beyond) Robinson's poems look to be understandable, their diction plain, their forms—sonnet, quatrain, blank verse—familiar and unthreatening. "I suppose that I have always depended rather more on context than on vocabulary for my poetical effects, and this offense has laid me open to the charge of oversubtlety on the part of the initiated and of dullness on the part of the dull," he wrote to a professor of English in 1917. No wonder most professors proceed directly to inform their restless students, who couldn't care less about Robinson, of what that poet is presumably "saying."

To insist as I am going to that the life and challenge of Robinson's poetry lie in its way of saying, rather than in the truth or relevance or wisdom of the idea communicated (frequently it is difficult to identify what exactly the "idea" amounts to) sounds unadventurous. As with any poet, where else should one look than to the particular sequences of words which somehow constitute a living voice? Yet Robinson's voice is often a consummately dead one, so discussion of the poems is all the more likely to take place with only cursory attention paid to those particular sequences. There is more point to making this insistence about Robinson than about either Yeats or Hardy, his two most significant poetic contemporaries. With Yeats the verbal surface is inevitably so arresting and dramatically aggressive in its behavior (as well as replete with gyres and other strange objects) that one is not likely to ignore the words on the page. And while Hardy's surface is typically less agitated, there is—particularly in the "Poems of 1912–13" and in many other ones early and late—a recognizably human being at the poem's center, brooding, speculating, questioning Nature or the Immanent Will, leaning on a coppice gate at the end of the nineteenth century and wondering what it all means.

Robinson, on the other hand, is invisible, does not in the main write directly out of his personal experience, does not attempt to dramatize the self, as did Yeats and Hardy in their very different ways. In a phrase used about him by a contemporary poet, the late L. E. Sissman, Robinson is "implicit in the inward town," whether Head Tide, Maine, where he was born, or the "Tilbury Town" of many of his poems. Often this means that we are to listen to a story being told about somebody named Vickery or Flammonde or Richard Cory, in which the teller aspires to a more generalized and objective account than any man in particular could hope for. Robinson's "invisibility" also means that the words of his poems take on a fascinating, sometimes a maddening life of their own, with the illusion that they are operating somehow independently of their creator's will; and that whatever they are engaged in, it is not merely or mainly to make responsible, sympathetically acute statements about a world which lies beyond them. "His life was a revel in the felicities of language," said Frost in his felicitous tribute to him. How strange the word "revel" sounds applied to this soberest and gloomiest of the poets—to the "prince of heartachers," as Frost also called him. Yet it is a profoundly right thing to say, and provides the best way in to Robinson's genius.

Of all the modern poets, Robinson was the least various in his activities, and if such were the measure of a poet's life he might be judged the least "interesting"—a man "almost without biography," as J. V. Cunningham has called him. Born in 1869 in Head Tide, Maine, and moved to Gardiner, Maine, the next year, he was the third son of parents who left him unchristened for six months. A first name was eventually found by drawing lots, on the suggestion of a lady from Arlington whose residing place then became Robinson's middle name. His older brothers, Dean and Herman, undertook careers in medicine and business: both succumbed to drugs and alcohol, failed in their careers and died prematurely. Robinson himself claimed that all he could ever do was write poetry. As a high school student he became associated with the "Club," a small group of local poets who met to read aloud from their works; and in 1891 he entered Harvard as a special student—as Robert Frost and Wallace Stevens were to do later in the decade. Some of his poems were published in the *Advocate,* while his letters to his boyhood friend Harry DeForest Smith reveal a course of varied, intelligently conducted reading.

Robinson's father died in 1892 and he returned home to a family in serious financial difficulties. His mother died in 1896, the year in which he had printed at his own expense *The Torrent and the Night Before,* his first volume of poems, followed in the next year by *The Children of the Night,* a revision and expansion of the earlier volume. His older brother Dean died in 1899 in depressing circumstances, after which Robinson settled in New York for the rest of his life. He spent the early years of this century in desperate financial straits, eventually taking a job as time-checker in the construction of New York City's first subway. But in 1905, the son of President Theodore Roosevelt called his father's attention to Robinson's second book of poems, whereupon the President invited him to the White House (he never went) and after further negotiations installed him as a special agent in the New York Customs House at an annual salary of $2000. "I want you to understand," said Roosevelt, "I expect you to think poetry first and your work in the Customs House second." (Roosevelt also wrote a review of Robinson.) The poet lived up to this injunction as his poems continued to appear; few acts of patronage in American letters look in retrospect as well-chosen as this one. Robinson resigned the post in 1909, but two years later spent the first of his summers at the MacDowell Colony in Peterborough, New Hampshire, where through the contributions of friends he was able to spend the remaining summers of his life as a guest.

The Town Down the River (1910) and *The Man Against the Sky* (1916) secured his reputation, which never slipped until after his death. In 1921 his *Collected Poems* won the Pulitzer Prize, the first of the three such awards he was to receive. Robinson had now begun to turn his attention to the writing of long poems (an attempt to write plays had been unsuccessful) and for the last fifteen or so years of his life produced relatively few short lyrics, the springs of inspiration (he said) having dried up. Of these long poems the three Arthurian ones, particularly *Tristram* (1927), were more commercially profitable than anything he had done and he was able to repay most of his debts and remain financially solid until he died in 1935 from an inoperable cancer.

One of the strangest of Robinson's early poems is "The Book of Annandale," a longish affair in two parts, ostensibly presenting the responses of a man (Annandale) and then a woman (Damaris) to the death of their respective spouses. Though Annandale has lived happily with his young wife for a few years, he finds himself after

her funeral rather calm, less interested in mourning her than in
contemplating the book he's been hard at work at for some time.
What is in this book? A hard question to answer, as we see by
inspecting lines like the following:

> It might be the book;
> Perhaps he might find something in the book;
> But no, there could be nothing there at all—
> He knew it word for word; but what it meant—
> He was not sure that he had written it
> For what it meant; and he was not quite sure
> That he had written it;—more likely it
> Was all a paper ghost. . . .

Yet this book is more real than the wife he has just lost.

It is a curious "poetry" Robinson is effecting here—with its
dashes and ellipses and monosyllabic mutterings—that asks to be
known "word for word" rather than "For what it meant."
Readers of "The Book of Annandale" have rightly found the
poem obscure, especially in its second section when Damaris, musing upon her pledge to Argan (her dead husband) not to remarry,
now suffers under that pledge in a style like this:

> And had she known the truth
> Of what she felt that he should ask her that,
> And had she known the love that was to be,
> God knew that she could not have told him then.

Granted this "means" something; yet one barely thinks about
meaning as, one by one, thirty-six monosyllables march by, creating a puzzling, dislocated apprehension of things. Eventually we
find out (though commentators are not in full agreement) that Annandale has written the book for Damaris and that somehow it is
a surrogate for himself. Whether or not Annandale earlier proposed to Damaris and was rejected (because of her vow to Argan)
is not clear. But the poem becomes extremely animated as it
moves to a climactic assertion in which Damaris suddenly understands all:

There were the words that he had made for her,
For her alone. . . .
They were eternal words, and they diffused
A flame of meaning that men's lexicons
Had never kindled; they were choral words
That harmonized with love's enduring chords
Like wisdom with release; triumphant words
That rang like elemental orisons
Through ages out of ages; words that fed
Love's hunger in the spirit; words that smote;
Thrilled words that echoed, and barbed words that clung. . . .

This passage makes Yeats's "For words alone are certain good" sound like an understatement. Clearly Robinson is very moved here, has pulled out all the stops to make us feel the marvel of what has happened. Yet what *has* happened? Yvor Winters, writing about the poem, declared with annoyance that "this is not art, but is rather a technique of systematic exasperation." One sympathizes with him, and it should be emphasized that it is the verse itself which not only exasperates but also teases us with its hint of something ever about to be revealed.

The "words" of which Annandale has composed his book do all sorts of impressive things: diffuse a flame of meaning, are choral and triumphant, ring like orisons and feed love's hunger, smite and thrill and cling. This diction is perilously close to the sort of "uplift" tradition of the Beauties of Poetry which Robinson staked his career on avoiding. An often-quoted letter about his forthcoming first volume (*The Torrent and the Night Before*) says proudly that "When it comes to 'nightingales and roses' I am not 'in it' nor have I the smallest desire to be," and that he chooses instead to sing "of heaven & hell and now and then of natural things . . . of a more prosy connotation than those generally admitted into the domain of metre." Robinson's attempt to say what he was doing is sincere enough, but needs to be qualified and refined, especially as we try to understand the "prosy connotation" of his work in the context of the nineteenth century's last decade. His contemporaries, Hardy and Yeats, and the slightly younger Frost, were each working out their own versions of how to be prosy at the expense of the poetical. Robinson's version is, I am convinced, the most extreme of the four.

Admittedly the Tilbury Town "portrait" poems from *Children of the Night* (1897) eschew the poetical, aspire to flatness and directness of unembroidered statement. Yet the most famous of these—the heavily anthologized "Richard Cory," often used in schools to attract young readers to poetry—wears out its welcome pretty quickly. As Winters commented about its last two lines ("And Richard Cory, one calm summer night, / Went home and put a bullet through his head"), "the poem builds up deliberately to a very cheap surprise ending; but all surprise endings are cheap in poetry." What is really wrong with the surprise ending, in the case of a sensibility like Robinson's, is that it does violence to the tenuous, inconclusive, word-filled atmosphere he is so good at charming us with, as Annandale's book charmed Damaris. And the most interesting poems in his first volumes are those which succeed in charming us by casting a spell:

> Go to the western gate, Luke Havergal,
> There where the vines cling crimson on the wall,
> And in the twilight wait for what will come.
> The leaves will whisper there of her, and some,
> Like flying words, will strike you as they fall;
> But go, and if you listen she will call.
> Go to the western gate, Luke Havergal—
> Luke Havergal.

Winters, whose vigorous attempt to discriminate among Robinson's poems is surely the best we have, thinks this poem a masterpiece, but in his 1922 review of the *Collected Poems* admitted that there was little to say about it, except that the poem's "longing for death" was its strongest emotion. Theodore Roosevelt also admired "Luke Havergal," while confessing that he didn't know why he liked it. But he was charmed enough to offer Robinson a sinecure; and so was Winters, so am I "charmed" into giving increasingly rapt attention to the voice that weaves its sound effects over the poem's four stanzas. One is tempted to behave in the manner of Edith Sitwell and expatiate on vowel sounds, echoing rhymes, and repetitions; most importantly there is the dragging pace of utterance:

> But go, and if you listen she will call.
> Go to the western gate, Luke Havergal—
> Luke Havergal.

What this poetry *means* (is something called "suicide" being recommended, and just where is the western gate located to which Luke should go?) is less determinate and important than its effect as, by phrase and by pause, it achieves itself. Similar remarks could be made about "The House on the Hill," a villanelle with its repeated "They are all gone away" and "There is nothing more to say." My own remembrance is that it filled me with inexpressible sadness until embarrassment set in. And there is "The Pity of the Leaves," a sonnet which begins in this appealingly desolate way:

> Vengeful across the cold November moors,
> Loud with ancestral shame there came the bleak
> Sad wind that shrieked, and answered with a shriek
> Reverberant through lonely corridors.

The old man who hears these reverberations hears "Words out of lips that were no more to speak— / Words of the past that shook the old men's cheek / Like dead, remembered footsteps on old floors."

The griefs which fill these early and attractively desolate poems are nameless, profound, "reverberant through lonely corridors" where one's buried life rises to confront one or where the past shrieks out of ancestral shame. At roughly age thirty-three, the composer of these lyrics was already a thoroughly haunted man, dedicated to celebrating loss in all its shapes and forms, well on his way to becoming the prince of heartachers of Frost's phrase. But to do this memorably Robinson had to avoid at all costs the clearly defined, clearly accounted-for motive; had instead to exploit the possibilities for melancholy, grief, and pain, by using words in ways that always hinted there was something beyond them, something deeper, incapable of being at all adequately rendered by language, by "mere" words.

We don't know in just what tone Robinson claimed that the writing of poems was "the only thing I was any good at": "If I could have done anything else on God's green earth, I never would have written poetry. There was nothing else I could do, and I had to justify my existence." The all-or-nothing remark can be taken straight as a profession of faith; or it can be seen as a complicatedly self-protective and self-mocking way of humorously making a case for the way one is. But there was at least one other thing Robinson could do and which over the years he did a great deal of. Alcohol, preferably neat whiskey taken in tumblers, was a necessity for him at certain periods of his life—at other times he gave it up entirely. In his biographical and personal record of Robinson, Chard Powers Smith reports him as admitting, during a stroll at the MacDowell Colony, that when he was young there was a "devil" in his family, and that he knew it would be the devil poetry, not the devil liquor, which "got" him. Smith's anecdotes of bibulous times with the poet suggest that among the other moderns only Hart Crane exceeded him as a drinker; which is to say that it was a factor in Crane's disintegration, while Robinson was able to control it.

It may be dangerously facile to suggest a connection between Robinson's drinking and his attitude toward words—his overriding commitment to the writing of poetry while life went on someplace else, while other people fell in or out of love. But when in "Mr. Flood's Party" the hero sets down his jug at his feet, "as a mother lays her sleeping child / Down tenderly, fearing it may awake," one feels Robinson's heart to be quite simply on his sleeve. In pouring a drink or putting words together into a line of poetry, one has the illusion of freedom—one is on his own. Crane was to write about the "imaged word" which is "the unbetrayable reply / Whose accent no farewell can know." Robinson's early reverence for and rapt absorption in words used for the sake of nothing more than the satisfying combinations they can make seems to me a similar faith and one that fits appropriately with the kind of drinker I imagine him (on the basis of Smith's account) to have been. Adjusting some lines from *In Memoriam,* words, like liquor, half reveal and half conceal the soul within.

The most sweepingly ambitious attempt to "explain" Robinson's character and see his life and work as all of a piece is found in Chard Smith's biography, which is sometimes maddeningly pompous and naïve, but sometimes revealing of the man he was so enthralled by. Put very simply, Smith argues that the pattern of Robinson's life and poetry was determined by his falling in love with Emma Shepherd, a young Maine woman who in 1888 married Robinson's brother Herman, she having been seduced into the physical, away from the pure love which existed or should have existed between her and young "Win." Smith says, rather melodramatically, that at the moment when Emma became engaged to Herman while Robinson sat alone in his vacation cottage at Boothbay Harbor, "American literature turned a corner." And he goes on to read most of Robinson's poems by plugging them into the hidden drama he feels is really their subject: the relationships among these three lovers.

Smith likes to "explain" poems by using them as illustrations of the secret life he thinks he has discovered Robinson to have led. If this procedure seems morally dubious it is also critically barren, since it can make no useful observations about how, in the particular case, Robinson is an arresting user of words. Yet—and again with Hardy and Yeats in mind—one sees how the personally unrevealing surface of Robinson's poems, in which no "I" displays the wounds we may take to belong to their author, might drive an interpreter to argue that there must be depths, secrets, profundities in which these surface goings-on assume important meanings. To be fair to Smith, he does not attempt to include all Robinson's poems within his explanatory scheme; even so, it is impossible to be at all satisfied with being asked continually to think about entities named Herman, Emma, and "Win," as we read arrangements of words.

My own understanding of Robinson's temperament and character would begin rather by considering his praise of another poet, in one of the letters he wrote home from Harvard to Harry De-Forest Smith:

> Excepting *The Task* I have read little during the past week. I wonder why it is that I like Cowper as I do? Something tells me that he is not, and never will be, one of the really great poets, although in occasional passages he is well nigh unsurpassable. . . . He is popularly and justly, I suppose, called feminine; but human nature has a word to say regarding such matters, and a little sympathy is not likely to be wasted upon this poet. His timidity was a disease, and the making of verse and rabbit-hutches, together with gardening, was his occupation. He was a strange man; and this strangeness, with its almost pathetic sincerity, go to make up the reason for my fondness for his poetry.

Is it not possible to see in this generous and accurate praise of Cowper some knowledge on Robinson's part of the kind of man he himself was turning out to be? As far as I know, he neither gardened nor made rabbit-hutches; but his drinking served as a substitute, and otherwise the description fits. Rather than expressing himself in a "pathetic sincerity," as Cowper did most memorably in the lines from *The Task*—

> I was a stricken deer, that left the herd
> Long since; with many an arrow deep infixt
> My panting side was charged, when I withdrew
> To seek a tranquil death in distant shades

—Robinson spun out parables, sad and humorous stories about losers in life's sweepstakes, and gave us what Frost in his essay referred to as a poetry of "griefs" rather than "grievances."

One of the most gratifying things about his remarkable essay is

Frost's perception of the "inner humor," or (as he calls it) the "fun" of Robinson's creation. On the basis of his first two volumes a reader might have thought Robinson mainly interested in portraying the aspirations and yearnings of lyric souls by embodying them in combinations of words with strong musical effects. Yet the writer of "Richard Cory" is clearly someone who relished ironic incongruities and was more than eager to exploit the discrepancies between what "we" or society or an observer say about X, and the strange secret truth of X's inner life. With the writing of the long poem "Captain Craig" and the publication (in the 1902 volume of that title) of "The Book of Annandale" and the expertly managed "Isaac and Archibald," Robinson revealed himself as capable of ruminative, humorous verse of a leisured and assured touch. "Captain Craig" is so long that its good moments tend to get buried; but "Isaac and Archibald" is exactly the right length. A young boy goes to visit his two old friends who separately warn him about the impending decay and senility of the other. Eventually they decide to drink some cider, and the movement down cellar is rendered in the following way:

> Down we went,
> Out of the fiery sunshine to the gloom,
> Grateful and half sepulchral, where we found
> The barrels, like eight potent sentinels,
> Close ranged along the wall. From one of them
> A bright pine spile stuck out alluringly,
> And on the black flat stone, just under it,
> Glimmered a late-spilled proof that Archibald
> Had spoken from unfeigned experience.

Not exactly "humor" and almost too quiet for "fun," so the term which Frost uses to end his essay must be brought into use. "The play's the thing" says Frost playfully; and this passage from Robinson is alive with the energy of noticings, with the playful thrustings of things on the consciousness, eager to be converted into lively words.

Frost reports that he and Pound laughed over the fourth

"thought" in "Miniver Cheevy" ("Miniver thought, and thought, and thought, / And thought about it") and explains the laugh this way: "Three 'thoughts' would have been 'adequate' as the critical praise-word then was. . . . The fourth made the intolerable touch of poetry. With the fourth, the fun began." This observation makes it possible to look with fresh eyes at the anthology-piece and see what an ingeniously artful piece of work it is:

> Miniver mourned the ripe renown
> That made so many a name so fragrant;
> He mourned Romance, now on the town,
> And Art, a vagrant.

Any reader will have his favorite effects; mine occur in this fourth stanza as "so" is repeated while the lines swing along in their attractive lilt; or the way it is casually, ruefully confessed that "Romance" has gone, alas, "on the town"; or the last line, dutifully five-syllabled as always, with its awkward-to-say "And Art," followed by a pause, then the only word that could rhyme with "fragrant."

Robinson took opportunities to insist on the importance, for due appreciation of his poetry, of the humorous faculty: "I am not suicidal, nor am I a vegetarian. I am not a pessimist or anything of the sort. My optimism and chronic appreciation of a joke, if it be a good one, are what will save me," he wrote in 1895, inviting us to note the use of "chronic" and the deadpan coupling of "suicidal" with "vegetarian." Or many years later: "Whatever merit my work may or may not possess, I fancy that it will always be a waste of time for any reader who has not a fairly well-developed sense of humor—which, as someone has said before, is a very serious thing—to bother with it." Referring to Hardy's poetry he opines that it "fares about as badly with a single reading as that of another spreader of sunshine whom I might drag in," by which the image of Hardy and Robinson as co-spreaders of gloom is nicely created. When some of his early poems were to be used in William Stanley Braithwaite's anthology, Robinson noted that "my uncomfortable abstraction called 'Luke Havergal' is also to be soused in anthological pickle—along with two or three others of the forlornly joyous breed."

Anecdotes about him similarly reveal an excellently wry sense of things. At one point he wrote a letter composing his own epitaph, imagining that fifty years after he died a "small paragraph somewhere" would begin like this: "He expected to die young and should have done so. Owing, however to some slight cosmic error, he was allowed to live beyond the logical time and to write divers books of verse, mostly about corpses and things, and lost illusions . . ."; later the epitaph allows that "He was unpopular during his life, on account of his incurable optimism. . . ." He signed the letter "Torquato Tasso." One of the few things he seems to have done while working at the Customs Office was to write (to the same correspondent) "Madam: in reply to your letter of the second instant I have to say that bananas and skeletons may be imported free of duty. I regret to inform you that there is a duty of ten (10) per centum on baked ant's eggs. Respectfully, E. A. Robinson." From a series of anecdotes in Smith's biography I quote just one, an incident at the MacDowell Colony in which a depressed young poet, having threatened suicide, was discovered in the grass in the center of the circular drive, alive but prostrate and silent, determined evidently to be run over. Surrounded by the concerned occupants of the colony, the poet made no response to their advice and wisdom. Finally Robinson joined them "and for a long time he considered the unhappy form. At last he spoke— 'The ants will get him.' "

These examples all seem to me more or less distinguished for their wit, and are dependent on a way with words, on feats of association, disproportion, grotesque and silly yokings together. Their creative life and impulse, their "play," is the same as the kind we see in "Miniver Cheevy" where the balancing act is performed so adroitly. It will not do to call the poem "light verse" in order to place it in a safe category. It is no more light, and no less serious, than "Luke Havergal"; yet neither poem can be defended long on the grounds that it makes significant statements about life, or bodies forth the interesting thoughts and feelings of a complex man with an expressive inner soul. This brings me to a judgment I hope is shared by others—that though these poems are verbal tours de force of impressive proportions, they neither of them seem quite as serious or central or "relevant" as we ask major poems to be. I want now to consider whether after 1910 Robinson went on to develop into a poet who wrote deeper and more humanly satisfying poems than these two ("Luke Havergal" was written in 1892, "Miniver Cheevy" sometime before its publication in *The Town Down the River,* 1910) and if so, then of what that "more" consists.

The volume on which Robinson's achievement can be judged to have deepened and extended itself is *The Man Against the Sky* (1916). After it he published very few short poems ("they just ceased to come"), and not many readers today are tempted to make an argument that the long poems—whether Arthurian or domestic-psychological—form a solid basis for appreciation. Occasional purple patches, fine lines here and there, but on the whole prolix, fussy, and somehow terribly misguided—the long poems are stone-dead. Winters has a lovely paragraph on Robinson as a "belated and somewhat attenuated example" of a certain sort of New Englander (Winters is viewing this from the Pacific hills) "in which ingenuity has become a form of eccentricity; when you encounter a gentleman of this breed, you cannot avoid feeling that he may at any moment sit down on the rug and begin inventing a watch or a conundrum." This characterization fits the humorous Robinson, but also the contriver of long poems, ingeniously spun out of whole cloth and really about nothing in particular. There is a habit of comparing him with Henry James, and indeed (remembering H. G. Wells's description from *Boon,* as well as other descriptions) it is superficially plausible if one considers late James generally, say the stories in *The Finer Grain*. But there is an important difference: much energy appears to have gone into the techniques of cultivated attenuation and reader-subversion James was intent on practicing. His narrative renditions of appearances and places are done with sweep and boldness, and there is much comedy in the dialogues among characters, for all their murkiness. Robinson's overall "flat" tone, the monotonous narrative presence at the center of his tales, keeps the cap on everything, allowing no voice to break free of it even momentarily; thus the poems drag their slow lengths along and feel extremely wearied.

In arguing that Robinson's reputation as a significant modern poet depends mainly on a group of lyrics and lyrical narratives from *The Man Against the Sky* rather than on the later longer narratives, I should also add that the title poem of the 1916 volume appears to me virtually unreadable, to be admired neither for its ideas nor for its eloquence. Flatulence seems instead the quality characterizing the endless maundering to which the problem we are supposed to care about (Where was the Man Against the Sky going? What does it all mean anyhow?) is subjected:

> Shall we, because Eternity records
> Too vast an answer for the time-born words
> We spell, whereof so many are dead that once
> In our capricious lexicons
> Were so alive and final, hear no more
> The Word itself, the living word . . .
>
> If after all that we have lived and thought,
> All comes to Nought,—
> If there be nothing after Now,
> And we be nothing anyhow,
> And we know that,—why live?

One feels that Groucho Marx is the appropriate person to respond to these questions. At any rate such "eloquence" should have had its neck wrung, the way Robinson was wringing it in shorter poems written at the same time.

My list of the poems for which Robinson should be most remembered and the nature of which needs to be defined more clearly in order to locate his peculiar kind of genius is as follows: "For a Dead Lady," from *The Town Down the River,* and the following ones from *The Man Against the Sky:* "The Gift of God," "Eros Turannos," "The Unforgiven," "Veteran Sirens," "The Poor Relation," and "Hillcrest." After 1916 only one poem, "The Sheaves," seems clearly in their class. This is basically Yvor Winters's list of "great poems, with "The Gift of God" added (which I am certain should be there) and "The Unforgiven" (about which I have more doubts). But Winters was unable or did not attempt to give a satisfactory account of why they were to be taken as great poems; he tells us that in general the writing is "distinguished" and that the moral vision (particularly in "Hillcrest," with its criticism of romantic escape into nature) is disenchanted and gravely sane. On the basis of these poems and a few other selected ones, Winters finds Robinson to be a much finer poet than Frost, insisting that although they bear a superficial resemblance—mostly on the grounds of their shared interest in colloquial speech and New England material—any comparison in terms of "greatness" is pointless, since Frost is so clearly minor and Robinson so clearly not.

The judgment might not be worth dwelling on, had it not been made again by two extremely intelligent critics of Robinson's work. Warner Berthoff, for example, finds Robinson's command of tone more consistently "major" than Frost's; while Irving Howe finds his dramatic poems superior to Frost's in their fullness of experience, tragic awareness, command of the "middle range" of life. These critics emphasize and share a sense of Robinson's "weight," as opposed to surface brilliances or the sudden felicities of which Frost is master; Robinson's pre-eminence is signaled by his larger and deeper authority. I myself find Frost both more interesting and "weightier" than Robinson, but am less concerned with arguing that case than with suggesting that three of Robinson's very best poems—"For a Dead Lady," "Eros Turannos," and "The Gift of God"—are remarkable for something other than weight or fullness of experience or complexity of moral feeling. In each of them I am struck by the simplicity of "content" or subject by contrast with the charming elaborations of form, the attractiveness they show as tuneful fables about all-too-human situations. With each poem one wonders, just briefly, whether there wasn't a trick in it somewhere, whether the narrating presence is really as calm, as wise, as understanding of life as it appears to be over the compass of the poem.

"For a Dead Lady" presents in its first stanza the special Robinson gambit that words, language, are inadequate to express the soul, the essence of a person—are inadequate to take the measure of any human being:

> No more shall quiver down the days
> The flowing wonder of her ways,
> Whereof no language may requite
> The shifting and the many-shaded.

Yet it must be said that the poet isn't interested in trying to express much about what this lady (supposedly "based" on his mother, Mary Robinson) was like. He tells us only that nobody else's eyes will "fringe with night / Their woman-hidden world" the way hers did; that her laugh is now silent; that her forehead and (a curious detail) her "little ears" have gone away; and that her breast has ceased to rise and fall. But the way in which the above-quoted lines work as poetry is themselves to act as a flowing wonder of words, artfully creating the dead lady's specialness by employing striking phrases which somehow seem just right, precisely the way to describe "it," but which also can't be expatiated on and which don't abide our questions about what exactly they mean. Just *how* were her "ways" a "flowing wonder"? Or how did this wonder "quiver," or what were the shifting, many-shaded tones she manifested? One does not pursue these questions, but they might need to be answered if we were to praise Robinson as a poet of moral depth and complexity of human presentation. Instead we are given the splendid third stanza:

> The beauty, shattered by the laws
> That have creation in their keeping,
> No longer trembles at applause,
> Or over children that are sleeping;
> And we who delve in beauty's lore
> Know all that we have known before
> Or what inexorable cause
> Makes Time so vicious in his reaping.

It is extremely satisfying to participate in a confession of our common ignorance when confronted by death the reaper. The perfect positioning of "shattered," "inexorable," and "vicious," the nice shift in the sense of ways in which the lady no longer "trembles," the weary certainty in the repetition of "Know all that we have known before"—above all, the seeming inevitability of the rhymes, the strength and simplicity of the rhythm—it is these basically verbal, rather than moral or psychological, effects which make us respond with grave assent.

The single most acute statement ever made about Robinson's lyrics was Conrad Aiken's in his 1921 review of *Avon's Harvest* as he identified the central characteristic of Robinson's verbal technique. Speaking of the poetry up through 1910, Aiken noted its "technical neatness" and also confessed to suspecting it of speciousness: ". . . what we suspect is that a poet of immense technical dexterity, dexterity of a dry, laconic kind, is altering and directing his theme, even inviting it, to suit his convictions in regard to style." Aiken is tempted to call it "padding" but decides against so harsh a word. At any rate it "took shape at the outset as the employment when rhyme-pattern or stanza dictated, of the 'vague phrase,' the phrase which gave, to the idea conveyed, an odd and somewhat pleasing abstractness." Thus Robinson's fondness for using Latinate words to achieve a "larger and looser comprehensiveness." Aiken goes on to say that in the early volumes this comprehensiveness was "often more apparent than real," that an "engaging magician" was performing his illusions for us. But with *The Man Against the Sky* volume the "vague

phrase" is "no longer specious but genuinely suggestive, and accurately indicative of a background left dim not because the author is only dimly aware of it, but because dimness serves to make
it seem the more gigantic."

Although I would not draw the line so clearly between the pre-
1910 poems where the "vague phrase" is speciously employed and
the immediately post-1910 ones in which it is "genuinely suggestive," Aiken's perception is brilliantly right for purposes of getting
at the life of Robinson's best lyrics. Consider the last stanza-and-
a-half of "The Gift of God," a poem about a mother's unshake-
able belief in her son's high destiny, even though "others"—"we,"
"the town"—know he's a good deal more ordinary than she can
see. Those others would "writhe and hesitate" if asked their opinion of him:

> While she, arranging for his days
> What centuries could not fulfill,
> Transmutes him with her faith and praise,
> And has him shining where she will.

Surely the magic in the word "transmutes" has something to do
with its un-ordinary weight; a baser metal has been turned into
shining gold through the uses of imagination, mother's and poet's:

> She crowns him with her gratefulness
> And says again that life is good;
> And should the gift of God be less
> In him than in her motherhood,
> His fame, though vague, will not be small,
> As upward through her dream he fares,
> Half clouded with a crimson fall
> Of roses thrown on marble stairs.

"Both nuns and mothers worship images"—Yeats's phrase from
"Among School Children" comes to mind. Robinson's way of
making the son's fame both vague and large at once is to use for
his main verb the rather indeterminate "fares," then to produce
the stunning and also mysterious "crimson fall" of those roses and
those marble stairs. Here one can say, in Aiken's phrase, that lan-

guage is being used in genuinely suggestive ways, as long as one doesn't have to specify exactly what those ways are.

There is finally the widely anthologized "Eros Turannos," a poem taken seriously in a way that even admiring readers of Robinson don't quite take "Luke Havergal" or "Miniver Cheevy." The presumption is that it exhibits psychological, even sociological penetration; and it is a poem for those who see Robinson as a deep and sensitive understander of the human heart. Winters called it one of the great short poems in the language, claiming for it "the substance of a short novel or of a tragic drama" and calling the writing (except for the fifth stanza, in which a "we" speaks for the town which is witness to the drama) beyond praise. The two middle stanzas describe the "securing" of the traitorous man by the self-deceiving woman in love with him:

> A sense of ocean and old trees
>   Envelops and allures him;
> Tradition, touching all he sees,
>   Beguiles and reassures him;
> And all her doubts of what he says
> Are dimmed with what she knows of days—
> Till even prejudice delays
>   And fades, and she secures him.
>
> The falling leaf inaugurates
>   The reign of her confusion;
> The pounding wave reverberates
>   The dirge of her illusion;
> And home, where passion lived and died,
> Becomes a place where she can hide,
> While all the town and harbor side
>   Vibrate with her seclusion.

Such handsome language for this "tragic drama," disposing itself in such a rhythmically regular way (the heavy rhymes, the audacity of rhyming "inaugurate" with "reverberate"!), the deft and rare metrical substitution of that final "vibrate"—may serve to conceal rather than more fully express the "human content" presumed to lie behind it. Here and at other moments in the poem, paraphrase feels hardly competent to translate the richness into a correspondingly subtle kind of sense.

As with other Robinson poems there is the feeling that everything has already happened somewhere a long way back, in myth or pre-history where one struggles with the god and accepts the god's triumph:

> Though like waves breaking it may be,
> Or like a changed familiar tree,
> Or like a stairway to the sea
>   Where down the blind are driven.

Robinson is the least "dramatic" of modern poets, if drama means a development in consciousness, a sense that the poem is entertaining choices even as it proceeds to its outcome. Instead the aim of "Eros Turannos" is to make the unknown background seem dim, gigantic, intensely suggestive, an object for us to wonder at, rather than penetrate or understand. It is all as inevitable and unchangeable as the hapless woman's fate in "The Poor Relation":

> With no illusion to assuage
> The lonely changelessness of dying,—
> Unsought, unthought-of, and unheard,
> She sits and watches like a bird,
> Safe in a comfortable cage
> From which there will be no more flying.

Robinson's individuality is not in question, though its nature has not yet been fully defined, nor has it in these pages. But James Dickey's introduction to the Macmillan *Selected Poems* (1965) comes so close to getting it right that it is worthwhile trying to say how he nonetheless gets it a bit wrong. Robinson's "new approach," which Dickey sees as one of modern poetry's most remarkable accomplishments, consists of "making of a refusal to pronounce definitively on his subjects a virtue . . . that allows an unparalleled fullness to his presentations, as well as endowing them with some of the mysteriousness, futility, and proneness to multiple interpretation that incidents and lives possess in the actual world." What this account leaves out, thereby misstating Robinson's specialness, is the willfulness and the cadence of the poems. From Dickey's account one might intuit a thoughtful, cautiously skeptical contemplator of experience, intent on not bending it to suit his own temperamental inclinations. The poems which issued from such an imagination would, on that account, feel more truly open, more (to use the unlovely Leavisian phrase) "exploratory-creative" than I take Robinson's to be—either at their most typical or at their best. At the risk of overstating the case in the other direction, I should call the "speculation upon possibilities" which Dickey finds central to the poems less a real than an apparent phenomenon. Robinson's reticence, his solipsism even, are real enough gestures of uncertainty, of how-can-we-say-for-sure-since-we-all-know-so-little; yet the poems' rhythms show no such uncertainty, no haltingness of mind and impulse—quite the reverse. The music carries us along, as if by magic.

Dickey goes on to call Robinson's poetry the kind of communication that "tells the more the more it is not told." Let us place the line in its context of his wonderful late sonnet "The Sheaves," the note on which to take leave of Robinson:

> Where long the shadows of the wind had rolled,
> Green wheat was yielding to the change assigned;
> And as by some vast magic undivined
> The world was turning slowly into gold.
> Like nothing that was ever bought or sold
> It waited there, the body and the mind;
> And with a mighty meaning of a kind
> That tells the more the more it is not told.

The octet moves along so smoothly and inevitably that one almost neglects to ask, what is being asserted here anyway? So that Robinson can pay tribute to the "vast magic" he invites us to notice, his gestures perform a beautiful hocus-pocus, tell us what "it" is not—not economic tender, not to be divined by human words, telling us "the more" but not telling us more. The mysterious promise of the last two lines is what makes the poem memorable, quotable, seemingly full of rich insight, if only we don't question it too closely.

Where then does the poet turn?

> So in a land where all days are not fair,
> Fair days went on till on another day
> A thousand golden sheaves were lying there,
> Shining and still, but not for long to stay—
> As if a thousand girls with golden hair
> Might rise from where they slept and go away.

The extraordinary thing about these lines—the sestet of the poem—is how really unpredictable they are; one could not possibly have imagined *this* as the outcome of the poem, anymore than one could have predicted the dash after "stay," then the final two lines thrown off "as if" they came by magic, by a sudden inspiration, on a charming whim. Frost alludes, in his introduction to *King Jasper,* to what he calls "the dazzle of all those golden girls" in "The Sheaves," and his language provides the right word for what the sonnet does. It dazzles by the purity of its concern, the pure poeticality of it, as if Robinson had no other motive in writing it than to write a poem. And although I wouldn't deny that "The Sheaves" is a special poem even for Robinson to have written, it shares that purity with his poetry generally: telling the more the more it is not told, folding in upon itself rather than gazing out with love or insight or moral reproof on an "actual world." That "infolding" has been seen as a tragedy, an indication of the poet's warped nature or insufficient growth as a human being; it may have been that, but it was certainly the condition for his very considerable, very strange achievement in poetry.

4

ROBERT FROST
Elevated Play

Robert Frost was born in San Francisco in 1874, son of a journalist who died young of tuberculosis and of a Swedenborgian mother who introduced him to, among others, the poetry of Wordsworth, Emerson, and William Cullen Bryant. A younger sister, Jeanie, was born in Lawrence, Massachusetts, while Isabel Moodie Frost was estranged from her husband; they were reconciled, but when William Frost died in 1885 the mother and children moved east permanently. Frost attended high school in Lawrence, where he graduated as co-valedictorian with the girl he was to marry, Elinor White. He entered Dartmouth College in the fall of 1892 but stayed for less than a semester, returning home to teach school while he tried to persuade Elinor, herself at college, to marry him. In 1894 he sold his first poem, "My Butterfly: An Elegy," which is all that remains in his collected work from the little book of five poems called *Twilight* he had a Lawrence printer make two copies of—for Elinor and himself. When she refused to marry him until after her college graduation, Frost headed south on a strange and desperate journey through Virginia's Dismal Swamp. They were eventually married, both taught school for a

109

time, then Frost entered Harvard as a special student, remaining there just short of two years. His health was uncertain and he rented a house in the country, tried poultry-farming none too brilliantly, then moved to a small farm in Derry, New Hampshire, which his grandfather bought for him and where, over the next nine years, he would write most of the poems that were to make up his first published volumes.

Frost alternated his farming with some years of secondary-school teaching; then in 1912, at age thirty-eight, in the great move which made all the difference to his life, he sold the farm and with his wife and four children set out for London, as if to seek his fortune. The family sailed from Boston to Glasgow, settled near London, and within two months Frost managed to place his first book, *A Boy's Will,* with a small London publisher, David Nutt. He also made the acquaintance of the poet F. S. Flint, who introduced him to Ezra Pound, who in turn reviewed both *A Boy's Will,* and *North of Boston* which followed it. The letters written from England back home to his American friends are particularly rich in Frost's formulation of the "theory" on which he felt his poems were getting written. Among English poets his sympathies were with the Georgian group, and he moved his family from Beaconsfield to Gloucestershire on the special urgings of Lascelles Abercrombie and Wilfrid Gibson, both of whom lived there. The deepest relationship he made, however, was his friendship with Edward Thomas, the two encouraging and sustaining each other's work until Thomas's death in World War I.

That war hastened the Frosts' return to America in 1915. Frost's re-entry was effected with highly successful introductions to the literary worlds of New York and Boston, with the solid support of the publisher Henry Holt, and with assurances from editors like Ellery Sedgewick at the *Atlantic* and anthologists like Braithwaite and Untermeyer that he had their interested backing. A third volume, *Mountain Interval,* published in 1916, revealed no falling-off from earlier standards. He bought a farm in Franconia, New Hampshire, then accepted Alexander Meiklejohn's invitation to become a member of the Amherst College faculty at the beginning of 1917. He stayed at Amherst for three years until, unhappy in the difficult circumstances of Meiklejohn's troubled reign, he resigned and moved to a larger farm in Vermont.

Meanwhile he had begun the practice of "saying" his poems to public gatherings, as if—at least in part—he needed to conquer his early terrors of being asked for such performances. The often exhausting occasions at which he would read, comment on, and reflect largely about his poems, life, and the world in general continued throughout his career. Particularly at colleges and universities he commanded the ears and frequently hearts of generations of students. His own association with the University of Michigan, with Dartmouth, with Harvard, most of all with Amherst, where at the time of his death he was still Simpson Lecturer; his further associations with the Bread Loaf School of English in Vermont; his Pulitzer Prizes and honorary degrees from universities; his term at Harvard in 1936 as Norton Professor of Poetry—these could only be eclipsed by the honor paid him in old age by President John Kennedy, at whose inaugural ceremony Frost read and who sent Frost to pay a call on Krushchev in 1962, an occasion that may have been too much for a man nearly ninety, even Frost, to handle.

As the triumphs piled up in the 1930's and as the poems continued to appear with no decline in quality, Frost's life was marked by a terrible series of family disasters. His first-born child, Elliott, had died of cholera at age four back in 1900; his sister Jeanie, never emotionally strong, was committed to a mental institution in 1920; his youngest and best-loved child, Marjorie, died at twenty-nine a slow and agonizing death from the puerperal fever she contracted after giving birth to her first child. His wife died suddenly in 1938, leaving him desolate; then just when it seemed he had pulled things together once more, his son Carol committed suicide. His daughter Irma lives still, but in a mental hospital. Only Lesley, the eldest daughter, survived her father without suffering the worst of physical and mental extremities; yet it is safe to assume that few of Frost's readers and listeners were aware either then or later of the shocks and bitter griefs he suffered from these events. After Elinor Frost's death, he lived for a time in Boston, then, with the devoted help of Kathleen Morrison, his secretary and companion, he established the routine which he followed with some regularity for the rest of his life: falls and springs at a new home in Cambridge; winter in Florida; summer at his newly purchased farm at Ripton, Vermont. The associations with Bread Loaf School continued (Theodore Morrison was the director), as did the public readings and the longer stays at Amherst and Dartmouth.

The last twenty years of his life show a falling-off in the amount of verse published: *Steeple Bush* (1947) and *In the Clearing* (1962) show also a lessening of some earlier intensities. Flattered by the attention paid to him by both Eisenhower's and Kennedy's administrations, he was willing to sound off on subjects not even his devoted admirers cared to hear him linger over. But the play of wit was unabated. In the late 1950's he made a triumphant and nostalgic return to England, where he received the warm regards of T. S. Eliot, among others. He expended his energies to have Pound released from St. Elizabeth's Hospital; he admired and encouraged younger American poets such as Robert Lowell and Richard Wilbur. His last reading was given to a large audience in Jordan Hall, Boston, in December 1962. The following day he entered the hospital for a prostate operation, suffered a severe heart attack while convalescing, then a series of embolisms, the third of which killed him in January of 1963.

In "The Study of Poetry" Matthew Arnold reminds us that there are various sorts of "estimates" we make of a writer, of which the historic (in which we appreciate a writer—usually for his contribution in the past—even though he may have lost the power to move us today) or the personal (in which we overpraise a writer—

usually a modern or contemporary one—because he speaks to us so strongly at the moment) may substitute for what Arnold calls the "real" estimate: in which we see the object, the poetry, as in it-self it really is. With respect to Frost I confess to worrying that what I hope is a "real" estimate may be a "personal" one rather, in Arnold's sense of the term. Frost was the first of this century's poets whom I read with pleasure and comprehension and respon-sive feeling; while through my association with Amherst College as a student and teacher, I came to know him and benefit from his conversation. Most of his poems are so well anchored in my head that the task of just valuation may be that much more difficult to perform. I shall be occupied here rather more with describing moments in his poetic career and making comparisons with some modern contemporaries than with the attempt to argue my convic-tion of Frost's pre-eminence, even when Yeats, Pound, and Stevens are included in the picture.

Since the appearance of Richard Poirier's definitively critical ac-count, *Robert Frost: The Work of Knowing* (1977), there should no longer be hesitation about taking the work as seriously as we take Eliot's or Pound's. Yet for many intellectuals and serious readers of modern literature there are still obstacles in the way of a full, unembarrassed appreciation of Frost's poetic virtues. The presumed simplicity, the folksy charm, the "New England" sub-ject matter—just as surely as these have drawn to Frost readers who have never heard of *Harmonium* or *The Tower,* have they also repelled or embarrassed more highbrow sensibilities. "The Pasture," "Stopping by Woods . . . ," "Birches," "Mending Wall"—haven't these poems been so much exclaimed over by peo-ple whose poetic taste is dubious or hardly existent, that on those grounds alone Frost is to be distrusted? For a time, after Jarrell's essays in the 1950's and Trilling's birthday tribute in 1960, one heard talk about the "dark Frost," the poet who possessed a vi-sion of evil after all, and was thus to be taken seriously. But such terms are of little interest twenty years later to readers looking for fresh ways of thinking about the poetry.

There persists also, even among some admiring readers of Frost, the doubt that he is either "major" or "modern"; that his lyrics, deftly and charmingly turned as often they are, still fall short of the larger ambitions and risks of a major writer; and that their old-fashioned contentedness with rhyme, syntax, and stanzaic patterns, with a sequential or logical mode of thought, disqualify him for a place in the modern pantheon. There is also the fact that he failed to write or even attempt a long poem—as Pound and Williams, Eliot, Crane, and Stevens succeeded in doing. I would admit that his work can be most comfortably and accurately placed in a literary context which includes Hardy, Yeats, and Robinson, rather than Pound and Eliot (although Poirier makes a very interesting comparison between Frost's and Eliot's early work). Like Frost, the earlier three writers were mainly un-modernist in their practices (even if Yeats employs many modernist trappings) and were at their best as writers of short lyric poems. As for Frost's failure to write a long poem, if (as I would argue) we care about the *Cantos, The Bridge,* and *Paterson* in fragmentary rather than entire ways, then we must regard with less reverence the epic ambition in poets whose virtues, like those of their predecessors, were essentially lyrical.

But appreciation of Frost's achievement is doomed to failure if it does not begin and end with something heard. We need to "look at the language," yes, but only in order to hear a voice; for Frost is no better than the sentence-by-sentence unfolding of the locally special postures he was committed to striking off. He is the most playful of modern poets—in his poems, in his prose utterances, in the wonderful letters he wrote. With him, it seems particularly important to resist being drawn off from the poems into talk about the pastoral myth, or American humor, or post-Romantic, post-Emersonian revisionism. His poems allow you, compel you, to stay with them longer than most. "The play's the thing. Play's the thing," he said in the Robinson preface. But if the play is really the thing, then it will exert more of a pressure against moving off into areas of "content" or substance or meaning than some readers can put up with. "Anyone who has achieved the least form to be sure of it, is lost to the larger excruciations": this is a promising and also a ruthless attitude to take towards the renewal of words.

Three months after the Frosts landed in Glasgow in September of 1912, they were established in their Buckinghamshire bungalow and the nearly thirty-nine-year old poet was writing home to a teaching colleague who had doubted the wisdom of his move to England: "We have had ice (a few times) on the rain barrel if that constitutes winter. And one morning early in December the papers were out with scare heads like this: ENGLAND IN THE GRIP OF FROST. I accept the omen, says I, I accept the omen. Better so than that Frost should be in the grip of England." This single sequence may be enough to indicate that the grip of Frost is a humorously and aggressively verbal one. Take one American farmer-teacher with aspirations to poetry, transplant him to a different land at the midpoint of his life, grant him the anticipation of having a small first book of poems published by a small English publisher— and then listen to the way he talks! The play here is in converting a melodramatic weather report into an omen, also converting any possibly stormy inner weather into a triumphant assertion of possibility, with just enough wryness to make it less than pompous: "I accept the omen, says I, I accept the omen."

Four months later, a few days after *A Boy's Will* was published, he was writing another New England friend, John Bartlett, about how Yeats had told "my dazzling friend Ezra Pound that my book was the best thing that has come out of America for some time" (one wonders how many books of American poetry Yeats kept current with) and how he had spent an evening in Yeats's "dark-curtained candlelit room" talking to him about, among other things, Yeats's play *The Land of Heart's Desire*. Frost assures his correspondent that Yeats ("Yates") "is the big man in poetry here of course." If the big man was in the grip of Frost's first book,

who might not follow? By the fourth of July, 1913, when Frost
wrote home to Bartlett one of his fullest statements about his poetry, there was more than humorous extravagance in the following
confidence: "To be perfectly frank with you I am one of the most
notable craftsmen of my time. That will transpire presently." It
did.

The letter to Bartlett proposed that poetry in English had come
to a dead end—"on the wrong track or at any rate on a short
track"—with the assumption that the music of words "was a matter of harmonised vowels and consonants." Frost cites Tennyson
and Swinburne as the poets who perfected this notion of poetry;
one presumes he had in mind "The Lotos-Eaters" and Ten-
nysonian lines like "The moan of doves in immemorial elms / And
murmurings of innumerable bees"; or a Swinburne poem like
"The Garden of Proserpine." Frost sets himself in principled opposition to this poetry under the following colors: "I alone of English writers have consciously set myself to make music out of
what I call the sound of sense." He goes on to call it "the abstract
vitality of our speech" which we get as if from voices heard from
behind a door that cuts off the words. To be a poet one must
break the sounds of sense "with all their irregularity of accent
across the regular beat of the metre." He concludes the letter by
warning Bartlett, and himself, "Never if you can help it write
down a sentence in which the voice will not know how to posture
specially."

Recall that in the very same year in which Frost made this pronouncement about how he "alone of English writers" had set himself to make music out of the sound of sense, Hardy was composing "At Castle Boterel":

> It filled but a minute. But was there ever
>   A time of such quality, since or before,
> In that hill's story? To one mind never,
>   Though it has been climbed, foot-swift, foot-sore,
>   By thousands more.

Yeats, whether or not Frost counted him as an English writer, had written "Adam's Curse," "No Second Troy," and the poems about to be published in *Responsibilities;* while D. H. Lawrence's first volume, *Love Poems and Others* (1913), contained many examples of the tension between irregular accent and regular meter. This is to say nothing of the sometimes successful efforts of Georgian poets like Gibson or Abercrombie, or the far subtler effects in speech-movement Edward Thomas was about to develop. On the basis of his 1913 comments Frost appears to have been familiar mainly with pre-1900 Yeats and to have read him for something other than his exploitations of the "sound of sense"; instead Frost can be seen admiring a line such as begins Yeats's "Rose of the World" ("Who dreamed that beauty passes like a dream?") for the way it "weeps defiance to the un-ideal"; or he remarks how "The Lake Isle of Innisfree" and other early lyrics "make the sense of beauty ache." And in his comments on Hardy's "My Spirit Will Not Haunt the Mound," whose first stanza shows very much the sound of sense ("My spirit will not haunt the mound / Above my breast, / But travel, memory possessed, to where my tremulous being found / Life largest, best"), Frost simply calls him an "excellent" poet and a great novelist.

I'm not suggesting that Frost consciously ignored what he might have reached out to in the efforts of contemporaries as confirming his own practice. Hardy and Yeats were institutions, or close to it, and the sort of heroic role Frost saw for himself, as working all alone on a new theory of poetry ("notable craftsman" that he was turning himself into), could only have been diminished by claiming institutions as allies. And he was already different enough from Yeats or Hardy, or from the Robinson whom he had by now recognized as *the* American poet to take seriously ("I wish sometime if you know Robison you could put me in the way of knowing him too," he wrote to a Maine book collector in 1913), so that his version of the speaking voice was truly his own. The first stanza of the first poem in *A Boy's Will* entertains the common

late-nineteenth-century notion of escaping through dream from
the real world:

> One of my wishes is that those dark trees,
> So old and firm they scarcely show the breeze,
> Were not, as 'twere, the merest mask of gloom,
> But stretched away unto the edge of doom.

"The Lake Isle of Innisfree" is also such a wish, but Frost speaks
uninsistently, permits us just to overhear an indulged youthful
fantasy, and doesn't make a nobly eloquent complaint out of it.

Pound, reviewing *A Boy's Will,* managed to patronize Frost ("a
little raw . . . a number of infelicities . . . the tang of the New
Hampshire wood") while praising the volume mainly in negative
terms: "He is without sham and without affectation." Actually by
the standards Frost was already setting for himself, and which he
lived up to in some of the work in *A Boy's Will,* these early poems
had their share of archaisms, used a less than direct syntax, and
contained posturings (rather than postures) Frost tried to get
round by providing each poem with an epigraph in which "I" became "the youth"—an exerciser of the boy's will in its long, long
thoughts who is to be regarded with some irony. Still, their charm
is not in any ironies Frost directs at his speaker (and they aren't
very extensive anyway) but in the statement of a mood or a moment when the imagination and "nature" exist together in lovely
cooperation. This octet from "The Vantage Point" is a good
enough example of what he managed to do with the sound of
sense in these early poems:

> If tired of trees I seek again mankind,
>   Well I know where to hie me—in the dawn,
>   To a slope where the cattle keep the lawn.
> There amid lolling juniper reclined,
> Myself unseen, I see in white defined
>   Far off the homes of men, and farther still,
>   The graves of men on an opposing hill,
> Living or dead, whichever are to mind.

The sort of accent that must (and must not) be given to "Well" here marks the "special posture" Frost insisted poets make sure their lines were signifying; as does the artfully placed dash in the second line, and the natural ease of commas in the fifth and the last line. Although this is a poem which toys with the idea that the "I" can do anything, turn whichever way he pleases and contemplate what or whomever he chooses, the tone is mild and unboastful, as if this were just the way things are and as if we were being vouchsafed nothing more than the facts:

> And if by noon I have too much of these,
>   I have but to turn on my arm, and lo,
>   The sun-burned hillside sets my face aglow,
> My breathing shakes the bluet like a breeze,
>   I smell the earth, I smell the bruised plant,
>   I look into the crater of the ant.

"The Vantage Point" plays with the egotistical sublime, but the last six lines—a single sentence to be delivered in one breath—don't make overmuch of the moment. It is enough to find that "The living part of a poem is the intonation entangled somehow in the syntax idiom and meaning of a sentence. It is only there for those who have heard it previously in conversation."

Critics of Frost's work have paid homage to the poet's skills in creating a voice which lives through the idioms and gestures of the sentences it speaks—through the sound of sense. But it is always dangerous, probably always inadequate, to accept a poet's own valuation of himself and allow that valuation—in Frost's case constructed through a number of carefully struck-off letters written in the year *A Boy's Will* was published—wholly to dictate the terms of understanding. There are other important things going on in his poetry, and highly visible in this first volume, which have not been so much noticed but need to be for a more inclusive account of the poems to emerge. If "The Vantage Point" is a good illustration of the sound of sense, other poems in *A Boy's Will* ("Ghost Houses," "My November Guest," "Love and a Question," "Wind and Win-

dow Flower," "In a Vale," and most grandly "The Trial by Existence") are more song-like in their appeal and not fully distinct
from the music of "harmonised vowels and consonants" Frost had
set himself against as it appeared in Swinburne and Tennyson.
Consider the final stanza of the lovely "Reluctance," last poem in
the volume:

> Ah, when to the heart of man
>   Was it ever less than a treason
> To go with the drift of things,
>   To yield with a grace to reason,
> And bow and accept the end
>   Of a love or a season?

And compare with a stanza from "The Garden of Proserpine":

> There go the loves that wither,
>   The old loves with wearier wings;
> And all dead years draw thither,
>   And all disastrous things;
> Dead dreams of days forsaken,
> Blind buds that snows have shaken,
> Wild leaves that winds have taken,
>   Red strays of ruined springs.

In the previous stanza Frost had even struck off a triple rhyme in-
volving "thither," "wither" and "Whither," and though in general
"Reluctance" is less elaborately worked for its sound combinations than Swinburne's poem, the two are not opposed in quality.
Much of the pleasure in A Boy's Will is of this old-fashioned "poetical" sort. Frost's vigorous attempts to present an image of himself as a poet of speech-rhythms shouldn't blind us to other kinds
of pleasures in these poems.

But there is a second, more important and more persistent quality to them which cannot be accounted for by insisting, as Frost
does, that each line must have its special posture, that poet and
reader must both "know how it goes." Here I call upon the
reader's memory of moments in Frost where it feels as if something important is being said at a crucial juncture in the poem;

where there is no particular syntactical or verbal difficulty to un-
snarl, but where the "sense" of the line seems to float large and not
quite defined in front of us; where we shrink from paraphrase
because to do so risks unduly narrowing the associations experienced in our reading. Admittedly such vagueness or indefiniteness
sometimes serves a dramatic function—as in the opening lines
from "Mending Wall," the first poem in his second book, *North
of Boston* (1914): "Something there is that doesn't love a
wall, / That sends the frozen-ground-swell under it." Here the
main accent could be on "Something," or "is" or "doesn't" or
"love" or "wall," or on all of them more or less equally. We wait
to see what will develop in the poem, and thirty-five lines later the
opening line appears again and at the close of a speech which the
narrator imagines himself giving to the old farmer who keeps saying "Good fences make good neighbors":

> "Something there is that doesn't love a wall,
> That wants it down." I could say "Elves" to him,
> But, it's not elves exactly . . .

and here the emphasis has to be on "Something," that which isn't
"elves exactly" but which by now we've gotten closer to the spirit
of.

"In "Mending Wall" the progress, as regards the sentiment in
this repeated line, has been from ambiguity to clarity. The sort of
effect I have in mind is quite different and usually occurs in his
poems after they have been going on for a time. For example in
"Mowing"—the poem in *A Boy's Will* about which Frost himself
said,"I come so near what I long to get that I almost despair of
coming nearer"—the first eight lines present a mower and his
scythe "whispering to the ground." The mower teases himself by
wondering what the scythe is whispering and says that at any rate
it wasn't an idle dream or the "easy gold" of magical revelations:

> Anything more than the truth would have seemed too weak
> To the earnest love that laid the swale in rows,
> Not without feeble-pointed spikes of flowers

(Pale orchises), and scared a bright green snake.
The fact is the sweetest dream that labor knows.
My long scythe whispered and left the hay to make.

The mower speaks through the poem, yet moves more and more outside himself to the point where he can refer to what he's doing as "earnest love" and can delicately place "Pale orchises" within a parenthesis. In another sense there is no "mower" here at all, only the poet arranging words in the artful simulation of sentence sounds in lines of verse. And by the penultimate line we can't at all precisely locate or describe a character from which this even pronouncement about fact, dream, and labor emanates; it is as if something in ourselves had been called forth to participate in a fresh realization of the nature of things.

Frost once wrote his friend Sidney Cox, a professor at Dartmouth, about how there should be more to the classroom than disagreement and debate:

> Clash is all very well for coming lawyers politicians and theologians. But I should think there must be a whole realm or plane above that—all sight and insight, perception, intuition, rapture. . . . Get up there high enough and the differences that make controversy become only the two legs of a body the weight of which is on one in one period, on the other in the next.

He is saying that a good classroom can on occasion be like a poem, at least have a poetic moment or two, not be wholly removed from possibilities for rapture. At such moments nobody would be expressing an "opinion," and disagreement would be no more appropriate or called for than agreement—one would just somehow be there, on a high plane. Such a "being there" occurs in the line from "Mowing" ("The fact is the sweetest dream that labor knows") where for a moment everything is held in contemplative cooperation and the large assertion floats "up there high enough." The reader is elevated too.

Those who knew Frost knew what a master he was at taking you to a high enough plane so that you felt unordinary. My own word for it is "elevated"; and it is perhaps because elevation was such a strong characteristic and consequence of his conversation, his teaching, his poetry, that the less noble figure who appears throughout Lawrance Thompson's biography—manipulative, petty, jealously aggressive in his impulses—should have so shocked and surprised readers who knew a different Frost. But the significant point with regard to his poetry is that no personality, no special posture or tone of voice, can be identified as characterizing these moments of impersonal perception or insight. The liberal speaker of "Mending Wall" is nowhere so colloquially unbuttoned, even cute, as when he tells us how he could teasingly have said "Elves" to his inflexible neighbor. But only a few lines later he gives us a picture of that neighbor quite different in tone and gravity:

> I see him there
> Bringing a stone grasped firmly by the top
> In each hand, like an old-stone savage armed.
> He moves in darkness as it seems to me,
> Not of woods only and the shade of trees.

The effect of these lines is to dignify the man and render him as an object, a myth even, to be contemplated and wondered at, rather than teased or despaired of. The speaker's voice takes on a corresponding largeness of impulse, refusing to be held down to a particularly identifiable tone of address. As in the classroom, the "differences that make controversy," that have been so pungently named by the "Something there is" line and the "Good fences make good neighbors" line, momentarily dissolve; or rather (in Frost's words about teaching) "become only the two legs of a body."

In a revealing letter to Braithwaite just after Frost returned

from England in 1915, he called *A Boy's Will* "an expression of
my life for the ten years from eighteen on when I thought I greatly
preferred stocks and stones to people," and said that he kept farm
"less as a farmer than as a fugitive from the world that seemed to
me to 'disallow' me." With the gift of retrospection he can now
see that "I went away to save myself and fix myself before I
measured my strength against all creation." This heroic version of
his commitment to poetry is immediately followed by the now familiar lecture on the sound of sense, of how we must get away
from "book language" to more varied tones—"We must write
with the ear on the speaking voice. We must imagine the speaking
voice." At this point in the letter Frost turns to his second book,
North of Boston. He has already claimed, somewhat exaggeratedly, that his interest in people was probably at first "no more
than an almost technical interest in their speech" (the "almost"
here is a safety valve) but that about ten years ago in writing "The
Death of the Hired Man" he discovered that he cared about not
only speech-tones but also the people who produced them.

I assume that Frost wants to imagine himself here as both an as-
tute listener to the "technical" sounds of sense and a decent
human being who knows there's more than just sentence sounds
to care about—that there are people whom these sounds don't
wholly express. At any rate it is *North of Boston* which remains
Frost's great book of people; in which the attempt, the necessity to
imagine the speaking voice is inseparable from imagining a life.
The best-known response to the volume is Pound's *Poetry* review,
which said more about what made Frost's work interesting than
did his previous review of *A Boy's Will,* though Pound was still
preoccupied with beating on American editors for not recognizing
a good American poet. One of his best remarks concerns the degree of interest and respect we give to the poet's imagined
speakers, mainly (in *North of Boston*) rural New Englanders in
diminished circumstances. Pound praises Frost for presenting them
"honestly and seriously," for taking "their tragedy as tragedy,

their stubbornness as stubbornness." In a fine sentence he insists that "I know more of farm life than I did before I had read his poems. That means I know more of 'Life.' "

Such a way of speaking would make style not just important, but of complete concern, since it would say that *any* subject matter is as good as another, that it is treatment which makes all lhe difference. Pound backs away from this radically modernist position later in the review when he says that "of course" nobody except "professors" thinks Jane Austen as interesting as Stendhal, and that a book about the dull lives of dull people (*Pride and Prejudice? North of Boston?*) "will never be as interesting as the work of some author who has comprehended many men's manners and seen many grades and conditions of existence" (*The Red and the Black,* doubtless). It depends on how cosmopolitan or internationalist you want to be—and Pound wanted very much to be both—but just as I think Jane Austen quite as "interesting" as Stendhal, so I don't think *North of Boston* or Frost's poems generally suffer when their back-country subject matter is compared with the citified, internationally varied one of *The Waste Land* or *Hugh Selwyn Mauberley.*

But even though Frost insisted that in this book (to which we may also add the dialogues or monologues of country life from his next one, *Mountain Interval*) he was performing in a language absolutely "unliterary," and that he was dropping to a level of diction which even Wordsworth in the *Lyrical Ballads* kept above, there is a trick somewhere in this protestation. No more than we can understand the style of Hemingway's *In Our Time* by claiming that this is the way people really talk, can we simply imagine Frost's voices as emerging from farmers, housekeepers, and deprived or distraught married people. And unlike Hemingway's, these characters talk in blank verse, making even more problematic the notion that the poems are written in a language "absolutely unliterary." Consider, for example, some homely lines spoken by the woman in "A Servant to Servants":

> . . . It seems to me
> I can't express my feelings any more
> Than I can raise my voice or want to lift
> My hand (oh, I can lift it when I have to).
> Did ever you feel so? I hope you never.
> It's got so I don't even know for sure
> Whether I *am* glad, sorry, or anything.

These probably represent about as pure an exploitation of colloquial emphasis and audible changes of pitch and tone, as one
could ask for; but let it be noted that when we talk of "hearing a
woman speak" we are making a metaphor—that there is no
"woman" here, that "she" is not "speaking," that Frost has artfully coaxed these utterances into a page of iambic pentameters.

A truism yet maybe one forgotten when we talk, as did Pound,
about how "real" the characters are. In fact at crucial moments in
many of these monologues and dialogues Frost's use of language,
rather than performing in a manner "absolutely unliterary" or at a
level lower than Wordsworth's, is elevated by a style which has
displeased some critics. At a crucial moment in the marvelous
"Home Burial," when the wife begins to reveal to her puzzled husband the sources of her animus toward him (he had grieved insufficiently over the death of their first child), she is made to sound
very "literary" and unordinary in the speech given her when she
responds to his annoyed cry "A man can't speak of his own child
that's dead" with

> "You can't because you don't know how to speak.
> If you had any feelings, you that dug
> With your own hands—how could you?—his little grave;
> I saw you from that very window there,
> Making the gravel leap and leap in air,
> Leap up, like that, like that, and land so lightly
> And roll back down the mound beside the hole."

Consonance, assonance, and extreme alliteration are unmistakably
to be noticed here, especially when taken in from the page rather
than read aloud; thus some principle other than realistic fidelity to

actual speech has to be invoked in describing the poetry. At such a moment one is more aware of Frost the poet than of "characters" or situation; and the moment is similar to those mentioned earlier in "Mowing" and "Mending Wall"—not describable as being delivered in a specific tone or a particular manner or "special posture." You cannot be merely reproaching someone if you are presumed to say, "Leap up, like that, like that, and land so lightly."

As remarked earlier, critics have objected to these "literary" passages as intrusive or distastefully genteel. Years ago Auden singled out for adverse comment the passage in "The Death of the Hired Man" (it begins with "Part of a moon was falling down the west") in which Frost does some pastoral scene-painting against which the woman's revelation to her husband about old Silas (" 'Warren,' she said, 'he has come home to die' ") takes place. And Poirier, on the lookout for moments when Frost caters to "readers who want their elevation in an easy chair," finds particularly cloying Mary's definition of "home" as "something you somehow haven't to deserve," a line which in its homey memorability has certainly been taken to heart by those prone to uplift in poems. Yet it is worthwhile remembering just how we encounter the line in the poem:

> "Home," he mocked gently.
>
> > "Yes, what else but home?
> It all depends on what you mean by home.
> Of course he's nothing to us, any more
> Than was the hound that came a stranger to us
> Out of the woods, worn out upon the trail."
>
> "Home is the place where, when you have to go there,
> They have to take you in."
>
> > "I should have called it
> Something you somehow haven't to deserve."

It's not just that, as in the other dialogues, both speakers are right, and that when something terrible happens—like the death of old men and young children—nobody is to blame. But there is also Mary's attempt to convince herself, by talking about the worn-out hound, that the hired man is really "nothing to us"; there are cool white spaces separating and etching the two definitions of home; and there are those definitions themselves, so studiedly arranged in the lines as to sound preternaturally natural. It is such a tour de force, so very literary a creation, that (for me at least) the poem is invulnerable to the genteel quality Poirier reproaches it for having. (Frost is not always so invulnerable, especially in some of the narratives from *New Hampshire* written after he resettled in America and was becoming a famous poet.) Pound may have thought he could make us sneer at merely accomplished poetry when in his review he said that Frost's was not "accomplished." But the longer poems in *North of Boston* and *Mountain Interval* are very accomplished indeed, not, to contradict Pound, because of their subject matter ("His stuff sticks in your head—not his words, nor his phrases, nor his cadences, but his subject matter"), but because of how they employ the language.

In somewhat insistently making a point about Frost's style as experienced in his early books, I don't mean to act professorially (professors of English care about language while real human beings care about life) at the expense of the writer's humanness. Almost the last thing he said in a letter written on the eve of his death was that "Metaphor is it and the freshness thereof." It was the freshness of metaphor he cared about in his poetry, his teaching, his friendship and love for others: for the renewal of words meant something more even than that words were to be made new. But, as he also once put it, it is "touch and go with the metaphor," and there is no single one large or good enough to impose on his own work, thereby bringing full explanation to it. Probably the metaphor of "play" is as good a one as any he left us; at least—of the modern poets considered here—Frost seems most naturally to be available for understanding through this term. In the language of the Robinson preface, one accepted the world as a place of griefs, not grievances, understood that "woes flat and final" were man's lot—"And then to play. The play's the thing. Play's the thing. All virtue in 'as if.' . . ." Or as he put it in his last lecture, "On Extravagance," delivered just before he entered the hospital for his final struggle, "poetry is an extravagance about grief."

Our ultimate judgment of how good or even great a poet Frost was will depend on how high we rate "play" or extravagance as the true and worthy end of all poetry, not as a means to something larger or just one more spicy ingredient in a stew of elements. It depends, that is, on how much we value something like this—one of Frost's merest trifles of a poem:

> Here come real stars to fill the upper skies,
> And here on earth come emulating flies,
> That though they never equal stars in size,
> (And they were never really stars at heart)
> Achieve at times a very star-like start.
> Only, of course, they can't sustain the part.

The essential Frost is everywhere present in "Fireflies in the Garden" as a cool, amused, aristocratic, incorrigibly inventive word-user; and it represents in concentrated form what goes on to one or another degree in all of his poems, whether ostensibly humorous or serious.

The play must have been central in his teaching also, or so we gather from these sentences in a letter to Untermeyer written in 1924 about teaching at Amherst:

> The boys had been made uncommonly interesting to themselves by Meiklejohn. They fancied themselves as thinkers. At Amherst you *thought,* while at other colleges you merely *learned.* . . . I found that by thinking they meant stocking up with radical ideas, by learning they meant stocking up with conservative ideas—a harmless distinction, bless their simple hearts. . . . They had picked up the idea somewhere that the

time was past for the teacher to teach the pupil. From now on it was the thing for the pupil to teach himself using, as he saw fit, the teacher as an instrument. The understanding was that my leg was always on the table for anyone to seize me by that thought he could swing me as an instrument to teach himself with. So we had an amusing year. . . . I was determined to have it out with my youngers and betters as to what thinking really was. We reached an agreement that most of what they had regarded as thinking, their own and other peoples, was nothing but voting—taking sides on an issue that had nothing to do with laying down. But not on that account did we despair. We went bravely to work to discover, not only if we couldn't have ideas, but if we hadn't had them, a few of them, at least, without knowing it. . . . So I put them on the operating table and proceeded to take ideas they didn't know they had out of them as a prestidigitator takes rabbits and pigeons you have declared yourself innocent of out of your pockets and trouserlegs and even mouth. Only a few resented being thus shown up and caught with the goods on them.

Frost was spared the educational cant of the sixties in which professors were asked to "learn" from their students, but he would doubtless have been equal to the situation. His letter crackles with the kind of "thinking" he was most interested in: the making of metaphor, comparison, witty reduction (thinking is voting), and the verbal extravagances of clowning, understatement, sarcasm. There is hardly a place to rest in these sentences, a quality that profoundly distinguishes Frost's letters, and often his poems, from those of both Yeats and Hardy. (Robinson has more of it, though in a diffuse, slowed-up way.) If, as I think the case may be, there are readers who find such behavior manic or overprotective or just too much unrelieved self-display, Frost has in a way anticipated them by remarking that "Humor is the most engaging form of cowardice," another juxtaposition worth some considering.

When his daughter Lesley went to Wellesley College in 1917 he wrote her a long letter about how to write a course paper:

. . . I pity you having to write essays where the imagination
has no chance, or next to no chance. . . . One way to go to
work is to read your author once or twice over having an eye
out for anything that occurs to you as you read. . . . There
should be more or less of a jumble in your head or on your
note paper after the first time and even after the second.
Much that you will think of in connection will come to nothing and be wasted. But some of it ought to go together under
one idea. . . . One idea and a few subordinate ideas—its to
have these happen to you as you read and catch them—not
let them escape you in your direct interest in your author.
The sidelong glance is what you depend on. You look at your
author but you keep the tail of your eye on what is happening over and above your author in your own mind and nature.

Most students will merely paraphrase what Hawthorne or Poe or
Emerson said or wrote, being incapable of the "over-and-above
stuff":

They are too directly intent on their reading. They can't get
started looking two ways at once. I think too they are afraid
of the simplicity of many things they think on the side as they
read. They wouldn't have the face to connect it in writing
with the great author they have been reading. . . . The game
is matching your author thought for thought in any of the
many possible ways. Reading then becomes converse—give
and take. It is only conversation in which the reader takes
part addressing himself to anything at all in the author in his
subject matter or form. Just as when we talk together!

This seems to me supremely interesting, and at least as imaginative, as poetical, as the description of teaching at Amherst. Like
the earlier quoted insistence on getting "up there high enough," or
on how poetry must deal with griefs rather than grievances, there
is the effort to free the life of mind and imagination from particular directives which have little of that life in them: write the paper
to pass the course to get the job; "vote" against apartheid or
genocide or the destruction of whales. When in the 1930's and

beyond Frost himself descended to particularities and, reacting to the liberalism he saw around him, especially in the academy, told us what to do with the New Deal or the United Nations or Fidel Castro, he lost his touch and sounded like a nag. The trouble was he hadn't been able to stick to his own advice about staying up there high enough.

The "elevated" Frost I am emphasizing is admittedly not the only one. Other Frosts encountered in the poetry include the homey, folksy speaker met with in relaxed performances where the style of ingratiation is to the fore ("The Gum-Gatherer," "Lodged," "The White-Tailed Hornet"); the anecdotal humorist of the longer fables and narratives; or the more directly identifiable entertainer who capers through the long poem "New Hampshire," or says in "Canis Major," "I'm a poor underdog, / But tonight I will bark / With the great Overdog / That romps through the dark." There is, most familiar to us in recent years, the "dark Frost" pointed to by Jarrell and Trilling and represented by "Acquainted with the Night," "Desert Places," or "Design," poems that have now had perhaps sufficient attention paid them. As compared with these, the presence I have been trying to describe is an elusive one, though quite distinct from that of any other modern poet. It is heard in the lines that form this "inscription for a garden wall":

> Winds blow the open grassy places bleak;
> But where this old wall burns a sunny cheek,
> They eddy over it too toppling weak
> To blow the earth or anything self-clear;
> Moisture and color and odor thicken here.
> The hours of daylight gather atmosphere.

"Atmosphere," the title of this little poem, is what Frost's poems have when they thicken, when they elevate themselves "over-and-above" the excitements of scoring hits against particular attitudes or institutions, when they are close to pure performance—the "performance and prowess and feats of associations" Frost in his *Paris Review* interview identified with poetry. The poem as pure performance cleanses our perceptions and takes us momentarily out of time, as in "Time Out":

> It took that pause to make him realize
> The mountain he was climbing had the slant
> As of a book held up before his eyes
> (And was a text albeit done in plant).
> Dwarf cornel, gold-thread, and maianthemum,
> He followingly fingered as he read,
> The flowers fading on the seed to come;
> But the thing was the slope it gave his head:
> The same for reading as it was for thought,
> So different from the hard and level stare
> Of enemies defied and battles fought.
> It was the obstinately gentle air
> That may be clamored at by cause and sect
> But it will have its moment to reflect.

The mastery comes out in so many ways, in the parenthetical "albeit," in the lovely botanical catalogue of line five, in the quiet delight with which the analogy between climbing and reading or thinking develops, in above all else the elegantly oxymoronic "obstinately gentle" as descriptive of the air "up there." And all to be found in a piece of "minor" Frost.

"Time Out" is from *A Witness Tree* (1942), published after Frost had been through the harrowing sequence of familial disasters mentioned earlier. There is of course no way to illuminate such a poem—and there are many such—by adducing the harsh events of his life in the later 1930's. He wrote the preface to Robinson's last poem in 1935, with its characterization of poetry as play in the face of "immedicable woes, woes flat and final," not long after his daughter Marjorie's sad death in 1934, and with the deaths of his wife and son lying ahead. In a letter to Untermeyer written the year Elinor died, Frost says, "She has been the unspoken half of everything I ever wrote, and both halves of many a thing from My

November Guest down to the last stanzas of Two Tramps in Mud Time." After Carol's suicide, the father's guilt—justified or not—can be imagined. Those years, probably the most turbulent and unsettled of his life, were rivaled by the uncertain ones spent at the Derry farm at the century's beginning; but they surpass them in shock and dislocation.

In the poetry of Hardy and Yeats we are brought up against an unabashed use of, or response to, personal catastrophe. Emma Hardy's death was the catalyst for the "Poems of 1912–13" with their detailed reference to remembered events from courtship and marriage and their passionate evoking of Hardy's suffering. Although Yeats often dressed things up with mythological analogues ("Was there another Troy for her to burn?") it is a commonplace how many poems derive from his unrequited pursuit of Maud Gonne, or how the *Last Poems* get their urgency from the impulses of the "foolish, passionate man" Yeats saw himself as. In both poets the relation between life and work seems relatively direct, at least as regards these converted moments of crisis and pain. It is instructive to compare Frost with them because, although the sequence of ten poems which opens *A Witness Tree* is the most sustained and powerful one in his work, its relation—more accurately, the relation of individual poems—to personal disaster is much more indirect, oblique, and elusive.

Here are the first ten titles from the volume, after the prefatory "Beech" and "Sycamore": "The Silken Tent"; "All Revelation"; "Happiness Makes Up in Height for What It Lacks in Length"; "Come In"; "I Could Give All to Time"; "Carpe Diem"; "The Wind and the Rain"; "The Most of It"; "Never Again Would Birds' Song Be the Same"; and "The Subverted Flower." Some of these were first published in 1938 and 1939, after Elinor Frost died; some, like "The Subverted Flower" and perhaps "The Wind and the Rain," had been around in one form or another for some time. But none of them is clearly "about" the death of his wife or daughter and indeed the best of them—perhaps "All Revelation," "The Most of It," and "Never Again Would Birds' Song Be the Same"—are about ultimate matters like knowing and sex and song and cosmic loneliness, in ways that are "over-and-above" any particular embodiment. For all the talk about Frost's marvelous sense of particularity, the concreteness of his speech and image, there is always something abstract, philosophical, bookish even, about the experience of the poems. This seems to me not a limitation but a mark of his special quality as a poet: "I refuse to match sorrow with anyone else, because just the moment I start the comparison I see that I have nothing yet as terrible as it might be."

Like Yeats, who declared that "Measurement began our might," Frost believed in the orders of syntax, stanza, and rhyme, but he was a more severe critic of what personal material should—or rather should not—go into those measures:

> Everybody knows something has to be kept back for pressure and to anybody puzzled to know what I should suggest that for a beginning it might as well be his friends, wife, children, and self. . . . Poetry is measured in more senses than one: it is measured feet but more important still it is a measured amount of all we could say an we would. We shall be judged finally by the delicacy of our feeling of where to stop short.

Nothing could be less Yeatsian than the last remark; or the first one: "Something has to be kept back for pressure." The presence of this truth that, supposedly, "Everybody knows" makes the whole statement so much more interesting than a mere directive to keep one's lip buttoned about friends and relations, or even one's self—insofar as that self may be sensationally and facilely expressed. In the year *A Witness Tree* was published, Frost sent Untermeyer his last version of a poem he had been tinkering with on and off for years. It begins "To prayer I think I go / I go to prayer" and continues with a dream-vision in which the "I" is abased and eventually finds his place in a "crypt," a "stony pavement in a slime of mould"; then it ends with this plea:

> O, if religion's not to be my fate
> I must be spoken to and told
> Before too late!

It is a very un-Frostian performance, and not at all the better for that; but—or is it because?—it came out of deep, painful, and un-mastered emotions. He told Untermeyer that "I decided to keep the matter private and out of my new book [*A Witness Tree*]. It could easily be made too much of."

There is no elevation in the "prayer" poem; it is all melodra-matic assertion and exclamation, ah woe is me. So it was kept back, but another one—"The Wind and the Rain"—was allowed in. In this latter poem an "I," much like the one who appeared many years before in *A Boy's Will,* feels he is being driven "death-ward" by the wind as it drives the last leaves of autumn. He reflects on what he has been doing:

> I sang of death—but had I known
> The many deaths one must have died
> Before he came to meet his own!
> Oh, should a child be left unwarned
> That any song in which he mourned
> Would be as if he prophesied?

Had he known then what he knows now . . . there is no complet-ing the sentence except with an exclamation. You can't but be melancholy in those early days before experience has fully marked you; nor can you suppress that melancholy in favor of a willed cheerfulness, and yet—

> And yet 'twould seem that what is sung
> In happy sadness by the young
> Fate has no choice but to fulfill.

The "happy-sad blend of the drinking song" was one of Frost's ways of characterizing the accent of true poetry.

But the poem becomes truly strange in its second part as it moves from "wind" to "rain" and the troubled speaker turns into a frenetic showman-rainmaker, inventing a global shower ("I would pick up all ocean less its salt, / And though it were as much as cloud could bear / Would load it on to cloud") while planning to get thoroughly soaked by it. The poem ends curiously:

> 'Tis not enough on roots and in the mouth,
> But give me water heavy on the head
> In all the passion of a broken drouth.
>
> And there is always more than should be said.
>
> As strong is rain without as wine within,
> As magical as sunlight on the skin.

Here Frost seems to flirt with the possibility of a personal revelation of grief, then to draw back from it with that isolated line ("We shall be judged finally by the delicacy of our feeling of where to stop short") into a more fragmentary, dissociated manner than is usual to him. Then he moves into the final six lines:

> I have been one no dwelling could contain
> When there was rain;
> But I must forth at dusk, my time of day,
> To see to the unburdening of skies.
> Rain was the tears adopted by my eyes
> That have none left to stay.

He had said in the Robinson essay that "grievances" should be expressed in prose, "leaving poetry free to go its way in tears," its subject matter "griefs." Yet I think it not excessive to say that this poem reveals the loneliness and profoundly unsettling consequences of being a poet, surrounded by your own verbal brilliancies, with nothing to do but "play" yet once more even as the world crumbles around you. Yvor Winters, who attacked Frost's deficiencies as a thinker, would say that such are the consequences of not laying claim to a coherent philosophy, a rational interpretation of experience; and other critics who have censured Frost for lack of "thought" might agree. If, as Frost did, you define poetry as nothing more or less than performance, there will come a moment, as there does in Yeats's "The Circus Animals' Desertion," when the poet confronts himself as one who has made up everything:

> These masterful images because complete
> Grew in pure mind, but out of what began?

Yeats goes on to claim that now that his stilts, his "ladder," has disappeared, he will have to lie down in the "foul rag-and-bone shop of the heart." Yet in saying that what has he done but to build another ladder?

The ultimate summarizing of a poetic career occurs in what one continues to think of as Frost's last important poem, even though after "Directive" (1947) he had fifteen more years of writing ahead. "Directive" has been much written about, and I wish to consider only its closing lines, in which the speaker-guide, having directed us "back out of all this now too much for us," shows us the imagined or imaginary remnants of a "village culture," the "house that is no more a house" with its children's abandoned "playthings," and a brook "Cold as a spring as yet so near its source / Too lofty and original to rage." He then makes a final offer to us:

> I have kept hidden in the instep arch
> Of an old cedar at the waterside
> A broken drinking goblet like the Grail
> Under a spell so the wrong ones can't find it,
> So can't get saved, as Saint Mark says they mustn't.
> (I stole the goblet from the children's playhouse.)
> Here are your waters and your watering place.
> Drink and be whole again beyond confusion.

At this point one has finished the poem, drunk of the waters even as the invitation was being made. "Here are your waters . . ."—it is the same place as Yeats's "where," "where / The body is not bruised to pleasure soul" or "where all the ladders start"; or as in Eliot's "To arrive where we started / And know the place for the first time." It seems to be the place where salvation is to be achieved.

But Frost's place of salvation is so odd as to make us think twice about what "salvation" means. The guide holds up a goblet, stolen from the children's playhouse; while the traveler-reader has been taken so far out of "this now too much for us" with which the poem began that anything goes. Is there any measure by which we can now distinguish between a solemn act of faith and a wild scheme of making-believe? Wherever we are, we experience it only through the accents of a voice that is priest, magician, rural humorist, child, and spellbinder by turns and ever more indistinguishably. It may well be that, bringing ourselves to the poem, the cast of our temperament will determine what it is we drink and how far "beyond confusion" we get taken. On at least one public occasion Frost invited a listener who had asked him whether he was ever confused to play a game with him called "Confusion." He directed the person to ask him whether he (Frost) was confused; the person did so, whereupon Frost answered "No." He then asked whether the questioner was confused: "Yes," replied the sincere person, and Frost shot back— "You lose."

My own way of seeing and hearing reveals a Frost who, unlike Yeats or Eliot, is never wholly caught up and taken in by his own offer ("I stole the goblet from the children's playhouse"): he lets us know, parenthetically lest we forget, that the broken goblet was only "like" the Grail and lest we think that at last we are in the presence of a metaphor which will never break down. When Eliot projects at the end of "Little Gidding" his "condition of complete simplicity / (Costing not less than everything)," the parenthesis is but a more solemn reinforcement of what is being urged or promised. With ("I stole the goblet from the children's playhouse"), who is to say how it should ideally be said? "I play euchre and he plays Eucharist," Frost once remarked about Eliot; "Poetry transcends itself in the playfulness of the toast," was his own way of putting it throughout his career. At the end of "Directive" one feels at any rate that there is nothing in or out of the world that can reduce Frost to a monotone, that can take the play out of his voice—not even a condition of complete simplicity. That simplicity would cost no less than everything, and would be too much to pay. "Earth's the right place for love; / I don't know where it's likely to go better"—as early as "Birches" Frost showed a healthy inclination to distrust his own elevations, even as he proffered them to us. If we have been rightly instructed by a lifetime of his poems, he trusts us to know how to drink from the waters at the watering-place, and to imagine, *only* to imagine, what it is like to be whole again beyond confusion.

5

EZRA POUND
Persistent Explorer

In 1921, having visited Ezra Pound in Paris, Wyndham Lewis directed the following questions to Agnes Bedford: "Was it you who stimulated Pound to the purchase of a BASSOON? And if so, do you think that is an action justified by the facts of existence, as you understand them?" Very little in Pound's life is justified by the facts of existence as they are ordinarily understood. He lived to the age of eighty-seven, standing with Frost and Hardy as one of the three patriarch poets of modern times. But it was a more loudly eventful life than either Hardy's or Frost's, since nearly everything Pound did or read or said was converted into public record. The books, the essays and reviews, the causes espoused, the thousands of letters, all went into the creation of a character which insisted upon being taken as extraordinary. Perhaps for that very reason there is as yet no fully satisfactory biography of him. The best of them, Noel Stock's, was published in 1970 before Pound died, and while it assiduously and intelligently gathers together the facts, the anecdotes, the innumerable publications, one comes away with a somewhat blurred picture, wondering how to put it all together, wondering whether it can or should be. At

141

seventy-four, with twelve more years to live, he told Donald Hall, interviewing him for the *Paris Review,* "you see—a man—in fragments." Perhaps the biographer should be properly wary, as was Stock, of putting them together into a coherent but simplified "character."

The man who loved Provençal, whom Eliot called "the inventor of Chinese Poetry for our time," was born, appropriately, in Hailey, Idaho, a bona fide frontier town where his father ran the federal Land Office. When Pound was eighteen months old his mother, Isabel Pound, moved him to New York in a trip across the country during the Great Blizzard of 1887, the trip made behind—so Pound liked to tell it—the first rotary snowplow. Eventually they settled in a suburb of Philadelphia, where Pound's father Homer became assistant assayer at the Mint and where Ezra attended a military academy, then Cheltenham Township High School. By the time he was fifteen, Stock tells us, he had decided to be a poet; Pound himself says that his examination of comparative European literature began in 1901 when he was sixteen and had just entered the University of Pennsylvania. He studied there until 1903, making friends with William Carlos Williams, a medical student at the university, who wrote a wonderful letter to his (Williams's) mother describing Pound's character, telling her why nobody liked him ("He is so darned full of conceits and affectations") but defending him as really a fine person. At Hamilton College, where Pound transferred, he studied more languages and wrote some of the poems which were to appear in his first book.

He returned to the University of Pennsylvania to take his master's degree, traveled in Europe, and planned to go on to write a doctoral thesis on Lope de Vega. In 1907 he secured an ill-fated teaching position at Wabash College in Indiana where, so the story goes, he befriended a stranded burlesque dancer and put her up in his apartment; she was then discovered by the landlady, who reported Pound to the authorities. Whether or not this is the way the irresistible tale happened, Pound was dismissed, soon after which he assembled his poems—a collection of forty—and sailed for Europe with, among other things, hopes of getting them published. He did this in Venice at his own expense: *A Lume Spento* (1908), one hundred copies. Later in the year he moved himself to London, landing there with three pounds in his pocket, and promptly began the astonishing series of literary operations which distinguished his next twelve years.

Procuring a lectureship at the Regent Street Polytechnic, Pound delivered the substance of his first work of prose, *The Spirit of Romance* (1910), about the troubadours and other contributors to the "Literature of Southern Europe." Meanwhile, strategically distributed copies of *A Lume Spento* procured the support of the publisher-bookseller Elkin Mathews, who published *Personae,* Pound's first collection printed in England, in 1909. The book was intelligently reviewed by Edward Thomas, himself not yet a poet; and Pound soon after made friends with the two men who were of most significance to his early poetic career—Ford Madox Ford (then Hueffer) and W. B. Yeats. With the particular help of Hueffer (who, Pound said later, once rolled on the floor in agony over the affectations of his third volume), he worked to chasten his style, while promoting the work of young poets in whom he discerned qualities of simplicity and unaffectedness not yet typical of his own work. Here his major finds, though he was not instrumental in their first publication, were Frost and D. H. Lawrence ("detestable person but needs watching," he said of Lawrence). He also reviewed Yeats's *Responsibilities,* Joyce's *Dubliners,* and boomed the early work of Eliot and Lewis. As European editor for Harriet Monroe's *Poetry* magazine, founded in 1912 and operating out of Chicago, he had—along with the many columns he wrote for the *Egoist*—plenty of room to express himself on literature and culture, past and present.

We shall later note some ways in which Pound's style developed and other ways in which it remained the same—from his early volumes through *Cathay* (1915) and its renderings of Chinese poems with the aid of Ernest Fenollosa's notebooks, then to the twin peaks of his achievement outside the *Cantos—Homage to Sextus Propertius* (1917) and *Hugh Selwyn Mauberley* (1920). These were years in which he spent much time with Yeats, acting as a sort of secretary, fencing partner, and stylistic consultant, while conducting vigorous campaigns on behalf of "The Men of 1914"—Joyce, Eliot, and Lewis—and of the sculptor Gaudier-Brzeska. In addition to his literary contributions he wrote art and music criticism pseudonymously for A. R. Orage's magazine *The New Age* and began to develop, under the influence of Major C. H. Douglas, his economic theories of social credit which a decade or so later became obsessional. He married Dorothy Shakespear (daughter of Yeats's friend Olivia Shakespear) in 1914 and lived with her in Kensington for the next five years. In 1920, Pound having prefaced his *Mauberley* by calling it "distinctly a farewell to London," he and his wife moved to Paris, and from thence to Rapallo in northern Italy where they stayed until the disruptions of World War II.

Meanwhile he had begun the *Cantos,* the first three of which (later much revised) appeared in 1917. This was his major venture in poetry throughout the remainder of his life; and of his many activities which contributed to their writing one could mention his work on Confucius, his musical studies (he composed an opera as well as played the bassoon), his general investigations into "Culture"—the main one of which became increasingly the diagnosis of economic depravities and the "money" issue. In the interests of straightening out the American public on this issue and on the true causes of World War II, he undertook the broadcasts over Radio Rome from 1940 to 1944 which later landed him in deep trouble. He was taken prisoner by Italian partisans in 1945, handed over to the U.S. Army, and sent to the Disciplinary Training Center near Pisa, where he was forced to endure a physical confinement which broke his mental and bodily health, though it also provoked (in the *Pisan Cantos*) his noblest poetry. Sent back to the United States to stand trial, he was declared legally insane and confined to St. Elizabeth's Hospital in Washington. For thirteen

years he lived there while working on Confucius and writing further cantos, seeing many visitors and extending his voluminous
correspondence, mostly by way of postcards. Eventually through
the efforts of Archibald MacLeish, Frost, and others, he was released on condition that he return to Italy. He spent most of his
remaining years in the Italian Alps, where he became increasingly
silent and, judging from reported comments, remorseful and uncertain about the value of what he had written. He attended
Eliot's funeral service in 1965; seven years later his own death
came. Whatever one thinks of his politics and, as he himself put it
late in life, his "cheap suburban prejudice" of anti-Semitism, there
is no denying John Reck's description of Pound's life as one "so
full of intellectual adventure, so distinguished for literary achievement—both in his own writings and in discovering and aiding
other writers—and so strange in its denouement, that there is really nothing like it in all modern literature."

No modern poet has received more intelligent critical attention
than Pound. The major examples of this attention are four books
written by two of the best critics of poetry in our time—Hugh
Kenner and Donald Davie; while many serviceable, useful studies
have illuminated various aspects of Pound's work. His biographer,
Noel Stock, has also written with an admirably balanced point of
view about his subject's successes and failures as a poet, particularly in the *Cantos*. This is to say nothing of the reams of explication and elucidation in countless articles, in such journals as *Pai-
deuma* or the *Pound Newsletter,* and in the *Annotated Index to
the Cantos* compiled by Edwards and Vasse.

    For this reason my treatment of Pound, unlike those of Hardy
and Robinson (to a lesser extent Yeats and Frost), will not attempt
to add much in the way of commenting on the best poems or discovering out-of-the-way ones (as is always possible with Hardy)
for admiration. There is agreement about where Pound is to be

seen at his poetic best, and it seems to me just. What I shall do instead is focus on a few aspects of the "Pound problem" as it shows itself in the early poems, in certain critical statements, in *Mauberley,* and in the *Cantos;* then try to form a more inclusive view of that problem. For I maintain there is a problem with Pound that does not exist with any of the poets considered so far: in my conversations with other readers of modern poetry I am aware of a yawning chasm between those for whom Pound stands as a great poet, perhaps—as for Kenner—the looming genius of this century's first half, and those for whom—however much they respect his critical work on behalf of modernism—his own poetry plays almost no part in their sense of what is moving and valuable in modern verse.

Note too that unlike those of other modern poets, Pound's name has been turned into a label to characterize his devoted readers: so-and-so is a Poundian (or sometimes Poundling), we are told. Whereas "Yeatsian" or "Frostian" is used as an adjective to characterize a quality of verse or of style, "Poundian" seems to mean something different. In reading criticism of Pound one notes how a defensive note is often struck by the critic who wishes to express something less than enthusiasm for the poetry but feels nervous about doing so. W. D. Snodgrass, reviewing the late *Thrones* sequence from the *Cantos,* called it "flash-card verse" (that is, like note-cards containing shorter and shorter significant phrases, flashed at us ever more swiftly), in responding to which he feared he would make the wrong answer, disgrace himself, and be held up as a bad example by the "superintendents"— Poundians like Kenner or Peter Russell: "Surely I will be sent to bed early, along and supperless, to sit up hours in the hope of doing better tomorrow." Or looked at from the other end, when George P. Elliott, in an essay critical of Pound, accused Kenner of failing to make clear why the recurrences in the *Cantos* were "structurally valuable," another Poundian, Christine Brooke-Rose, came to the defense with a terse, dismissive footnote—"Fails to make clear to G. P. Elliott."

It would be wrong to make overmuch of these instances of critical intimidation, or the nervous fear—expressing itself in a defensive humor—that one may be chastised for not appreciating or understanding Pound well enough. But there seems to be nothing comparable going on with respect to Yeats or Eliot or Stevens or Frost. One notes also that whereas the sense of Yeats's or Eliot's major poems slowly builds and complicates itself, is fed by a wide series of responses from all sorts of readers, often arguing with or qualifying each other, Pound's work has not undergone comparable enrichment. So much of the writing about his poems has been approving commentary from within the Poundian fold that outsiders like Snodgrass or G. P. Elliott end up shaking their heads and saying, "I just don't see what you see, or see why you think it is so valuable."

But the Pound problem is also my Pound problem. For good or ill, I was introduced to this body of poetry through the eyes of critics, Kenner and Davie especially, rather than through unmediated engagement with the poems themselves. Much more than with the other poets in this book (though to some extent with Eliot also), the critics are in my way; and I confess to moments when reading Kenner on the *Cantos* is a more exhilarating activity than banging my head against the thing itself. There is also the problem of how many languages the critic of Pound must lay claim to. He himself had no doubts about it when in 1913, in "The Serious Artist," he laid down the law that "Every critic should give indication of the sources and limits of his knowledge. The criticism of English poetry by men who knew no language but English, or who knew little but English and school classics, has been a marasmus." (A marasmus is defined as a "wasting of the body.") Surely my own nervousness about Pound's work has some, though not all, of its roots in my knowing no language but English, in any sense of the word "know" that matters. And as Davie says truly if exaggeratedly in his short book on Pound, the *Cantos* are not written in English. There is no comparable difficulty with any other modern English or American poet—by now only the beginning student is likely to be bothered by the presence of other languages in *The Waste Land*. Reading Pound is a different story. In the vignette mentioned above, Snodgrass imagines himself as raising his hand to testify, about a passage from the *Cantos*, "I *can* translate the Greek," but then has to admit failure when the instructor asks him to relate it to the Chinese character also in the passage.

If the "language barrier" is an important source of uneasiness about Pound, a more serious one was pinpointed by Yeats in his preface to the *Oxford Book of Modern Verse* when he said of Pound that "Even where the style is sustained throughout one gets an impression, especially when he is writing in *vers libre,* that he has not got all the wine into the bowl, that he is a brilliant improvisator translating at sight from an unknown Greek masterpiece." A poem of this sort is "The Return," which Yeats both included in the *Oxford Book* and used to conclude his preface to *A Vision*. This much-admired piece was published in *Ripostes* (1912), the volume in which Eliot detected a maturing in Pound's style:

> See, they return; ah, see the tentative
>   Movements, and the slow feet,
>   The trouble in the pace and the uncertain
>   Wavering!
>
> See, they return, one, and by one,
> With fear, as half-awakened;
> As if the snow should hesitate
> And murmur in the wind,
>   and half turn back;
> These were the "Wing'd-with-Awe,"
>   Inviolable.
>
> Gods of the wingéd shoe!
> With them the silver hounds,
>   sniffing the trace of air!
>
> Haie! Haie!
>   These were the swift to harry;

These the keen-scented;
These were the souls of blood.

Slow on the leash,
    pallid the leash-men!

Pound said "The Return" was representative of the kind of poem
he wrote "which is an objective reality and has a complicated kind
of significance," and he compared it to pieces of sculpture by Epstein and Gaudier-Brzeska. We are not to ask what such a poem is
"about," as did the lady looking at the piece of carving. Gaudier's
sculpture *Boy with a Coney,* which Pound names in analogy, will
not be more truly grasped if we think of it as about a boy and a
rabbit. So commentators on "The Return" seem agreed that, for
purposes of guide-book summary, it can be said to be about how
far away we are historically and spiritually from the Greek gods,
from any organic myth. But neither the poem's particular details
nor its rhythm are helpfully elucidated by so saying. While to
claim, as Pound does, that it possesses a "complicated kind of significance" is also to say quite legitimately that he is not about to
unpack and simplify the complication by isolating this or that element for our better understanding.

This leaves the commentator in a rather tricky situation, not un-
common when reading Pound. At about the same time as he composed this poem (rumored to have been accomplished in fifteen
minutes), he cooked up an interview with F. S. Flint which
then—as "A Few Don'ts for Imagists"—appeared in *Poetry* in
March 1913. This now-familiar document announced that Pound,
along with H. D. and Richard Aldington, had agreed on "Direct
treatment of the 'thing' whether subjective or objective"; also had
agreed "to use absolutely no word that does not contribute to the
presentation" and "to compose in the sequence of the musical
phrase, not in sequence of a metronome." Presentation, not description, is what Pound repeatedly insists on, misquoting some
lines from *Hamlet* ("the dawn in russet mantle clad") to illustrate

what he means. "The Return" is as good an exhibit of what the imagist should *do* as anything Pound ever wrote; and if we line up key words from the "manifesto," then juxtapose them with the poem, which he included in his anthology *Des imagistes,* we find a similar difficulty in dealing with each.

Perhaps "difficulty" is the wrong word; the point is that there's not very much to say about either the manifesto or the poem, and almost before one begins one has said too much. First of all, from the manifesto, we are to admire "direct treatment of the 'thing' " (that entity placed in quotation marks), and we understand "direct" to mean no fuss, frills, ornament, not many words, not "indirect," not like Milton or Shelley—it is "presentation" not "description" that counts. As for the poem's rhythm, it must be musical ("in the sequence of the musical phrase") not metronomic. Here Pound baldly simplifies, speaking as if rhythm *must* be one or the other—either a mechanical iambic "swat" or a subtle and various "musical" expressiveness. To go no further than Frost is to see how much more dialectical and satisfactory is the latter's insistence that the speaking voice strike its "tunes of meaning" against the rigidities of meter, against the metronome; while Yeats's practices, in the poems from *Responsibilities* he was writing at this time, are similarly oriented. When Pound says, as he did five years later in reviewing Eliot's first book of poems, "I do not believe that Chopin wrote to a metronome," he is still simplifying the issue, as if every Chopin waltz did not have three beats to each measure against which regularity the rhythm of a melody defines itself. However much he and Eliot were later to deplore the flabbiness which free verse soon fell into, Pound's invocation of the "musical phrase" is really an invitation to such anarchic flabbiness: to every poet his own ear, to every poem— every line—its individual rhythm. One man's musical phrase may be—and turned out to be, as much bad free verse got produced— another man, or woman's, chaos.

The best way to explain terms like "direct treatment," "presentation," and "musical phrase" is to point to a particular poem like

"The Return" and say about its first stanza and the component individual lines—now *that* is what is meant, *that* is a musical phrase: do you hear its rhythm? *That* ("the tentative / Movements, and the slow feet") is "direct treatment of the [objective] 'thing.' " Yet critics or teachers who can find a lot to say about a speech from *Othello* a Donne sonnet, a Pope satire, or a Wordsworth lyric will have difficulty (if my own case is typical) in coming up with much of interest to say about this poem of Pound's. As far back as 1951, Kenner (in *The Poetry of Ezra Pound*) diagnosed the teacher-critic's problem in exactly these terms, by comparing one of the *Cantos* with Hamlet's speech about the "delicate and tender prince," Fortinbras:

> It is obvious how much more the critic can find to say about the example from *Hamlet*. . . . But this order of complexity . . . bears no *necessary* relation to the inherent voltage, to the value of the work in question as a human product. The assumption that what can be taken apart equals what has been put together has accustomed the analyst and his victim the reader to a brilliant but drastically limited range of emotional complexes: abrupt, wry, witty, and so on. . . . Hence by such criteria, Pound's poetry, before *Propertius* and after *Mauberley,* simply isn't there.

This impressive defense is none the less so for its inadvertent flattering of the philistine reader who is against "all this dissection and analysis" and thinks he can appreciate poems "for themselves." Put in the language we have found useful in speaking about Frost or Yeats, there is no specifiable "voice" in "The Return" and nothing to be gained from investigating the "tones" in which things are said. It is an undramatic poem, revealing of no "speaker" with emotions and attitudes toward something, which emotions and attitudes "develop" over the course of the lines. When Kenner comes, in his book, to write about "The Return," he sums it up this way: "It exists primarily in and for itself, a lovely object, a fragment of Greek frieze, the *peripeteia* of impalpable huntsmen too firmly-drawn to be wraiths in a dream, set in

verse delicate, clear, and word by word inevitable." Yet this splendid tribute must draw upon words like "inevitable" and "clear,"
which are as resistant to further development as Pound's own
terms discussed above.

In *The Pound Era* Kenner returns to "The Return" and directs
his remarks about it wholly at its rhythms. And indeed as early as
1917, in "Ezra Pound: His Metric and His Poetry," with its em-
phatic positioning of "Metric," Eliot discussed the "technical accomplishment" of early Pound—up to and including *Ripostes*—as
pre-eminently the thing to call attention to in reading this poet for
the first and later times. My own favorites from Pound's early
(1912 and before) volumes—"Sestina: Altaforte"; "Na Audiart";
"Planh for the Young English King"; "The Spring" ("Cydonian
Spring with her attendant train")—surely ask for such attention,
each of them being an exercise in literary form or rhythm in which
Pound has an "archeological" interest; and as Eliot argued in
another of his essays about Pound, this poet is most original when
he is most archeological. Eliot also claimed that to be able to
penetrate "the life of another age" was to penetrate the life of
one's own; therefore (the argument would run by extension)
Pound is also a valuable analyst and diagnostician of the modern
world, at least as "personal" as those of his contemporaries less
interested in wearing personae, or "masks of the self" as he called
them.

Pound must have wondered, in moments of less than full conviction and self-confidence (presuming he had any such in his earlier career), just what sort of poet he was not only in relation to
what, as Mauberley says, "the Age demanded" but as compared
to other contemporaries he admired—Yeats, Hardy, the young
Eliot. Some of this wondering gets into one of the most interesting
and accomplished of his early poems, "Portrait d'une Femme,"
which may be as much about the poet as about the lady he draws.
Written in blank verse, it has an enjambed continuity of sweep
that makes it unique in Pound's work as well as somewhat of an
embarrassment (it was written in 1912) to those who would

champion only the revolutionary aspects of his rhythm and ver-
sification:

> Your mind and you are our Sargasso Sea,
> London has swept about you this score years
> And bright ships left you this or that in fee:
> Ideas, old gossip, oddments of all things,
> Strange spars of knowledge and dimmed wares of price.

With a mixture of affection and condescension toward the lady,
the voice goes on to portray her as not quite this and not quite
that, as "second always," as "a person of some interest" whom
one visits and from whom one comes away with "strange gain":

> Trophies fished up; some curious suggestion;
> Fact that leads nowhere; and a tale or two,
> Pregnant with mandrakes, or with something else
> That might prove useful and yet never proves. . . .

Very cautiously, elaborately, in the manner of Henry James, the
poem winds its way to a concluding salutation:

> These are your riches, your great store; and yet
> For all this sea-hoard of deciduous things,
> Strange woods half sodden, and new brighter stuff:
> In the slow float of different light and deep,
> No! there is nothing! In the whole and all,
> Nothing that's quite your own.
>   Yet this is you.

More and more the lady turns out to be a perfect Jamesian consciousness, a "Sargasso Sea" on or in whom nothing is lost, and
who, rather than going about expressing her "self"—that self
which in the usual case is filled with opinions, ideas, an inner light
of personal conviction—"pays" rather in stranger, more subtle
ways.

Is it a distortion of the poem to read it as also, perhaps even
centrally, a self-portrait of the Poundian artist who asks to be
treasured for what he has managed to adhere to and bring to art
from the past, rather than for his uniquely interesting personality?

If I am reading back into the poem Eliot's doctrine from "Tradition and the Individual Talent," published seven years after "Portrait d'une Femme," it is certainly the way Eliot saw Pound and accounted for his absence of a personal center, of an individual voice which shows consistency from one poem or one year to the next. That sort of voice we hear very loudly and entertainingly in Pound's letters, though its concerns are almost wholly professional and "shop"—there is no time for confessional revelations about love, life, and other of the deeper, inward things. So Pound, like the lady he portrays, is most personal when most archeological, as Eliot put it. And like the lady, "he" is an elusive presence who, whatever criticisms he may incur as sometimes less than a great archeologist (here one would raise the question of translation versus "imitation," or how "creative" a translation should be), cannot be criticized—as Yeats or Lawrence can—on the basis of a self, projected and dramatized within his poems.

Pound's arguably most brilliant feat of escape from the personality of an Idaho wild man (a "frenzy behind a beard," as Kenner wittily called him) is in the *Cathay* volume of 1915, consisting of poems translated from the Chinese with the use of Ernest Fenollosa's notes. I make no attempt here to tell the fascinating story of how Fenollosa's widow decided that Pound was the man to make contemporary poems out of these ancient ones, nor to assess Pound's success by comparing them with versions by Arthur Waley and other translators. The fact which interests me and which is important for understanding Pound's character as a poet is that of all the poems he wrote the Chinese ones are the most universally admired. Whatever one's reservations about *Mauberley,* or the *Cantos,* or one's possibly less than intense interest in the early poems up through *Ripostes,* it seems generally agreed that "The River Merchant's Wife: A Letter," "Poem by the Bridge

at Ten-Shien," "Lament of the Frontier Guard," as well as other
favorites from *Cathay*, show the poet at his most delicate and
imaginative.

Donald Davie has usefully described what Pound did in these
poems to the traditional English "line": by avoiding enjambment
he also avoided building up "larger units of movement" in the
verse. Rather than striving for these larger conglomerates, Pound
treated the line as the basic unit of composition, and with the line
so isolated he broke it from within into even smaller units, as in
the beginning of "Lament of the Frontier Guard":

> By the North Gate, the wind blows full of sand,
> Lonely from the beginning of time until now!
> Trees fall, the grass goes yellow with autumn.
> I climb the towers and towers
>   to watch out the barbarous land:
> Desolate castle, the sky, the wide desert.
> There is no wall left to this village.
> Bones white with a thousand frosts,
> High heaps, covered with trees and grass;
> Who brought this to pass?

The passage, written by the poet who fulminated against Milton,
is properly simple, declarative, concentrated on naming, on *presenting;* while its purity and lack of any self-exploration on the
speaker's part do not invite correspondingly complicated activities
on the reader's.

This surely has something to do with why "Lament of the Frontier Guard" and the *Cathay* poems generally can safely be admired
in a way more self-exploring, self-dramatizing lyrics cannot. If,
that is, one praises a lyric by Yeats or Frost for the achieved quality of its feeling or dramatic posture, one must be prepared to
have another reader, pointing to the same gesture or tone, call it
posturing rather—whereupon an argument about the poem may
ensue. No such argument is possible about the frontier guard
lament or the other Chinese poems, since the only possible re-

sponse to them is sympathetic (and silent) admiration at the toneless (how would one know what tone to take?) iteration of perceptions:

> You dragged your feet when you went out.
> By the gate now, the moss is grown, the different mosses,
> Too deep to clear them away!
> The leaves fall early this autumn, in wind.
> The paired butterflies are already yellow with August
> Over the grass in the West garden;
> They hurt me. I grow older.

Some lines from the often-anthologized "The River-Merchant's
Wife: A Letter" illustrate the declarative purity of these Chinese
poems. But it may be emphasized that, attractive as they are, nobody runs any risk in admiring them; for how could one possibly
disapprove of such delicate, modest accuracy of statement? "These
things are great art because they are sufficient in themselves,"
Pound said of the sculpture of Epstein and Gaudier at about the
same time. Whatever reservations one may have about the *Cathay*
poems as "great art," they are brilliantly sufficient in themselves—lines, colors, and shapes arranged on a flat surface.

How much weight should be assigned the lines, colors, and
shapes of Pound's early poems, plus the *Cathay* and *Lustra* (1916)
volumes? The last-named seems one of his least essential ones,
containing many squibs and a cultivated "insolence" directed à la
Whitman at the philistines—the "general public":

> Come, my songs, let us speak of perfection—
> We shall get ourselves rather disliked.

There is less fun for the reader in this affected jauntiness than
Pound might have thought. Yet *Lustra* contains the excellent "The
Lake Isle," in which Yeats's "Innisfree" is guyed, and the amusing
"Ancient Music" ("Lhudde sing goddam"), poems in which
Pound reveals his very special talents as a cleverly ill-bred wise
guy, "vurry Amurrikan" (as he once said of Frost) and not above
the ribald. It is fair to say that as high as he mounts in lyric purity,

in the arrangements of lines and colors striven for in the Chinese poems, in "The Return," and occasionally in the *Lustra* volume (especially in "The Coming of War: Actaeon"), just so far does he cultivate a relaxed sinking into very broad "satire" indeed.

These comic and satiric bits, the inverse of lyrical utterances, are like them in that neither genre demands substantial, engaged pondering; each is unambiguous in its significance. Writing in 1933, after he had seen *A Draft of XXX Cantos,* R. P. Blackmur called the unambiguous performances he observed throughout Pound's work "great verse" rather than "great poetry," and went on to say acutely what he found in that work:

> When you look into him, deeply as you can, you will not find any extraordinary revelation of life, nor any bottomless fund of feeling; nor will you find any mode of life already formulated, any collection of established feelings, composed or mastered in new form. The content of his work does not submit to analysis; it is not the kind of content that can be analyzed—because, separated, its components retain no being.

Six years previously, in the "Revolutionary Simpleton" section of *Time and Western Man,* Wyndham Lewis had given, in looser and more amusing terms, a similar account of his friend and admirer:

> Pound is that curious thing, a person without a trace of originality of any sort. It is impossible even to imagine him being any one in particular of all the people he has translated, interpreted, appreciated. . . . By himself he would seem to have neither any convictions nor eyes in his head. There is nothing that he intuits well, certainly never originally. Yet when he can get into the skin of somebody else, of power and renown, he becomes lion or lynx on the spot. This sort of parasitism is with him phenomenal.

This parasitic ability was why Lewis titled his section on Pound "A Man in Love with the Past"—"He has really walked with Sophocles beside the Aegean; he has *seen* the Florence of Cavalcanti." And, Lewis added, this person is an untrustworthy commentator on things present, who never "intuits" originally. Yet

only a few years before Pound had intuited Lewis well enough to
call him one of "the great instigators and great inventors of design," and had coupled *Tarr* and Joyce's *Portrait of the Artist* as
the most significant novels of the century's second decade. As a
critic at least, his intuition of the best new writers was impressive.

Lewis and Blackmur were nevertheless onto something important about Pound, as was Eliot when he asked the famous question "What does Mr. Pound believe?" "It is not the kind of content that can be analyzed"—Blackmur's remark may be extended
from its application to a poem like "The Return" to take in the
larger matter of how in general Pound is resistant to analysis.
Homage to Sextus Propertius, apart from the question of to what
degree it is or is not a translation of the Latin poet, and whether
Pound made "errors" in the rendering or was fully aware of what
he was doing, is a prime example of a poem upon finishing which
the only significant response may be to read it again. Consider a
single passage from the fifth section:

> Yet you ask on what account I write so my love-lyrics
> And whence this soft book comes into my mouth.
> Neither Calliope nor Apollo sung these things into my ear,
>   My genius is no more than a girl.
>
> If she with ivory fingers drive a tune through the lyre,
>   We look at the process.
> How easy the moving fingers; if hair is mussed on her forehead,
> If she goes in a gleam of Cos, in a slither of dyed stuff,
> There is a volume in the matter; if her eyelids sink into sleep,
> There are new jobs for the author;
> And if she plays with me with her shirt off,
>   We shall construct many Iliads.
> And whatever she does or says
>   We shall spin long yarns out of nothing.

This is why Propertius doesn't care to celebrate war or the Em-
peror. And "this" constitutes the substance of the poem, along
with reflections on our human subjection to time and death. When
Blackmur came in "Masks of Ezra Pound" to discuss this poem he

praised it for the "elegance" of its language, by which (he explained) he meant the "craftsmanship" with which Pound employed words. It was, Blackmur went on to decide, a "tough elegance" (recalling Eliot's remark about Marvell), and he preferred the poem to *Mauberley* because Pound was at his best (argued Blackmur) when craftsmanship was enough. As it is enough for minor poets, writers of great verse rather than great poetry.

Propertius, like the Chinese poems, is mainly respected and admired. But *Hugh Selwyn Mauberley* is a different story, since nowhere in Pound's work is divergence of opinion about whether he writes "great poetry" or something else stronger than with respect to this "farewell to London." We have Eliot's testimony that it is a great poem, though Eliot was less than a searching critic where his friend was concerned. We have F. R. Leavis's insistence that it is virtually the only significant poem Pound wrote, and that it is great as a whole, "both tragically serious and solemn," says Leavis in not the most fortunate language. At any rate *Mauberley* is the poem which presumably comes to some sort of terms, unaccommodating as they must be, with London, the "modern stage," and—as we have learned too easily to call it—the commercialization and trivialization of modern culture. More unambiguously and directly than does *The Waste Land, Mauberley* sees nothing in contemporary experience but vulgarity and venality; John Espey's careful study of it finds the poem "always pertinent . . . fused with Pound's personal emotion" and says that it "comments without obliqueness on the contemporary scene."

Yet it seems that this "pertinent" poem is becoming more and more a curiosity to be investigated mainly by teachers of literature "doing" Pound, and probably—as with Robinson—doing him in an American Literature survey course where he is allotted one or two class hours. The "extraordinary subtlety" of the verse, which Leavis insisted on, seems not at all obvious; or rather seems more clever, more a tour de force, than the expression of (as Leavis claimed) "a pressure of experience, a compulsion from deep within." Here, from the introductory *"E. P. Ode Pour L'election de Son Sepulchre"* and from poems II and III, are typical stanzas in which Pound-Mauberley's "criticism" of the modern world is rendered:

> Unaffected by "the march of events,"
> He passed from men's memory in *l'an trentiesme*
> *De son eage;* the case presents
> No adjunct to the Muses' diadem.
>
> . . .
>
> The "age demanded" chiefly a mould in plaster
> Made with no loss of time,
> A prose kinema, not, not assuredly, alabaster
> Or the "sculpture" of rhyme.
>
> . . .
>
> All men, in law, are equals.
> Free of Pisistratus,
> We choose a knave or an eunuch
> To rule over us.

Each of these stanzas gives pleasure, but it is very much the pleasure of observing a neatly turned rhyme or line ending, or reading off the clipped inventory of what "we" in the modern world have settled for. Surely Pound thought it a clever stroke to rhyme "Pisistratus" with "us," and certainly it is. But even at the beginning of the poem, such effects, plus the insistent quotation marks, may result more in surface fireworks which go off with more or less successful bangs than in trenchant criticism of life springing from deep personal pressure.

The fullest-scale attack on *Mauberley* as a great poem or even as an interesting one was made by A. L. French in the service, he said at his essay's conclusion, of a more general re-examination of the claims of modern poetry—primarily Pound, Eliot, Yeats—to greatness. The excesses of Eliot's and Leavis's praise drove French to the opposite extreme, and he was concerned to show how each

section of the poem is unfocused or *simpliste* or crude in its tone—
with the result that his essay is a bit too much like a demolition
job. But there are many good remarks and just queryings of the
poem, one of the best of which is French's refusal to accept
"tragic" as the right way to describe Pound's apprehension of
things:

> The poem continually implies that the situation of the artist
> in modern England is tragic; but nowhere is the sensibility of
> anything approaching a tragic quality. For all its apparent
> subtlety, indeed, Pound's moral sensibility bears a striking re-
> semblance to Voltaire's.

And French goes on to compare the poem to *Candide*.

Only if one comes to *Mauberley* with the expectation that here,
finally, Pound touched new depths of feeling in a "self" which
was there, waiting to be expressed, now no longer a persona but a
person, will one be immensely disappointed and accept French's
criticism as a devastating indictment of the poem. It took something as shattering as confinement in a cage at the detention center
in Pisa to bring a shock to Pound's buoyant and boundless energies sufficient to inspire the corresponding pressure from within
which informs the great moments in the *Pisan Cantos*. In *Mauberley*, unlike his aesthete-poet persona whose poem "Medallion" is
the only thing he leaves behind him (this poem concludes the second half of *Mauberley*), Pound is exhilarated by writing about the
dreadfulness of modern social and intellectual culture—and not in
"tragic" ways. The moral sensibility of a Voltaire may not be as
fine as Dante's or Samuel Johnson's, but neither is it a disgraceful
thing to possess:

> Faun's flesh is not to us,
> Nor the saint's vision.
> We have the press for wafer;
> Franchise for circumcision.

These lines are so pointedly and cleverly turned that no one, including the speaker, is likely to be overcome with grief at what

"we" have lost. And since, sixty years later, we can all plug ef-
fortlessly into any denunciation of the media (though the press
now gets higher grades than television) or can be cynical about the
virtues of the "franchise," these lines come across as purely verbal
exercises in wit with a context that is of historical interest only.

I am saying that *Mauberley* as a serious, even tragic, poem
about the terrible state of modern culture, the substitution of en-
tertainment or anodynes for Art, is not available to us—whatever
was the case for Leavis or other readers half a century ago. What
remains strongest in the poem, aside from its Voltairean satiric
parts in which simple oppositions are played off against each
other in an agile, sardonic, and uncomplex manner, are the denun-
ciatory passages directed at the Great War as a useless sacrifice of
life and the relaxed portraits of various figures from the nineties
and from contemporary London. In these parts of the poem
Pound's attitude is admirably complex or terribly muddled, depending on one's degree of tolerance for unresolvedness in poetry.

The invective against war (poems IV and V) is the sort of thing
which asks to be declaimed when one is alone, in the highly "bitter" manner that Pound manages in his Caedmon recording of
parts of the poem:

> Died some, pro patria,
>
>   non "dulce" non "et decor" . . .
> walked eye-deep in hell
> believing in old men's lies, then unbelieving
> came home, home to a lie,
> home to many deceits,
> home to old lies and new infamy;
> usury age-old and age-thick
> and liars in public places.

In the next poem we are asked to see this sacrifice as made "For a
botched civilization," also "For two gross of broken statues, / For
a few thousand battered books." The rant against liars and usury
is exciting but perhaps also rant; and as one declaims it the feeling

grows that perhaps the "serious" diagnostics, the truth to be stated, is slightly at odds with the rhetorical kick one gets out of performing it. A. L. French makes the good point that it's really not clear whether the sacrifice in young men's lives was worthless because civilization is "botched" and usury prevails (as the *Cantos* would demonstrate at length), or whether that sacrifice, insofar as it went to preserve Art—statues and books—was still a heroic one. I myself am more ready than French is to welcome Pound's possibily uncertain state of mind here, since his major limitation as critic and poet is his penchant for too clear-cut, oversimplified distinctions.

The most assuredly successful parts of *Mauberley* are more disinterestedly comic in their impulse; in them Pound becomes an elegantly sophisticated presenter, without comment or animus, of social manners—*"Moeurs Contemporaines,"* as he titled a series of poems about Mr. Hecatomb Styrax and other worthies. Consider the stanza from the section of *Mauberley* titled *"Siena Mi Fe; Disfecemi Maremma"* where a "Mr. Verog" describes the death of Lionel Johnson "By falling from a high stool in a pub":

> But showed no trace of alcohol
> At the autopsy, privately performed—
> Tissue preserved—the pure mind
> Arose toward Newman as the whiskey warmed.

A. L. French finds the passage just "flippant," but that word is inadequate to describe the lovely way this ideal fate is imagined for Lionel Johnson, a devout Catholic who was found never to have developed sexually. It is really much funnier, more genial, and done with more brio than anything in Eliot's quatrain poems, written at about the same time. But whether it contributes anything to a feeling for *Mauberley* as a unified poem with a large point about the modern world is problematic indeed. As is the significance of poem X, presumably written with Ford Madox Ford in mind:

Beneath the sagging roof
The stylist has taken shelter,
Unpaid, uncelebrated,
At last from the world's welter

Nature receives him;
With a placid and uneducated mistress
He exercises his talents
And the soil meets his distress.

The haven from sophistications and contentions
Leaks through its thatch;
He offers succulent cooking;
The door has a creaking latch.

Pound has never written better, and never with less of a chip on his shoulder. The "stylist's" rural paradise is neither sentimentalized nor deprecated; it *is* a haven, and the roof leaks, and the food is marvelous, and the door creaks. Put these facts together and you get nothing more than a nicely various image of life—an ideogram if you will.

Whatever one's opinion of *Mauberley* it is surely Pound's most solidly realist piece of work, his attempt to "condense the James novel" perhaps to be compared to Joyce's *Portrait* and Lewis's *Tarr*. With that work he broke the mold and never did anything like it again. Ronald Bush's recent book on the genesis of the *Cantos* most usefully and carefully studies the literary interactions between Pound and Eliot in the closing years of the century's second decade, and their responses to Joyce's *Ulysses* as it emerged section by section in the *Little Review*. Bush says that "To a contemporary observer, the work in progress of Pound, Joyce, and Eliot as it emerged from 1919 to 1922 must have seemed part of a contest whose prize was to be awarded for the work of the greatest impenetrability." How do the works from those years by those three modernists look to the latter-day observer?

An answer to the question might be that it depends how much of a Poundian that observer is, for no work has been more explicated and revered by some readers nor has frustrated, bored or annoyed others more than the *Cantos*. It is important to distinguish the poem from *Ulysses* and *The Waste Land:* Joyce's novel has been explicated and revered, but it is also read often intelligently and with pleasure by large numbers of literary people. Eliot's poem probably touches a smaller audience, as tends to be the case with poetry, but—and here my own experience is relevant—students are invariably fascinated by the puzzle element, the sheer rhetorical brilliance of *The Waste Land;* it is also short enough to reread and thus become accustomed to. The *Cantos* on the other hand tend to attract young readers who think of themselves as fiercely literary, or as poets, or as at odds with the order of things, or who are looking for a master or an exclusive club to join. Their interest often seems to come from sources other than a "pure" response to the poetry itself.

Of course the *Cantos* should not be held suspect because of some of the readers they attract—in fact they could use more readers. Almost thirty years ago Kenner laid down the challenge, asking why Eliot and Joyce were so much more read than Pound by students of modern literature. The situation still prevails: aside from a few tags like the Homeric opening, the forty-fifth "usura" canto, the "Pull down thy vanity" section from #81 in the *Pisan* section, the poem for many is largely an unvisited mausoleum whose contents are forbidding and unfamiliar. And one has to admit that there are good reasons why after all these years they should have remained unvisited, or why so many readers should have been turned away by the sensibility, by the *person* of Ezra Pound, who is visible, certainly audible, under all the ideograms, juxtapositions of "luminous details," namings and summonings of the sacred places and people (as well as the obscene ones) in this long poem. It was in the *Cantos* that he answered fully Eliot's question about what Mr. Pound believed, and thereby left himself open to the following charge by Sir Maurice Bowra, whose opinions about modern poetry are not generally of significance: "The unceasing rattle, the chaotic flow, the pointless gossip, the feeble generalizations, the 'knowing' air, the inside information, the culture . . . Pound, after all the fuss and trouble, is nothing but a bore and an American bore."

Aside from the Oxonian bluster of this charge, it is objectionable and irresponsible in that it takes no account of the fine parts of the poem which have been accurately identified and admired by a score of critics and reviewers. Yet it does force us to recall the tedium of so many other moments. Even Kenner, whose defense of the poem is often more entertaining and enlivening than what he's defending, cannot convince us to take as interesting and significant what hardly feels so as we read. Here the testimony of other scholars and critics of Pound must weigh heavily: so one is relieved to hear Davie supporting one's sense of Cantos 53 to 61, the "Chinese" Cantos, by saying that "There is no alternative to writing off [this] whole section of Pound's poem as pathological and sterile." And one finds especially valuable Noel Stock's procedure of moving through the poem with us and asking about its worth here or there as *poetry*, rather than as a record of Pound's "ideas" or a juxtaposed interpenetration of "themes" or "recurrences."

It has been a critical habit to talk about certain works of modern writing as "heroic failures," especially long poems like Crane's *The Bridge,* Williams's *Paterson,* above all Pound's *Cantos.* Always impatient with such ways of talking, I find myself wanting to ask—"if this is *failure,* what could success possibly be?" I take it that as regards Pound, the answer is that "success" would be to write the poem Hugh Kenner so vividly delineates in two books on the poet. This would be a poem which possessed total relevance, each of whose parts existed in dynamic relationship to all the other parts; a poem in which Pound had brilliantly applied the disciplines of nineteenth-century French prose writers Stendhal and Flaubert, as sifted through the practices of Conrad and Ford Madox Ford: thus we would read the *Cantos* by attending to time-shifts and juxtaposed historical periods, legends, stories, and heroes. It would further be a poem whose center of ideas is unwobblingly Confucian, its dramatis personae to be understood as "artists, warriors, statesmen, sages, . . . engaged in parallel activities, faring forward, making successive statements with reference to details set in order," and in which Pound and the reader discover "verbal equivalents for the 'inarticulate heart's tone' of successive phases of civilizations." Finally, a poem in which it seems inevitable and right to think of Pound as Odysseus, the hero of a modern "plotless" epic; in which from the earlier cantos surveying Hell and Purgatory, we emerge in the *Pisan* sequence and the ones beyond to a vision of Paradise.

With the help of Kenner and other critics of Pound's long poem, I have attempted to read the *Cantos* in this "total" way—and failed. What seems a magnificent feat of imaginative concentration and energy as one reads about it in Kenner seems something else again when I take up the actual poem. Though I can juxtapose passages from different parts of the poem, bringing them before my eyes and mind in exciting and compelling ways, as I read along canto by canto, trying to make the appropriate correspondences, I am at least as often defeated as successful. This defeat may reveal nothing more than that I am simply unresourceful, or unwilling to do the requisite "homework" so as to bring the poem into vivid life. Yet that homework has largely been done, Pound's poem as explicated as anyone could desire, and still it remains frequently unavailable and unconvincing—all allusions identified as they may be.

Conflicting advice has been provided on how best to read the *Cantos* and on what pace is likely to enhance one's experience of the poem. Davie suggested recently that the best way to proceed was to read them fast, swatches at a time, with attention to their rhythms—we should be alert to the passages which sound most distinctive and attractive. By contrast Kenner has emphasized how slowly one must go if coherence is to be achieved; how the separate blocks must be perceived in their intricate relationships with the other blocks, and how this means taking time over intuiting their individual natures. Both pieces of advice are admirable, if not easily reconcilable. But I should like to offer advice of my own, not so much on how to read the *Cantos* as how to read Pound generally—though with special reference to the work on which he spent half a century.

My conviction, I believe a shared one, is that we are dealing with a man who throughout his life had a penchant for making strong, incisive distinctions, like a sculptor impressing on his material the form of a mind; a poet who—because he believed that poetry should "present" things, and whose virtuous terms were "simplicity," "juxtaposed images," "hardness," "clarity of definition," the *mot juste*—needed to condemn Milton ("the worst sort of poison") and Virgil before him, found Wordsworth mainly "a dull sheep," took Shelley's "The Sensitive Plant" to be the "lousiest" poem ever written, and while dismissing almost all of nineteenth-century English poetry and fiction, told us we could learn everything about language we wanted to know by reading the first half of Stendhal's *Chartreuse de Parme* and the novels of Flaubert. If he knew what literature was "nutritive" and what was bad for one, his political and economic ideas were equally clear-cut; as were his ideas about music, about sculpture, probably about tennis also. The list of subjects on which he pronounced authoritatively and unambiguously could be extended. But the point is that with a poet of such temperament and proclivities, it is a bad mistake for a critical reader to try to behave likewise, or to try to take over the insights of a Kenner and read Pound as if all his rights and wrongs, yeses and no's were not sometimes brilliant, sometimes just wrong, sometimes mainly cranky and boring— after all, what if an Elgar symphony or *Middlemarch* appeals to us more than a Bach cello sonata or *L'Education sentimentale?* It would be healthier and more interesting, better for both poet and reader, if we admitted our difficulties and reservations about the *Cantos* rather than trying to iron them out or banish them by further study of the allusions and method. Why should we not admit to feeling ambiguously about this most unambiguous of poets even to the point of cultivating uncertainties and tentativenesses of response, since his own responses are so untentative and certain of their acuity?

The sheer amount of interest contained in Pound's work taken as a whole, with all the criticism and letters included, is massive and not likely to be exhausted in our lifetimes. In one important sense he is larger than the poets considered thus far; for we can more easily and successfully address ourselves to the various fine, but mostly short, lyrics which Hardy, Yeats, and Frost produced in their later careers. The *Cantos* are an undertaking of a quite different scale from the writing of poems even as good as "The Circus Animals' Desertion" or "Directive" or "After a Journey." Whether or not Pound "succeeds" in enforcing a parallel between himself and Odysseus, the very idea of his trying it at all is worth more than a little admiration.

So this counsel for reading the *Cantos* is a simple one: proceed by impulse, keep the poem handy to pick up and read here and there as the spirit moves. It never stays still, never seems quite the same from one time to the next. Its "big moments" do not inevitably and always come through as marvelous; while, with any new reading, previously unnoticed ones throw off unexpected light and pleasure. For no other poem is Blackmur's remark about the critic of poetic performance so apposite: "He knows that the institution of literature, so far as it is alive, is made again at every instant. It is made afresh as part of the process of being known afresh; what is permanent is what is always fresh, and it can be fresh only in performance—that is, in reading and seeing and hearing what is actually in it at this place and this time."

With this reminder a reader might attempt to "know afresh" the last three pages of Canto LXXX, the sequence beginning with "O to be in England now that Winston's out," running through references to the Magna Carta, the invocation to "watch a while from the tower" (earlier, Yeats's line "Is every modern nation like the tower half dead at the top?" was answered by Pound with

"Dear WBY, your ½ was too moderate") and see if the fields are tilled, or lie in "rust, ruin, death duties and mortgages" under the present economic system. Personal memories of forty and more years ago pass through the prisoner in his tent, while other prisoners pass by; then things are gathered together in the magnificent "Tudor indeed is gone and every rose" lament-song. The canto ends in a manner both elegiac and comically ironic: Pound observes a lizard stalking a green midge and juxtaposes it with other sorts of "green elegance" and with memories of "my London your London."

The sequence, representative of many in the poem, is particularly attractive in its openness and variety, in how much "play" (to bring back the Frost term) is involved in knowing the work afresh, in "performing" it. Embarking on a reading of the *Cantos,* it is not nearly enough to study the guidebooks and identify the references, though usually the more one knows the more one wants to know. The important thing is to become even in a small way, a voyager yourself, never clear just where you're going to end up, the likelihood a distinct one that you will be thrown up on some shore you had not planned to visit. Shipwreck is certainly a possibility. But at least, in the language of Coriolanus, "There is a world elsewhere." Pound's epic poem, his career of discriminations and preferences, throws us up against that realization as does the work of no other modern poet, no matter how finished and perfected his individual poems.

6

T. S. ELIOT
Superior Amusement

The reviewer of an anthology of contemporary poets published in 1919 distinguished three generations of "verse-producing units" to be observed in Great Britain:

> The first, the aged, represented by the great name of Hardy, but including several figures in process of oblivescence; the middle-aged, including Mr. Yeats and a small number of honoured names; the ageing, including the Georgian poets and the curious shapes of Mr. Eliot and Mr. Pound: all these ages have already lined their nests or dug their graves. We could, at will, pronounce a fitting obituary over any one of these writers except the first mentioned.

At the time he made this witty pronouncement, T. S. Eliot was thirty-one years of age, the author of a book of poems (*Prufrock and Other Observations*, 1917), an unpublished doctoral dissertation on the philosophy of F. H. Bradley, and a great deal of periodical journalism written mainly over the preceding three years. Aging fast, ready if challenged to produce a fitting obituary for himself, he still provided that self with a named place in the landscape of British poetry along with Hardy, Yeats, and Pound.

171

Various other figures of oblivescence, honored names, and Georgians would go unspecified. But what might have been merely an amusing bit of arrogance, quite remote from later, different estimates of worth in literary reputations, turns out in retrospect to have been absolutely accurate about the English scene. Meanwhile in America, Robinson had completed his best work; Frost was establishing himself ever more solidly; the main achievements of Stevens, Williams, and Crane lay ahead and were accomplished with no assistance from England, where in 1919 W. H. Auden was a schoolboy, age twelve.

The paragraph is typical of the critical writing Eliot was turning out during the years just before and after the end of World War I. One is struck by the civilized humor tending toward mordancy, expressing itself sharply in particulars of diction and idiom; as in choosing an automation-like phrase, "Verse-producing units," to neutralize the creative pretensions of all these poets; or "oblivescence," imparting a suavely gentle air of decline to the "aged"; or "ageing" as a mock-weary epithet for himself and Pound (both in their early thirties) and with a nod to the Georgian poets of whom everyone (such is the air) is by now tired. Finally there is the one-two punch of yoking these "units" together, all of them having "lined their nests or dug their graves"; and the concluding boast about how the reviewer could write an obituary for any of them, except of course—in a graceful bow—Hardy, "the first mentioned." The surface of this prose is so engaging and resourceful, the reader feels so flattered to be addressed in such a knowingly urbane way, that he is unlikely to have much interest in disputing Eliot's distinctions even when they are more disputable than the ones brought forth here. Two years later he attempted to describe "wit" as he found it in Marvell's poetry, using words that could gloss much of his own critical prose: "tough reasonableness beneath a slight lyric grace . . . the recognition in any experience of other experiences that are possible."

By 1919 Eliot was well on his way to becoming a great critic, one who would effect massive changes in the way people thought about literature, particularly English literature. Sixty years later it seems proper to place him at the end of the list which begins with Dryden and includes Johnson, Coleridge, and Arnold. Eliot takes his place in this list as, like the rest of them, a poet-critic whose prose judgments must always be considered at least in part in relation to his own creative aims and productions. Whatever reservations and complaints one has about the literary essays, or the introductions to other books and writers he wrote in his later years—and they are more measured and fussy, less combative and unsettling than those written in the 1917–23 period—I think it fair to claim that even without them Eliot is still a major critic. His work will be returned to endlessly for specific judgments and tips, as well as for a general challenge to one's own critical powers.

Is there a similar agreement about the greatness, the indispensable and endlessly rewarding character of Eliot's poetry? Perhaps the question need not even be asked; yet it does seem that, by contrast with recent responses to Stevens, Frost, Hardy, or Yeats, there is a certain deadness to be observed in the criticism of that poetry. "Who has a first-hand opinion of Shakespeare?" he asked in 1918, "Yet I have no doubt that much could be learned by a serious study of that semi-mythological figure." A similar question might be put with respect to his own work, not in the interests of renewed explication which would settle its meaning once for all, but to speculate on whether, as our century draws to its end, readers will continue to read, argue about, share their pleasure in "Prufrock," *The Waste Land, Four Quartets,* and a few of his other poems.

Quite literally, there are no more than a "few" other Eliot poems on which his reputation can rest. One of the guarantees of Hardy's or Stevens's or Yeats's likely persistence as poets who will continue to be read is the sheer number of individual poems by each. Their collected works are thick with more individually appealing lyrics than our minds can take in—we never sit down to reading them through once more without finding some poem we had never quite known was there. This is simply not true of Eliot; indeed (excepting Hart Crane, whose career was such a short one) he is the only one of these modern poets whose work one can thoroughly know, even have largely committed to memory, sit down to of an evening and rise later on having read through the volume. This relative slimness of output is a fact not enough remarked upon, since it makes a difference in the nature of our response. On the one hand Eliot can be admired for the critical discipline he has exercised on his own oeuvre, for how few poems he has let into it: as Donald Davie called it, when the 1963 *Complete Poems* was published, "a fantastic achievement . . . of judgment, taste, self-knowledge, self-control." On the other hand, rightly or wrongly, it is fatally easy to decide that one "knows" these few poems, has heard them all before and will never be surprised by what comes next; that surprising as "Prufrock" or "Gerontion" or *The Waste Land* were when published, they are thoroughly unsurprising now, because thoroughly familiar. One may be a fairly devoted reader of Yeats, yet not know "1919" as well as "The Second Coming," or "A Bronze Head" as well as "The Municipal Gallery Revisited." There is no comparably possible situation with respect to Eliot—either you know them all, or you haven't read them. This fact could contribute to a conceivable future in which Eliot, like the Ben Jonson he wrote so brilliantly and defensively about, becomes a "frozen, unread classic"; not, as with Jonson, because there is dauntingly so much, or because none of it attains the "third dimension" (to use Eliot's term about him), but because there is so little.

Having said as much, let me speak of my own reading of Eliot over the past twenty years. Possessing a good memory and musical sense, I find these poems are very much in my head; to put it somewhat exaggeratedly, I can almost "read" him without picking up the book. In my experience this is not true of the other modern poets: no matter how much Frost or Yeats I have committed to memory, there will always be a poem there on the next page that I know only slightly and delight to read as for the first time. But I find often that, preparing to talk to a class about, say, "Gerontion" and sitting down dutifully once more with the text, I find that the poem in my ears jumps ahead of and completes itself before the poem there on the page as read by eye. With Eliot it is particularly hard to think about, to perceive, what is in front of one. What is? Thankfully in the classroom these difficulties largely vanish. Reading aloud steadies concentration; the presence of other minds to whom the poem is unfamiliar exerts a useful check on too-rapid mental transit; and the questions one asks and is asked help to direct and locate the subject.

Beyond that, it may be said that students are fascinated by Eliot's poems. Despite the publicity about how his reputation was declining in the late 1960's, my experience detects no waver in the lively response younger readers make to the art of "Prufrock," *The Waste Land, Four Quartets.* It's not a matter of instantaneous approval, the reader deciding upon perusal that the poem is assuredly a great one, but a matter of pure curiosity rather. What is going on here? And how on earth is one going to say anything about it which someone else might find to be of interest or help? My point is that Eliot's poetry will continue to count as a living force insofar as we keep the poems open, prevent their hardening into meanings which make them easier to handle only because they are no longer fluid, problematic, and alive. With that aim in mind we may divide the career into three stages, the earliest one containing "Prufrock" as its main poetic exhibit; the second culminating with *The Waste Land* issuing forth from a mass of invaluable articles and reviews, also a nervous collapse; the third, the "Christian" period of which *Four Quartets* is the distinguished fruit.

Eliot was born in St. Louis in 1888, the youngest of seven children, with a mother, Charlotte Stearns Eliot, who was herself a poet of some idealistic fervor. In her informative book on Eliot's early years, Lyndall Gordon tells us that the youngest child had a congenital double hernia, and that Eliot's mother, fearing it would rupture, forbade him to take part in any strenuous sports. It is almost too pat that the enforced spectator grew into the author of Prufrock's love song. Eliot attended private schools in St. Louis and then Milton Academy, from where he entered Harvard in 1906. There he was introduced to Arthur Symons's *The Symbolist Movement in Literature,* which had the effect of turning him toward French poetic models, in particular Jules Laforgue, whose influence on his early poetry has been well noted. Upon Eliot's graduation from Harvard he spent a year in Paris, presumably with the intention of becoming a poet. But in the late summer of 1911 he returned to Harvard to pursue a career as a graduate student in philosophy, and in that summer his notebooks show that he had composed most of the poem we now know as "The Love Song of J. Alfred Prufrock," a poem which was published four years later in *Poetry* and which shaped the title for Eliot's first volume, *Prufrock and Other Observations* (1917).

The poem deserves its pre-eminence among Eliot's early works. Its irresistible name has doubtless played a part in its notoriety, somewhat as has that of Caspar Milquetoast, hero of a once-admired comic strip from the *New York Herald Tribune*'s Sunday funnies, "The Timid Soul." The notion of an indecisive, conscience-ridden male, particularly uneasy in his relationships with women, has exercised much fascination over literary people; one encounters short stories about a professor of literature who, at the climactic moment of the tale, discovers that he *is* Prufrock, that the character he has been talking about in class is the prototype of his own real-life self. There are also the ensuing questions about whether this figure shall part his hair behind, or dare to eat a peach—activities which we, in our liberated vigor, could naturally perform in a moment, if we felt like it. It does seem then that one way of reading the poem, by following along, in a rather patronizing manner, the fortunes of its hapless protagonist, corresponds to the way Pound originally described it to Harriet Monroe when he wrote angrily in answer to some objections she had raised: "a portrait satire on futility can't end by turning that quintessence of futility, Mr. P. into a reformed character breathing out fire and ozone."

In fact it is "Portrait of a Lady" (along with "La Figlia che Piange" it makes the strongest claim, after "Prufrock," for major status among Eliot's early poems) which manifests qualities as a "portrait satire," in this case a satire of attitudes refined beyond the point of civilization, as Eliot once said Boston was. When the lady remarks about the concert she and the young man have just attended,

> "So intimate, this Chopin, that I think his soul
> Should be resurrected only among friends
> Some two or three, who will not touch the bloom
> That is rubbed and questioned in the concert room,"

we have no difficulty in taking the proper measure of such "cultivated" silliness. In case we did, the narrator is immediately on hand to inform us that their conversation proceeds "Among velleities and carefully caught regrets." This "portrait" then is first made up of its heroine's own words, after which follows a cautious, eventually tormented commentary about her by the narrator ("Well! and what if she should die some afternoon"), whose detachment Eliot both prizes and seeks to undermine so that the poem can end in irresolution, in the subtlety of ambiguous feelings. But this carefully maintained separation between the narrator and the lady, his assurance to us about how, when she goes too far in conversation, a "dull tom-tom" begins inside his head, serve to tie the poem down to a relatively conventional mode of procedure, for all the felicities of its conversational mode. Increased familiarity with "Portrait of a Lady" does not much deepen our feelings about a poem which seems more "period," more attractively minor, than would a truly disturbing one.

"Prufrock" by contrast manages to stay strange even after many readings; and it may be that while Eliot knew pretty clearly what he was up to in "Portrait," the same was not necessarily true of

the later poem. This indecision is an index of "Prufrock's" openness, its refusal to present us with the character as filtered through
a narrator's knowing ironies to be relished by sophisticated
readers. Instead from the very opening of the poem there is no
privileged vantage point for us to take.

> Let us go then, you and I,
> When the evening is spread out against the sky
> Like a patient etherised upon a table;
> Let us go, through certain half-deserted streets,
> The muttering retreats
> Of restless nights in one-night cheap hotels
> And sawdust restaurants with oyster-shells:
> Streets that follow like a tedious argument
> Of insidious intent
> To lead you to an overwhelming question . . .
> Oh, do not ask, "What is it?"
> Let us go and make our visit.

Much commentary has been expended upon these lines by way of
insisting that this is Hell (the poem's epigraph from the *Inferno*
lends support) or that the etherized patient is a particularly "modern" image, or that the atmosphere conjured up is a sinister or
degraded one. Yet the basic truth about this "character" was enun-
ciated by Hugh Kenner in a brief sentence: "Prufrock is a name
plus a voice."

The trouble—which is also, luckily, the fun—is that this voice
doesn't speak in any particular tone, and provides no tips on how
to regard the streets, the hotels, and the oyster-shells of its acquaintance. If we should ask whether the "insidious" argument
has already begun within these lines, there is no one to stop us
from so doing, but likewise no one to confirm our suspicion.
There is an opportunistic, even perverse character to the end
rhymes: that "shells" happens to go with "hotels" seems but a
clever and momentary notion, as does the rhyme of "visit" with
its last four letters—"is it." There is finally the pregnant ellipsis
after the "overwhelming question" to which it is promised we will
be led if we follow along.

This opening invitation sets out the whole poem in miniature in

that it promises everything, but nothing in particular. A hundred
lines later the same voice is still going on, speculating, turning
words and phrases around, importuning us in its now eloquent
manner:

And would it have been worth it, after all,
Would it have been worth while,
After the sunsets and the dooryards and the sprinkled streets,
After the novels, after the teacups, after the skirts that trail along the
    floor—
And this, and so much more?—
It is impossible to say just what I mean!
But as if a magic lantern threw the nerves in patterns on a screen. . . .

Here, rather than at the end of the poem with the mermaids, or in
the "Prince Hamlet" passage which precedes it, is found the "wisdom" of "Prufrock" and the outcome of a journey through streets
that wind insidiously to a moment of exclamation—"It is impossible to say just what I mean!" This very modern revelation or cry
occurs when Matthew Arnold's "dialogue of the mind with itself"
has been carried into the nerve ends; or, as Eliot described what
Donne looked deeply into, the cerebral cortex. "But as if a magic
lantern threw the nerves in patterns on a screen": these lines illustrate and most fully embody the voice of "Prufrock" which Kenner splendidly identified and which has been further described by
Barbara Everett as "Holding us by the authority of its own spellbinder's charm, its largely entertaining intelligence." That largely
entertaining intelligence makes the poem continuously engaging
even while it provides no permanent wisdom for us to carry away
from it.

   Or perhaps it does, if not of the most durable sort. Eliot wrote
the poem just after entering his twenties; I remember memorizing
it at age twenty on a bus bound for Albany, New York. It was an
extremely useful poem with which to convert late-adolescent feelings of inadequacy into satisfyingly romantic posturings: "I could
a tale unfold . . . , that is if I decided to speak as Hamlet or
Lazarus or Andrew Marvell. But (For I have known them all al-

ready, known them all) there is no one sufficiently sensitive to understand what I have to say, especially if the 'one' is female. And to tell the truth I don't quite know what it is myself (It is impossible to say just what I mean) since it stems from feelings too deep and mysterious for any adequate verbal expression." It was some time before Eliot formulated the doctrine of the objective correlative, but "Prufrock" foreshadows it. Barbara Everett thinks the poem edges "toward a beautiful but distinctly ad hoc conclusion" but that it "surely began as above all a poem of exploration, even if it ended as 'The Love Song of J. Alfred Prufrock.' " This seems to me exactly the right thing to say in pointing up "Prufrock's" special quality, as well as constituting a general truth about Eliot's best poetry.

Taking leave of the poem, it is probably right to be uncertain about just how "dark" a poem "Prufrock" is, even whether it justifies being described as, like Eliot's other early work, manifesting what Bernard Bergonzi calls "an intense sense of erotic failure and bewilderment." Uncertain, because this erotic failure and bewilderment, no doubt experienced by the young Eliot, as it has been by most of us, feels so much different when it is transformed into the irresistible cadences of Prufrock's love song. For song it is, and as we learn to perform its recurrences and its sudden novelties, its pauses and ellipses and blank spaces—the silences which surround the song—we may begin to think more of mastery than of bewilderment, of artistic success woven out of a failure in life. Twenty years after he wrote the poem, Eliot remarked in *The Use of Poetry and the Use of Criticism,* that the Coleridge of *Biographia Literaria* was already a "ruined man"; but, said Eliot, "to be a ruined man can be a vocation." Already in "Prufrock" there is an analogous fulfillment.

In the early 1920's Eliot wrote a number of "London Letters" for American readers, published in *The Dial.* They contain some of his best expatiations and deadpan effects, as in the following pronouncements from a July 1921 *Dial* letter, written as *The Waste Land* was being coaxed into shape. The first pronouncement said that "What is needed of art is a simplification of current life into something rich and strange"; the second passed along the good news that "A new form of influenza has been discovered, which leaves extreme dryness and a bitter taste in the mouth." Since Americans had just suffered through the terrible influenza epidemic of 1919, Eliot's revelation about the "new form" could hardly be considered vital news, yet the stating of this "discovery" evidently provided some sort of complicated satisfaction for the writer. As for his recipe for art as "simplification of life," it was made in the context of discussing Diaghilev's ballet. But Eliot had been making the same point over the past five years in his periodical journalism.

This journalism appeared mainly in the pages of the *Egoist* (in 1917–18), the *Athenaeum* (1919–20), and the *Times Literary Supplement* (1920 and beyond). Although his first book, *Prufrock and Other Observations,* was not published until 1917, the poems it contained were well behind him by the time Eliot entered upon his dazzling years as a critic. His work as a graduate student in philosophy at Harvard and the writing of his dissertation on F. H. Bradley coincided—as Lyndall Gordon has shown us—with a fascination with the lives of saints and the writing of some poems which never found their way into his collected works. In further pursuance of his Bradley studies, Eliot decided to spend the year 1914–15 at Oxford, and it was during that year that he met both Pound, the man who was to launch his career as a poet, and Vivien Haigh-Wood, the woman he was to marry in 1915—the year "Prufrock" appeared in *Poetry.*

Wyndham Lewis's description of first meeting Eliot in Pound's "triangular" flat is finely etched:

> As I entered the room I discovered an agreeable stranger parked up one of the sides of the triangle. He softly growled at me, as we shook hands. American. A graceful neck I

noted, with what elsewhere I have described as "A gioconda smile." Though not feminine—besides being physically large his personality visibly moved within the male pale—there *were* dimples in the warm dark skin; undoubtedly he used his eyes a little like a Leonardo. He was a very attractive fellow then; a sort of looks unusual this side of the Atlantic.

[Ezra] kept steadily beneath his quizzical but self-satisfied observation his latest prize, or discovery—the author of *Prufrock*. The new collector's piece went on smiling and growling out melodiously his apt and bright answers to promptings from the exhausted figure of his proud captor. His ears did not grow red, or I am sure I should have noticed. Ezra then gave us all some preserved fruit, of which it was his habit to eat a great deal.

Lyndall Gordon settles on March 1916 as the moment when this agreeable stranger decided not to go back to Harvard to defend his newly-finished doctoral dissertation, but to be a poet instead. Eliot assembled his early poems in the *Prufrock* volume, then devoted his compositional energies to writing, with Pound's encouragement, the satiric Quatrain poems ("The Hippopotamus," "Whispers of Immortality," "Mr. Eliot's Sunday Morning Service") while pursuing journalistic activities with a vengeance. In 1917, as his significant critical work began to appear with amazing frequency, he also began work at Lloyd's Bank, perhaps in some ways a less taxing job than the schoolteaching he had been doing at High Wycombe and at Highgate. Only extensive quotation can reveal the many delights and surprises of Eliot's periodical journalism; but certain concerns emerge and recur, as often he uses the books at hand for review as a peg on which to hang them. Some examples from the *Egoist:* in July 1917, reviewing John Butler Yeats's letters edited by Pound, Eliot quotes with approval the following remark by the elder Yeats in praise of the poet as solitary: "Poetry is the voice of the solitary, as resonant and as pure and lonely as the song of the lark at sunrise." This lonely purity is something other than humanly comforting and heart-warming. In October, Jean de Boschère is admired for aiming directly "at emotions of art," for "his obstinate refusal to adulterate his poetic emotions with human emotions." Although this refusal limits the number of his readers, "The effect is sometimes an intense frigidity which I find altogether admirable"—a vivid anticipation of what he was to argue more teasingly in "Tradition and the Individual Talent" two years later. In December 1917 Turgenev is praised for not getting "lost" in his characters: "[he] could not become possessed by the illusion that any particular creation was, for the time being, the center of the universe." Turgenev's "austere art of omission," his "vigilant but never theoretic intelligence" may prove, Eliot suspects, "most satisfying for the civilized mind."

These three writers are praised for what they avoid, for their refusal to be entrapped in "human emotions," in other people, in the overpowering fascination with a particular novelistic character. Perhaps the most famous of such refusals is to be seen in the example of Henry James, to whom, in the *Egoist*, January 1918, Eliot delivered his famous tribute. James was notable for "his mastery over, his baffling escape from, Ideas; a mastery and an escape which are perhaps the last test of a superior intelligence": in the memorable phrase, James had a mind "so fine no idea could violate it." On the other hand, the Georgian poets were full of "ideas," of earnest beliefs about nature, England, and beauty. So Eliot took every opportunity to mock "the annual scourge of the Georgian anthology" (May 1919), unfavorably contrasting it with the *Wheels* anthology (featuring the Sitwells), praised for its "dilettante effect, refreshing after the school-room." Unlike the sincere Georgians, the *Wheels* contributors "are not the good boys of the Sixth Form."

Lewis's *Tarr* was published in 1918, an occasion Eliot took to remark that no one lives in so thick an environment of "stupidity" as the Englishman; that "The *intelligent* Englishman is more aware of loneliness, has more reserves, than anybody else"; and that the "humour" Tarr is cursed with (as is, one might add, T. S. Eliot) is "the instinctive attempt of a sensitive mind to protect beauty against ugliness; and to protect itself against stupidity." In May 1919, writing now in the *Athenaeum,* this sensitive mind has acquired capital letters and been metamorphosed into the "hypothetical Intelligent Man who does not exist and who is the audience of the Artist." A month later Stendhal and Flaubert are singled out as great examples of intensity and of the "consequent discontent with the inevitable inadequacy of actual living to the passionate capacity, which drove them to art and to analysis." They were aware of "the indestructible barriers between one human being and another."

Eliot's favorite metaphor of "simplification" for expressing what, in his eyes, the artists he most admired are engaged in, is in keeping with the general impulse of his critical remarks toward avoidance, exclusion, escape *from* ideas, or togetherness, or simple sincerity, or too-eloquent "characters" from one's own creations. The word "simplification" is used more than once and always in an honorific sense: "The greatest novelists dispense with atmosphere. Beyle and Flaubert strip the world. . . ." If current life is marked mainly by "stupidity," "torpor," by new forms of influenza which leave intense dryness behind, then art's only justification lies in its ability to transform life into something rich and strange: as Pound had managed to do, almost by virtue of his metric alone; as Lewis was doing in his paintings and in parts of *Tarr;* as Joyce was doing (though "simplification" seems hardly the word for *Ulysses*) in the sections which had been appearing from his new novel.

Meanwhile Eliot was writing the most problematic of his poems—the Quatrain ones and "Gerontion." Pound's account of his own poetic output in the years 1917–19 would have us believe that he and Eliot, annoyed that *vers libre* and what Pound called "general floppiness" had gone too far, set about writing in "rhyme and regular strophes": thus Eliot's *Poems, 1920* and Pound's own *Hugh Selwyn Mauberley.* If this looks like an artistic simplification of the sort admired in Eliot's reviews of that time, the resemblance may be only a superficial one. Yet in the Ben Jonson essay written in 1919, Eliot attempted a rehabilitation of the word "superficial," using it, along with "simplification," as a way of characterizing Jonson's art. Certainly the Quatrain poems offer no satisfyingly available depths of meaning; and, unlike "Prufrock," these depths are not even gestured at by a resonant voice. An exception to the rule would be the evocation of the singing nightingales and the death of Agamemnon, at the end of "Sweeney Among the Nightingales." This poem, as obscure as anything Eliot ever wrote, is nonetheless wonderfully memorizable. Since he himself told us that poetry can communicate before it is understood, we may say that "Sweeney Among the Nightingales" does indeed communicate something: an attitude of knowing superiority to the puppets who are moved around by these expertly paced, brilliantly allusive stanzas. In fact Eliot's style puts the showman on display in a manner similar to one he had just praised in Lewis's *Tarr,* in which the antic dispositions of wild bodies are exhibited with cool mastery by the detached artist.

Fifteen years later, after he had become an Anglican, Eliot remarked (in *After Strange Gods*) with respect to Pound's "Hell" Cantos that "Mr. Pound's hell is for the other people." If this is a criticism of Pound's moral complacency, it could be turned back on Eliot's own satirical exercises composed in these emotionally turbulent years of his life, with too much work and too little time to do it in, and with his wife's and his own health deteriorating. (Valerie Eliot in her edition *The Waste Land* quotes a letter in which T. S. Eliot complains he has no time to get his teeth fixed.) All the more then, in the Quatrain poems, did Eliot separate the suffering man from the creative artist. These airtight pieces which curl their lip at most human emotions are undeniably smart displays whose wit initially dazzles and excites, but on repeated readings is less likely to do so. For all their obscurities and ingenuities they effect a "simplification" of life which comes to feel more like a reduction of it, as the simplifications Eliot admired in Turgenev, Stendahl, and Ben Jonson do not.

The most important poem from these years, "Gerontion," is a

different matter, and I have attempted in a previous work to describe its status as a poem that is all "voice," with even the pretense of a followable narrative dropped, therefore impossible to make sense of the way we make sense of most poems. In the interest of devoting more time to *The Waste Land* I will slight it here, only saying that "Gerontion" seems to me ever more the strangest of Eliot's poems and the one whose survival as a poem that will continue to be read is most uncertain. It has two moments of high rhetoric—the passage on history beginning "After such knowledge, what forgiveness" and the echo of *The Changeling* beginning with "I that was near your heart was removed therefrom"— which are extremely moving, though to exactly what end it is hard to say. Elisabeth Schneider, in her perceptive remarks about it, suggests that we look to the *Hamlet* essay also written in 1919 for a clue to what is strange and ultimately unsatisfying about "Gerontion": that in it Eliot was struggling to communicate deep and disturbed feelings but was unable to find an adequate "objective correlative" for them. At any rate the interest of *Hamlet* has hardly been lessened by Eliot's strictures on it; it may be that "Gerontion" in a smaller way will survive as a curious and undeniably individual piece of work, written with *The Waste Land* imminent (Eliot once thought of using "Gerontion" as a prologue to it) and taking on power from its proximity to that monument.

The monument appears to be in excellent repair and can now be seen more truly for what it is, and not another thing, than in the accounts of a few decades ago. It is doubtless a mistake to praise the critical perceptions of one's own times at the expense of past ones; still there has been some good criticism of this particular poem over the past decade, probably because of the attention focused on it by the publication of the manuscript facsimile, and because it became a half-century old in 1972. But something more than these facts was involved in enabling us to see the poem more clearly. My own sense of it is that the standard pioneering commentaries on *The Waste Land*—by Leavis, by F. O. Matthiessen, by Cleanth Brooks—had exhausted their usefulness by having become so thoroughly assimilated that they also became no longer interesting, no longer useful in helping readers see the poem freshly—"in performance," as Blackmur insists all good poems must be constantly reseen in order to stay fresh.

The older commentaries were agreed in treating the poem as a richly allusive criticism of the modern world, using the "positive" standards of myth, legend, and art to provide heroic, passionate versions of life (Philomela, Ophelia, Ecclesiastes) in comparison to which modern urban types like Sweeney, Mrs. Porter and Mr. Eugenides, the typist and her young man carbuncular, looked sordid or petty or grotesque. The Fisher King–Grail myth was taken seriously (particularly by Cleanth Brooks) as an explanatory myth or scaffolding to help us make sense of the poem's development from initial dryness up to the coming of the rains in its final section. In general, these commentaries treated the poem with great seriousness, often with solemnity, and had the effect of helping make it a sort of Sacred Book that was nourishing—like "Prufrock"—to readers who were excited by the sense of being "disillusioned" with the world in which they lived. But as it became a text to be studied, or puzzled over, its possible unity or possible fragmentedness a matter for debate, it also became less entertaining, less a pleasure to read. Joyce's *Ulysses,* which might be thought to provide a parallel case, was much less damaged by a comparable load of exegesis, since it was indisputably larger and more variously entertaining a work of comedy. By comparison *The Waste Land,* like J. Alfred Prufrock, appeared in danger of being "pinned and wriggling on a wall."

That the poem broke free and is now very much alive can be attested to by the astonishing way it remains receptive to yet undefined by its commentators. I shall single out three recent versions of how it works that are original and interesting, yet so far from a last word on the subject that one begins to suspect *The*

Waste Land may be as inexhaustible and undefinable as great poems tend to be. The first version is my own and makes its way into the poem through Eliot's essay on Ben Jonson, published in November 1919 when *The Waste Land* was germinating. In the Jonson essay, Eliot's interests as expressed in the periodical journalism over the last three years came to a head as he praised Jonson's art for its simplifications, its "stripping" of the world, its "flat distortion of the drawing . . . an art of caricature, of great caricature." Jonson's characters do not have the "third dimension," nor do they possess or arouse swarms of inarticulate feelings (as Shakespeare's do); his art is "superficial" but its superficies is a strong and solid one. Jonson's characters "conform to a logic of their own"—"the worlds created by artists like Jonson are like systems of non-Euclidean geometry." And his "satire" has a tenuous and indirect relation to the real world; it is a "titanic show" which is only obliquely a criticism of life. This account still seems to me to fit most of *The Waste Land,* especially the character portraits, whose referential aspect is extremely tenuous. For example, when Mr. Eugenides, the Smyrna merchant, is introduced—"with a pocketful of currants / C.i.f. London: documents at sight"—the vivid strokes by which he is etched are much more memorable and interesting than anything he might be said to "stand for" or "refer to," such as the theme of sterility or perversion or the decline of fertility cults. My argument is that reading *The Waste Land* should be essentially a matter of appreciating the "titanic show" by immediately taking in and admiring the *poetry* of the different sections, rather than worrying about what it all adds up to, indeed whether it "adds up" to anything.

A second version is Hugh Kenner's demonstrating that the poem began as an attempt to write about London in the manner of an early 1920's John Dryden (Eliot's essay on Dryden was published in 1921), but that, through the excision of long passages by Pound, it turned into a poem of Urban Apocalypse rather than of satiric detachment. Kenner was thus able to account for the character of the poem's fifth section, "What the Thunder Said," in a way my version does not. That last section, probably written during Eliot's rest cure at Lausanne in 1922, was untouched by Pound and reads as if it had come in a burst of visionary necessity. That it could not be cobbled together with imitation neoclassical accounts of a lady rising in the morning—the long passage on "Fresca" deleted by Pound—is seen as the strange and fortunate destiny of a master poem.

Finally, although lip service is paid to Eliot's indebtedness to symbolist poets, few critics of *The Waste Land* have taken seriously the consequences of such indebtedness. One who has is Donald Davie, by claiming that Eliot stands centrally in the symbolist tradition in which words have meanings, but not references to a real world outside the poem. Recently Denis Donoghue has provided a strong development of this approach to Eliot's poem in an essay titled, revealingly, "The Word Within a Word." Donoghue argues that the language of *The Waste Land* effects an "absence in reality," and that what fills up the vacuum is words:

> At first, the words seem to denote things, *sensibilia* beyond the lexicon, but it soon appears that their allegiance to reality is deceptive, they are traitors in reality. So far as the relation between word and thing is deceptive, so far also is "objective" reality undermined. The only certainty is that the absence in reality has been effected by the words, and now the same words are enforcing themselves as the only presence. What we respond to is the presence of the words.

Because of this, Donoghue argues, lines from the poem reverberate, seeming to carry more authority than can be "objectively" demonstrated:

> A woman drew her long black hair out tight
> And fiddled whisper music on those strings
> And bats with baby faces in the violet light
> Whistled, and beat their wings
> And crawled head downward down a blackened wall
> And upside down in air were towers
> Tolling reminiscent bells, that kept the hours
> And voices singing out of empty cisterns and exhausted wells. . . .

These climactic lines from "What the Thunder Said" mark as intense a moment of perceiving as is found anywhere in the poem; yet it is not at all clear what a relevant response to them—at least one expressed in words—would be. The mythical superstructure would dictate that we have arrived at the Chapel Perilous, with the quester about to undergo his crucial test. Yet at least one reader—R. P. Blackmur—despairing of this abstractly "thematic" way of accounting for the poem's power—testified in his *Anni Mirabilis* (1956) that "for myself, I muse and merge and ache and find myself feeling with the very senses of my thought greeting and cries from all the senses there are." Is there no middle way between intellectual thematic abstraction and a wholly sensuous merging and aching? There is surely no "tone" in which a believable "speaker" makes this and that pronouncement; no dramatic progression, as in Yeats or Frost; no punctuation to guide us in connecting one event to the next; no qualifications or degrees of emphasis. The "woman" who draws her hair out tight, the "violet light" which so strongly rhymes with it, the bone-dry "exhausted" wells and cisterns—these taken together form an apotheosis of much else in the poem. If we do not choose to speak tonelessly and without punctuation, what other possible manner of description or accounting for is left us to embrace? Like Blackmur, and in good company, we may prefer just to muse, merge, and ache.

In any case, whether one takes the poem as a series of brilliant set-pieces, a Jonsonian "titanic show" which entertains and thrills—as does the portrait of Mr. Eugenides or the bats crawling head downward down a blackened wall; or as a satire gone apocalyptic; or as a symbolist poem whose meanings are wholly internal to it—one will have to engage with "the poetry," about which (to paraphrase Eliot on another subject) one must find not the right thing but the least wrong thing to say about it. It also seems to me to represent, more than any other poem Eliot ever wrote, the sort of "simplification" he had been crying out for; not least in its hospitality to many approaches and its refusal to yield itself up to any single understanding, as a "complex" work like Yeats's "Meditations in Time of Civil War," published in the same year, will ultimately do. Eliot was later to write in *Four Quartets* that "the poetry does not matter." In *The Waste Land* it is the only thing that matters, and in every possible sense.

Eliot's years between *The Waste Land* and the publication of "Burnt Norton" in 1935 are marked by a religious conversion, an increasingly distinguished public career, and a private life with a woman whose nervous illness grew progressively worse. On the public side, he was editing *The Criterion* (1922–39) and (beginning in 1925) working at the publishing house of Faber & Faber. In 1932 he visited the United States and delivered the Norton lectures at Harvard, published as *The Use of Poetry and the Use of Criticism* (1933), and the Page-Barbour ones at Virginia, published, though never reprinted, as *After Strange Gods* (1934). In general his critical prose dealt ever more frequently with matters of religion, politics, and society, for which concern his conversion to Anglicanism in 1927 provided the main impetus. The final break with his wife Vivien came in 1933 when Eliot, returning from his American speaking engagements, took up residence in a cottage in Surrey rather than returning to their flat in South Kensington.

Since, for me, the fact of *Four Quartets* overshadows the other poems and plays Eliot wrote during the late 1920's and the thirties, I neglect these latter in order to devote more time to the long poem and to some of the continuing arguments about it. But at least passing mention should be made of "Marina," one of four "Ariel" poems (as Eliot later titled them), in which the visionary possibility of transformation is most hauntingly suggested. The vain desires and pleasures of this world, of "Those who suffer the ecstasy of the animals, meaning / Death")

> Are become unsubstantial, reduced by a wind,
> A breath of pine, and the woodsong fog
> By this grace dissolved in place

> What is this face, less clear and clearer
> The pulse in the arm, less strong and stronger—
> Given or lent? more distant than stars and nearer than the eye
>
> Whispers and small laughter between leaves and hurrying feet
> Under sleep, where all the waters meet.
>
> Bowsprit cracked with ice and paint cracked with heat.

I quote these lines from "Marina" to demonstrate the sureness and subtlety with which Eliot employs language in a suggestive, symbolist manner (though "symbolism" seems a crude label for the delicate procedure) while suggesting that there has to be a way out of symbolism, since there are realities "out there" which can be named, pointed to by the words working together. Of course the poem plays off others by Eliot; the pulse "more distant than stars" beats faintly in "The Hollow Men"; the risky, internal rhymes of "grace," "place," and "face" are employed even more riskily (and I think unsatisfactorily) in "Ash-Wednesday"; the "small laughter between leaves" will be heard again with the children in the apple-tree, in "Burnt Norton" and "Little Gidding."

"Marina" is affecting and successful, touching us as if by sudden magic, partly because it is also short, can make its elusive music heard and as quickly be gone. A similar music is heard at moments in "Ash-Wednesday," most beautifully in the climactic passage from the sixth section when "the lost heart stiffens and rejoices / In the lost lilac and the lost sea voices." Whether one can read through the entire six sections and feel a compelling development, or be satisfied with and stirred by the power of invention of the separate parts, is more doubtful: properties such as the three white leopards, the lady, the dry bones, the jewelled unicorns, the fiddles and the flutes, all of which make their brief appearances, strike at least this reader as possessing less inevitability and force than corresponding images or stage properties employed in "Prufrock" and *The Waste Land*. Granted that in the main Eliot is now no longer exploiting a dramatic rhetoric which sweeps us up with Prufrockian or Gerontion-like eloquence, or dazzles and scares us with the unnameable voice which narrates *The Waste Land*. In reading "Ash-Wednesday" rather, one finds himself (in the language of "Portrait of a Lady") "Doubtful, for a while / Not knowing what to feel or if I understand / Or whether wise or foolish. . . ." In no other poem Eliot ever wrote do we occupy such a strained position, looking on uneasily as certain private impulses attempt to find satisfactory expression in various scenes, images, and verse-forms. There is a disembodied air about much of the proceedings; the word "experimental" comes too quickly to mind as an unsatisfactory way of labeling a poetic behavior one never feels comfortable in responding to.

If these remarks about "Ash-Wednesday" have any truth—and they may reveal only that I am incapable of responding adequately to it—they can not be applied to *Four Quartets*. There is still no consensus about this poem. Some who think *The Waste Land* a supreme achievement consider the *Quartets* to be comparatively low in energy; flatly and sometimes pompusly discursive; a betrayal of or at least a falling-off from Eliot's powers. Others think that here finally, and perhaps only here, does Eliot achieve the difficult "sincerity" (the word is Leavis's) of speaking in his own, troubled, complex voice. With the publication of Helen Gardner's authoritative and fascinating study of their composition, we know about as much as we will ever know of their lineaments; but how much further we are toward just evaluation, toward seeing the object as in itself it really is, is unclear. What does seem clear to me, and why I regard this poem as a wholly fitting, "inevitable" conclusion to the career, is that more than any other modern poem *Four Quartets* causes us to think again about our deepest attitudes toward poetry—to question, in fact, whether we have such attitudes, and if so how deep they are. "The poetry does not matter": this famous line, plucked from its contextual situation in "East Coker," serves in a concentrated form as the sort of challenge I am talking about. How much to us—to the individual reader, not the confirmed or putative Christian voice in the poem—does "the poetry" matter? And to extend the metaphor, what kind of salvation do we expect to find by the perusal of patterns of words in various formal combinations which surprise and delight?

One way of answering these questions is to direct attention to passages, perhaps the finest ones in the *Quartets*, where Eliot's "first voice" of poetry can be heard: that of the poet speaking to himself with no design other than finding the right words to express the "obscure impulse" he is seized with. These passages are all the more affecting and moving for the way they emerge out of a very different sort of poetry—the public, pontificating, qualifying-and-explaining ruminations of Eliot the man of letters and Christian aspirant to humility:

> And what there is to conquer
> By strength and submission, has already been discovered
> Once or twice, or several times, by men whom one cannot hope
> To emulate—but there is no competition—
> There is only the fight to recover what has been lost
> And found and lost again and again. . . .

So when, after these sanely balanced homilies, the first voice of the poet asserts itself, as if by sudden impulse, the result is electric:

> Home is where one starts from. . . .
> Old men ought to be explorers
> Here and there does not matter
> We must be still and still moving
> Into another intensity
> For a further union, a deeper communion
> Through the dark cold and the empty desolation,
> The wave cry, the wind cry, the vast waters
> Of the petrel and the porpoise. . . .

It is in a movement such as this one from "East Coker" that the poem's deepest energies are felt.

Here I would like to put aside this matter, and also such well-rehearsed ones as the "musical structure" of the *Quartets*, the repetitive patterns obtaining in each of the four poems, the counterpointing and echoing of words and concepts; also questions of taste such as are provoked now and then by Eliot's tone (how for example one responds to the "or even a very good dinner" confidence in "The Dry Salvages"), in favor of a more problematical question, the one perhaps most involved with our continued reading of the *Quartets*. It is the problem of belief, and was recently raised by Leavis in one of his last sustained pieces of criticism— the hundred or so pages he devotes to the *Quartets* in *The Living Principle* (1976). With some repetitiveness and heaviness of vocabulary, Leavis nonetheless succeeds with admirable particularity in making the poem more alive by questioning its recommendation, its commitment to the "wisdom of humility," its inability (he argues) to celebrate the great creative achievement of English language and literature—in short, its anti-humanism. Leavis's answer to the poem is a considered "No," which *Four Quartets* is then praised for its capacity to elicit.

Since my own conviction is that one's attitude toward the *Quartets* is an expression of one's larger attitude toward Eliot's work generally and the kind of temperament revealed in it, I think the poem calls for no special pleadings or qualifications as an object exceptional to the canon. There have been attempts (Davie's on the opening of "The Dry Salvages" is one of them) to demonstrate that the "poetry" simply doesn't matter enough; that the master of technique fell into slack and tired formulations in *Four Quartets,* which even if they are taken as necessary to the poem's dialectic—they show the inadequacy of mere words by being merely words—still inflict grave damage on it. Yet whereas it is possible with older long poems to show how certain parts of them aren't as strongly composed, as "interesting" as others—*In Memoriam* or Wordsworth's "Immortality Ode" might be cases in point—this distinction is hard to make with Eliot's poem. Its style is so various, its extremes so musical and prosaic writing so blatantly evident, that one may expose little more than one's wish that the poem were more consistent with the particular style one prefers. Such consistency is exactly what Eliot sought to undermine by writing this adventurous poem. It is true that certain high points, most notably the Dantesque section from "Little Gidding" ("In that uncertain hour of the morning"), are praised by almost everyone; but what about the sestina section from "The Dry Salvages"—are the rhymes disastrous? Or the "wounded surgeon" lyric from "East Coker"—is it brilliant, or embarrassingly vulgar? There is of course no reason why critics should agree about the quality of different passages; yet disagreement about the poem has not led to a more inclusive understanding of it.

When I turn away from the commentators and read the poem instead, I find myself as always caught up and fascinated by certain moments, moving rather quickly over other, familiar ones which no longer challenge me; making one or two new connections I hadn't made before; trying to imagine what it would be like to speak in this voice, in these voices—to take Eliot's view of this world and of that other "reality" which humankind cannot bear very much of. And I finish the poem convinced that, as with *The Waste Land,* there is nothing like it in modern poetry. In an effort to specify further the "it," consider a single passage, various enough and "inconsistent" enough with itself so that it can fairly stand for the poem taken as a whole. The section is also from "East Coker" and follows the "What is the late November doing" lyric in section II:

> That was a way of putting it—not very satisfactory:
> A periphrastic study in a worn-out poetical fashion,
> Leaving one still with the intolerable wrestle
> With words and meanings. The poetry does not matter.
> It was not (to start again) what one had expected.
> What was to be the value of the long looked forward to,
> Long hoped for calm, the autumnal serenity
> And the wisdom of age? Had they deceived us
> Or deceived themselves, the quiet-voiced elders,
> Bequeathing us merely a receipt for deceit?
> The serenity only a deliberate hebetude,
> The wisdom only the knowledge of dead secrets
> Useless in the darkness into which they peered
> Or from which they turned their eyes. There is, it seems to us,

At best, only a limited value
In the knowledge derived from experience.
The knowledge imposes a pattern, and falsifies,
For the pattern is new in every moment
And every moment is a new and shocking
Valuation of all we have been. We are only undeceived
Of that which, deceiving, could no longer harm.
In the middle, not only in the middle of the way
But all the way, in a dark wood, in a bramble,
On the edge of a grimpen, where is no secure foothold,
And menaced by monsters, fancy lights,
Risking enchantment. Do not let me hear
Of the wisdom of old men, but rather of their folly,
Their fear of fear and frenzy, their fear of possession,
Of belonging to another, or to others, or to God.
The only wisdom we can hope to acquire
Is the wisdom of humility; humility is endless.

The houses are all gone under the sea.

The dancers are all gone under the hill.

First of all, *what* was a way of putting it? No doubt the just-concluded lyric with its roses and thunder, Comets and Leonids, hollyhocks and icecaps. But Eliot leaves open the possibility that any "study," any poetic fashion or style, is vulnerable to charges that it is "periphrastic" or "worn-out" or "poetical": there is this sense in which "the poetry" doesn't matter. Especially when, looking ahead to what follows, we see that the subject is old age and poems about old age like Browning's "Rabbi Ben Ezra" ("Grow old with me / The best is yet to be") which deceive and are self-deceiving, examples of just more "poetry." The parenthetical interpolation in the fifth line is no accident, at least we may presume Eliot thought twice about whether he wanted it at all, whether in or out of parenthesis; thought about whether such clearing of the throat was desirable when critics of the poem could then say, and have said, look at how lamely he cranks up the engine. Having thought about it, he persisted.

There follows the passage about old age with its grim dismissal

of "autumnal serenity" and the "quiet-voiced elders" who told us
about age's wisdom; yet even as the poetry warms to this chilly
vision and takes on amplitude and authority, there are odd effects
that pull towards the artificial: the word "hebetude" for example,
or the daring (is it misconceived?) inner rhyme of "receipt" with
"deceit." Then with another change of gears and clearing of the
throat Eliot begins to sound like a committee ("There is, it seems
to us, / At best, only a limited value" provides another moment, it
has been said, of "lameness") only to rise to the strong "And every
moment is a new and shocking / Valuation" and the fanciful evoking of the grimpen and the fancy lights (out of *The Hound of the
Baskervilles*). Then comes the fine salute to old men's folly
(Yeats's "Why Should Not Old Men Be Mad?" is brought to
mind), and the passage closes with an obeisance to the "wisdom
of humility" which has set at least Leavis's teeth on edge. A pause,
a space, a line about where the houses have gone; a pause, a
space, a line about where the dancers have gone.

The poetry then is anything but seamless. Although *Four Quartets* more than once puts me in mind of Johnson's great poem
"The Vanity of Human Wishes," Johnson had no problem with
maintaining an absolutely consistent manner of speaking throughout the poem. By contrast Eliot's modernity in *Four Quartets*—
and it is something other than the exemplary "modernism" of *The
Waste Land*—consists in his willingness, or his perhaps necessary
destiny, to write disjunctive, reflexive poetry, which eschews the
creation of what a contemporary poet, A. R. Ammons, speaking
of short lyrics, calls "those little rondures / splendidly brought off,
painted gourds on a shelf." I mean quite simply that the powerful
moments in the *Quartets* would not be what they are without the
presence of lower-keyed, even dull or pompous ones, in which a
voice struggles to get going, stops, starts again, apologizes for
repeating itself, speaks in a tone we may not always find congenial
or appropriate. I am aware of the dangers of talking this way
(does the poem about confusion have to be confused?) and I do
not mean to make a theoretical point—only to say that Eliot's

poem demands an individual response. Leavis's response was to say, "Yes-but-No": "Yes" to the creative brilliance of language; "No" to the negative attitude toward life, the espousal of "humility," the failure of nerve and failure of language manifested in these. By contrast, my own attitude is instead to accept it all, to marvel at the ways the poetry challenges us in outrageous terms, which terms taken in themselves it is very tempting to say No to, but which when taken together result in a poem I would not have any different than it is.

Kenneth Burke once said about Eliot's life that he had gone from being ordinary Tom from St. Louis to become St. Thomas à Becket. There were other, intermediary stages of naming: someone called T. Stearns Eliot composed his very first reviews; and there was also T. S. Eliot, known to all as author of a strange poem, *The Waste Land.* Eventually there was Mr. Eliot ("Possum" to Pound), winner of the Nobel Prize in 1948, who is commemorated in Westminster Abbey and whose ashes are buried in East Coker, the home of his English ancestors. This progression has served as fair material for gibes from the unfriendly, from those who see Eliot's career less as a heroic effort than as a series of suave accommodations which furthered his prestige. I would not begin to distinguish what in him was deepest and most sincere from what was role, pose, affectation, or impersonation. Certainly he was a remarkable ventriloquist. Kenner's book on him is titled *The Invisible Poet* and is filled with insight into the consummate skill with which Eliot played different parts as the occasion demanded; especially as an anonymous reviewer who produced in the *Times Literary Supplement* the great essays on the Metaphysicals, Marvell, and Dryden. Kenner's later account (in *The Pound Era*) of a Garrick Club luncheon with Eliot in 1948 when the Invisible Poet came to an elaborate confrontation with a wheel of Stilton cheese is the best of numbers of excellent anecdotes about his behavior as a complicated humorist. In comparison, stories about Yeats and Pound are louder and more melodramatic; and among the modern poets only Frost ("I play euchre and he plays Eucharist") has provoked a comparable fund of lore. The poet Donald Hall tells of visiting Eliot in his Faber offices when Hall was preparing to spend a year at Oxford. Eliot, pointing out that young Hall, like the young TSE of fifty years before, was moving from Harvard to Oxford, suggested that he should offer some advice. Meditating, while Hall anticipated a revelation, Eliot finally brought it out: "Have you any long underwear?" As always, it was not the expected; and Hall reports that he purchased the underwear. Eliot did seem to have an influence on other people, other poets.

What lay "under" all this play? Lyndall Gordon's bold statement may provoke, in its sweeping certainty, some demurs; but it is as good an attempt as I know of to name the central impulse of Eliot's life:

> Eliot's personality was self-centered enough to assume that the world and its vicissitudes—its women, its wars, seasons, crowds—existed as signals for his private conduct. The isolation and the absence of signs . . . brewed also a certain wilfulness. . . .
>
> [He] passed his youth walled-in by shyness and vast ambition. His adult life may be seen as a series of adventures from the citadel of his self in search of some great defining experience. He made expeditions across a perilous gap that divided him from the great world, and ventured into society, into marriage, into religious communion. He tried to maintain the polite, even curiosity of an explorer far from home, but each time had to withdraw—shuddering from the contact—to his citadel, where he would then labour to record, as precisely as possible, his strange encounters.

Eliot would not have liked that use of "shuddering," but "Prufrock" and "Portrait of a Lady," "Gerontion," The Waste Land, "Ash-Wednesday," and Four Quartets are surely believable in these terms. And it is a preferable and more sympathetic way to understand the poet than by stating merely that his is a poetry largely of "negative" emotions, and that our fascination with his work must in part be an expression of our fascination with our own share in those emotions—"anti-life" ones, if by life is meant all that is positive and affirming.

But perhaps Pound deserves the final word, his words about Eliot as contained in the tribute to him after Eliot's death:

> His was the true Dantescan voice—not honoured enough, and deserving more than I ever gave him. . . . Who is there now for me to share a joke with?
>
> Am I to write "about the poet Thomas Stearns Eliot" or my friend "the Possum"? Let him rest in peace. I can only repeat but with the urgency of 50 years ago: READ HIM.

It was that same friend and critic who once said, referring to Eliot's manner when visiting Pound's flat, "He doesn't come in *here* sounding like Westminster Abbey."

7

WALLACE STEVENS
Poet of the Academy

Wallace Stevens was born nine years before Pound, thirteen before
Eliot, yet in the story of modern poetry his place seems to be after
them. It is not that his work is explicitly a response, as in part
Hart Crane's was, to challenges and principles set or affirmed by
the revolutionary expatriates with their commitment to tradition,
their piety toward the "Mind of Europe," and their patronizing
condescension to most native American poets. Stevens regarded
Eliot as a negative force, and seems to have avoided Pound's work
quite successfully, but my guess is that he never considered his poetry as a corrective of theirs. Yet if we look at the course of American poetic reputations over the years since Eliot's death in 1965,
it is clear that Stevens and William Carlos Williams have been put
forth as the two American poets who make claim to a centrality, a
local identity, a human expressiveness more inspiriting than either
Pound's or Eliot's.

For example, we heard in the late 1960's that Williams was
"in" and that students were responding to the freedoms of his
verse and the democratic warmth of his sympathies, in contrast
with Eliot, the chilly anti-lifer whose stock was diminishing in

value. Williams seems to have been rediscovered after his death in 1963; but quite the opposite occurred with Eliot—it was as if people were relieved at last to put down the poems they had spent so many hours in explicating. That possibility, and the rhetoric of "liberation" heard so often in those years, may have been responsible for whatever shift in relative valuing took place. The Williams boom was relatively short-lived. But the rise of Stevens to a commanding position as *the* modern American poet has been more gradual and is likely to prove more lasting, at least insofar as academic critics call the turn. For it is evident that some of the best or most influential critics of poetry at this time—Helen Vendler, Denis Donoghue, Frank Kermode, and especially the Yale triumvirate of Harold Bloom, Geoffrey Hartman, and Hillis Miller—concur in an exalted estimate of Stevens's contribution and of his place in the hierarchy of American poetic tradition: he is the legitimate successor to Emerson and Whitman, and he presides (so at least Bloom would argue) over the most important American verse written today.

I call this an exalted estimate because it maintains itself by accepting Stevens's uses of language as in the main brilliant, richly and imaginatively satisfying. Although these critics don't agree on which is his best long poem—it may be "Notes Toward a Supreme Fiction" or "The Auroras of Autumn" or "Esthétique du Mal" (it will not be "Sunday Morning")—they do not question the overall authority and splendor of these poems, seeking rather to interpret more fully the meanings as they emerge. It seems to be agreed that these meanings are significant, and that Stevens's concern generally with the imagination and reality, with the "fiction" of the poem in its many guises, is to be taken with some reverence as perhaps the most dignified and worthy of modern poetic concerns. It may also be observed, as an indication of this reverence, that critics of Stevens often write sentences about the poem under question by quoting (or merely incorporating) lines and phrases from other Stevens poems, as if to insist upon (I will now employ the same technique) the omnipresent "total grandeur of a total edifice."

It is all a bit like going to church, but presumably much more exhilarating and free-breathing than going to church with T. S. Eliot. But as there were always those who refused to worship Eliot's poems, so there have been early and later dissenters from the canonization of Stevens. Yvor Winters, writing in the 1940's, judged that this poet's hedonistic philosophy was the cause of his downfall and deterioration after the early masterpieces in *Harmonium*. A few years later Randall Jarrell lamented Stevens in the guise of philosopher ("G. E. Moore at the spinet") and the resultant aridities found particularly in *The Auroras of Autumn*. More recently, the author of one of the best appreciations of "Sunday Morning," J. V. Cunningham, wrote an essay for the purpose, he said, of rescuing Stevens from "himself and his friends." In aggressively polemical terms, Cunningham made the following charge:

> The situation is this: there are over twelve thousand lines of poetry, almost four hundred separate titles, and much of this is junk, and most is repetitious. There is, furthermore, an immense body of commentary which is, with some notable exceptions, scandalously wrong, irrelevant, and confusing, much of it consisting of centos of phrases from the poetry.

He compared the reader of Stevens to one of Emily Dickinson; each will have "gotten his hands inextricably involved in the taffy—oversaturated, bewildered, unable to tell the good from the bad, snatching at this poem and that, this passage and that, to save something from the confusion." Cunningham's conviction is that, like Dickinson, Stevens was an amateur with "a homemade machine for the endless production of poems," written, again and ever again, to convince himself he was a poet.

I should like to promote the rescue of Stevens from his more uncritical disciples and interpreters by specifying further than Cunningham does the undeniable pleasures of those poems which stand out from the "junk" and are not just repetitions of ones written earlier. But there is no way to read Stevens repeatedly over numbers of years without getting yourself thoroughly, if not inextricably, involved in the taffy. He became involved in it himself, as is testified to by his long letters to exegetes who queried him about this line or that stanza from various poems. Unlike most poets, at least in our century, he was willing to go on at great length, making modest and sensible paraphrases which nevertheless induce weariness in us if we try to read them through; he must have thought that his poetry presented a challenge to the rational intelligence sufficient to justify these explanatory labors in its behalf. Going further, and to make my own bias clear: I propose that no other modern poet, not even Pound in the *Cantos,* can be as exasperating an acquaintance, as trying of our patience. Stevens, not the moon, is the "Arabian" of "Notes Toward a Supreme Fiction," "With his damned hoobla-hoobla-hoobla-hoo." And yet he can also make us feel, as at the end of this section in the poem, that "life's nonsense pierces us with strange relation."

The significant life of any poet is probably an inner one, but the remark in Stevens's case sounds like the feeblest of understatements; since the outward events of his life are so few and so mild, while the inner world—as he reports it in his journals and letters—is full of longing, delight, and fanciful play. He may have inherited some of the play from his father, an attorney in Reading, Pennsylvania, where Wallace was born (1879) and grew up. When the son, attending Harvard as a special student (as did Frost and Eliot), was elected in 1899 to the Signet Club (of which he came to be president, as he did of the Harvard *Advocate*), Garrett Stevens began a letter to him as follows: "Just what the election to the *Sig*n*et* sig*n*ifies, I have no sig*n*. It is sig*n*ificant that your letter is a sig*n*al to sig*n* another check that you may sig*h* no more." And so on, through various other embroideries, dedicated to illustrat-

ing the truth of a line his son was later to write—"Yet in excess
continual there is cure of sorrow."

The poems Stevens published at Harvard were conventional in
sentiment and unadventurous in form. He remarked in later life
that "One's early things give one the creeps," and looking back he
might have felt creepy about this sestet of a sonnet published in
the *Advocate* in March 1899, which began, "If we are leaves that
fall upon the ground." Since such is our destiny,

> Then let a tremor through our briefness run,
> Wrapping it with mad, sweet sorcery
> Of love; for in the fern I saw the sun
> Take fire against the dew; the lily white
> Was soft and deep at morn; the rosary
> Streamed forth a wild perfume into the light.

For all the perfume, it is essentially the idea which will inform
"Sunday Morning" sixteen years later; that death is the mother of
beauty and that the "tremor" attendant on this perception makes
all the difference to what we feel and see.

The most interesting part of Stevens's life, as a reader constructs
it from his journals and letters, is unquestionably the period spent
in New York after his Harvard career: from 1900, when he tried
journalism and soon gave it up to enter New York Law School in
the next year, to 1909, when he married Elsie Moll, a young
woman from Reading, and settled into the insurance business.
Part of the pleasure in this early prose is in watching the young
man discover New York, and on foot too, fighting off his loneliness, his tendency to smoke too many cigars (Stevens was convinced that smoking affected his constitution in immediately dele-
terious ways), indulging himself in strawberries, or perhaps
brandied peaches. The very best moments occur on Sundays, particularly in the carefully set-down details of typical Sunday morning activities: "I've had a handsome day of it and am contented
again. Left the house after breakfast and went by ferry and trolley
to Hackensack over in Jersey. From H. I walked 5½ miles on the
Spring Valley road, then four miles to Ridgewood, then another

mile to Hoboken and back towards town 7 miles to Paterson."
Or, full of sausages and buckwheats, he sets out at 5:00 A.M. and
walks almost to West Point. Perhaps the finest of all his walks was
taken after he and Elsie were married, as he writes to her, "I
walked from Van Cortlandt Park (the Broadway end of the Subway) to Greenwich, Connecticut—say, by my route and judging
from the time it took, roughly, thirty miles." There he meets "two
creeking [sic] stages full of negroes, returning from a pic-nic, with
their arms, etc. all intertwined." Stevens is exhilarated, the "sorrows, and civilities" of New York having disappeared.

His discovery, on one walk, of a "solitude" in the Palisades is
expressed with especial delicacy: "Silvery ropes of spiders' weav-
ing stretched over the road, showing that my retreat had had no
recent visitors . . . no litter of broken bottles or crushed egg-
shells on the brown needles—but a little brook tinkles under a
ledge into a deep ravine—*deep* en vérité": he promises himself he
will spend much time there. Another refuge from the busy hum is
St. Patrick's Cathedral, indeed churches generally where, as a
spectator not a participant in the service, Stevens can meditate.
But often, too often, other people get in the way, as in one church
where he perceives "a doddering girl of, say, twenty—idiot eyes,
spongy nose, shining cheeks. . . . One sees the most painful people wherever one goes. Human qualities, on an average, are fearful
subjects for contemplation; I can't make head or tail of Life. Love
is a fine thing. Art is a fine thing, Nature is a fine thing; but the
average human mind and spirit are confusing beyond measure."
And he writes to Witter Bynner, describing his "idea of life": "a
fine evening, an orchestra, + a crowd *at a distance,* a medium dinner, a glass of something cool + at the same time something
wholesome + a soft, full Panatela."

Statements like these and others in the letters harmonize with,
though they do not explain, the sentiments and tone of Stevens's
first important poem, "Sunday Morning." The romantic idealism,
the nostalgia and loneliness, the shrinking from average human
minds and spirit (are human minds necessarily "average" for

him?), the wholesomeness of the aspirations which too much drink or smoke or a sedentary life might contaminate, the generally Protestant sensibility seasoned with much grace and high style—these qualities are very much present in the poem's cadences and diction. It was Yvor Winters who adduced William Cullen Bryant as an American "source" for this sensibility—Bryant who in "Thanatopsis" spoke nobly of

> The hills
> Rock-ribbed and ancient as the sun,—the vales
> Stretching in pensive quietness between;
> The venerable woods—rivers that move
> In majesty, and the complaining brooks
> That make the meadows green; and, poured round all,
> Old Ocean's gray and melancholy waste. . . .

This is surely very close, in mood and diction, to the "nature" of Stevens's final stanza and of our "island solitude, unsponsored, free, / Of that wide water, inescapable."

But Bryant's poem is seamless, moving from beginning to end in a logical fashion with one declarative statement following another. Although compared to most poems Stevens was later to write, "Sunday Morning" is direct in its procedure and unambiguous in its implications, still its manner of proceeding is quite different from Bryant's or from any conventionally argumentative poem. When Harriet Monroe accepted it for publication in *Poetry* in 1915 she proposed to delete three sections (II, III, and VI), presumably because she felt them divergent or digressive from the main argument. Stevens, doubtless eager to have his poem published even at a little cost, made no objection but stipulated that the stanzas to be published follow an order different (I, VIII, IV, V, VII) from the one in which they appear in the *Harmonium* version we know.

It is a shock to read this earlier version of the poem, with its omissions and alterations of stanzaic order; yet one could argue that there are benefits gained from the transposing. For example, to follow the pigeons of the eighth stanza sinking "downward to darkness on extended wings" with the woman's contentment in the "wakened birds" of stanza IV is a satisfying continuity, and there are others. Then one realizes that even if the eight stanzas were shuffled and dealt out in a number of ways, one could nevertheless proceed to make various plausible connections among the parts. Omitting a stanza here or there would not result in a spoiled poem; the surviving body could be found to possess its own structure. The most suggestive attempt to identify that structure was made by R. P. Blackmur in his pioneering (1931) essay on Stevens's language. Blackmur compared him with Pound and Eliot, poets who condense and compress; by contrast Stevens's tropes were "neither visual like Pound nor dramatic like Eliot": "His visual images never condense the matter of his poems; they either accent or elaborate it. His dramatic statements, likewise, tend rather to give another, perhaps more final, form to what has already been put in different language."

The justness of Blackmur's perception may be seen clearly by considering the following stanza (V) from "Sunday Morning":

> She says, "But in contentment I still feel
> The need of some imperishable bliss."
> Death is the mother of beauty; hence from her,
> Alone, shall come fulfilment to our dreams
> And our desires. Although she strews the leaves
> Of sure obliteration on our paths,
> The path sick sorrow took, the many paths
> Where triumph rang its brassy phrase, or love
> Whispered a little out of tenderness,
> She makes the willow shiver in the sun
> For maidens who were wont to sit and gaze
> Upon the grass, relinquished to their feet.
> She causes boys to pile new plums and pears
> On disregarded plate. The maidens taste
> And stray impassioned in the littering leaves.

We observe that the voice which intones "Death is the mother of beauty" and subsequent truths does so in something quite other than a dramatic mode of response (as in a Frost dialogue, say) to "her" quoted statement. The modulation into another, deeper key is absolute; one feels that her statement is there merely as a pretext for the meditation to follow; that the poet is not really of two minds about this matter, is not really attempting to explore possibilities and see where they take him. The strewn leaves of obliteration had been worked previously by Stevens in the *Advocate* sonnet ("If we are leaves that fall upon the ground"); they now fall on our "paths" and, though this is scarcely a visual image at all, Stevens expands on the sorts of paths he has in mind. In Blackmur's terms, he accents and elaborates the matter, he presses home the point.

Harriet Monroe had trouble with the phrase "disregarded plate," and Stevens told her he had in mind "so-called family plate," fallen into disuse, but renewed and released by the perception of death. But he also allowed that her criticism was well-founded and proposed a possible rewriting:

> She causes boys to bring sweet-smelling pears,
> And plums in ponderous piles. The maidens taste
> And stray (etc.)

Fortunately the editor didn't insist that he make this change, so we were spared the plentitude of "p's" and the unfortunate locution "ponderous piles." But it's entirely possible that Stevens *might* have come up with something better, not worse, than "disregarded place"; the point is that there is much less inevitability about the image than, say, Pound's "Your mind and you are our Sargasso Sea"—surely the only way that mind could have been presented. With regard to "dramatic" statements like "Death is the mother of beauty," Blackmur's formulation is also right: the statement puts into another, more final form matter that has already been expressed otherwise, in different language. Stevens didn't, that is, discover what he had to say as he was writing the poem—as the author of "Prufrock" (published in the same year as

"Sunday Morning") must have. He had, instead, an idea, and with beauty, eloquence, and gravity he proceeded to set down the great humanist truth he was possessed by for much of his life: that we are the measure of all things, and that we know how to measure because we know we will die.

The best word Blackmur, somewhat apologetically, could find to describe the form of a Stevens poem was "rhetorical," though he quickly insisted that Stevens's language had much concrete experience in it. A way of expressing the difference between Stevens's poetic temperament and that of Eliot is to observe that the latter thought of rhetorical moments in poems or plays as ones in which a speaker saw himself in a dramatic light or was interested in achieving a large "impressiveness" of language. So Eliot wrote "Prufrock" and "Gerontion," in which these speakers attempted such impressive gestures ("No, I am not Prince Hamlet"; "I would meet you upon this honestly") and the reader was left to decide how feelingly or skeptically to give or withhold his sympathies. Such decisions almost never need to be made in reading Stevens; certainly not in "Sunday Morning," which is all rhetoric (or "eloquence" as Harold Bloom calls it) and calculated to overwhelm attempts at discrimination or relative valuation of parts.

By this I mean—and the point could be made as well about such later poems as "Notes Toward a Supreme Fiction" or "Esthétique du Mal" (my own favorites among the longer poems)— that, given Blackmur's sense of "rhetorical" activity as an accenting, or elaborating, a putting-it-another-way of a large statement about how we should live, or how vital is the imagination, or how we must transform reality yet not transform it too much—that it is not only exceptionally difficult but also of small use to find *this* elaboration admirable, while *that* one not so good. Stevens himself began a charming poem called "Table Talk" in the following manner:

> Granted, we die for good.
> Life, then, is largely a matter
> Of happens to like, not should.

Some critics happen to like different parts of different poems very much; others not so very much. Bloom finds the phrasing of "Death is the mother of beauty" "unfortunate," but doesn't say why, or doesn't make me reconsider my own sense of the statement as an extremely fortunate way of putting it. There seems no way in which a standard of good taste or decorum can be applied to this poet of excess ("in excess continual there is cure of sorrow") who boasts in "The Weeping Burgher" that he comes "as belle design of foppish line." If a sober reader finds in "A High-Toned Old Christian Woman" that "such novelties of the sublime, / Such tink and tank and tunk-a-tunk-tunk" go too far, are insufficiently adult or serious, he will be left alone with his high-toned moral sense of things.

"Sunday Morning" is of course a more traditional, generally an easier poem to get hold of than are most of the ones Stevens published in his *Harmonium* of 1923 (a second edition in 1931 added fourteen poems). At least it appears to have a logical structure, an argument which goes somewhere. Yet Stevens's poems have a way of appearing to go somewhere, while they circle back upon themselves, or issue in statements which seem to mean more than can be stated in a paraphrase. (For example, how does one "translate" the final assertion of the stanza from "Sunday Morning" quoted earlier: "Death is the mother of beauty, mystical, / Within whose burning bosom we devise / Our earthly mothers waiting, sleeplessly"?) Again Blackmur is of some use here as, in discussing some slighter, more obviously fanciful poems from *Harmonium,* he introduces the word "nonsense" and speaks of it both as "sleeping knowledge" which wakes in the poem, and as having "a persuasive force out of all relation to the sense of the words."

Consider what happens in apparently one of the most lucid and impeccably argued, also least ornate and "excessive," of Stevens's early poems. "The Snow Man" has received much admiration and comment, but not to the point where its curious manner of proceeding, the way it delivers its "message," becomes any less strange and resistant to paraphrase:

One must have a mind of winter
To regard the frost and the boughs
Of the pine-trees crusted with snow;

And have been cold a long time
To behold the junipers shagged with ice,
The spruces rough in the distant glitter

Of the January sun; and not to think
Of any misery in the sound of the wind,
In the sound of a few leaves,

Which is the sound of the land
Full of the same wind
That is blowing in the same bare place

For the listener, who listens in the snow,
And, nothing himself, beholds
Nothing that is not there and the nothing that is.

Commentators agree more or less that this is a poem about perceiving reality, or nature, without attributing human meanings and feelings to it, without making the "ambiguous undulations" of "Sunday Morning." Or it is a poem about how, to perceive in this way, "one" would have to become a snow man, refraining because of one's extremely cold constitution from hearing and thinking of "misery" in the sound the wind makes. So far it is similar to the doctrine of Frost's "The Need of Being Versed in Country Things," which ends with the speaker surveying a ruined scene, specifying that the birds are still visiting it, yet musing that "One had to be versed in country things / Not to believe the phoebes wept." Stevens's poem begins with a strong grammatical construction, "One must have . . . and have been . . . To behold . . . and not think of," but rather than developing into the sort of carefully measured and qualified assertion made by Frost's poem "The Snow Man" does something odder and more difficult to pin down.

Stevens's own explanation of its meaning, made years later, speaks of the poem as providing "an example of the necessity of identifying oneself with reality in order to understand and enjoy it." This seems to me of no help, especially as it drags in the word "identify"; nor is help to be found in the contorted dialectics about "being" and "nothing" engaged in by Hillis Miller in his account of the poem; at least they seem all out of scale—as does Bloom's long commentary—with the quietly skillful turns made by "The Snow Man." It is particularly important in reading any Stevens poem that we pay attention to "the listener"—ourselves as we read the poem—and try to describe what we are hearing. And the point here at which something most certainly is heard comes in the moment after the semicolon near the middle of the poem, as the voice begins to warm to its task of expressing how only a very cold mind would not think

> Of any misery in the sound of the wind,
> In the sound of a few leaves,
>
> Which is the sound of the land
> Full of the same wind
> That is blowing in the same bare place. . . .

The intoning becomes more pronounced, the repeated word "sound" making sure that what we attend to is something heard rather than seen or thought about—a matter for the ear not the intellect. "He is always trying to put down tremendous statements; to put down those statements heard in dreams," said Blackmur, with the proper auditory emphasis.

"Is the function of the poet here mere sound / Subtler than the ornatest prophecy, / To stuff the ear?" asks Stevens in "Academic Discourse at Havana." If we take this question seriously and treat the "mere sound" of "The Snow Man" as absolutely important, then what happens after the wind's sound fills the land is a good deal subtler than any statement about how one sees or should see reality. Somehow this wind is blowing

> For the listener, who listens in the snow,
> And, nothing himself, beholds
> Nothing that is not there and the nothing that is.

Not the snow man, but "the listener," who by this point in the poem if he is paying attention finds himself wholly caught up in the voice's turns and surprises. One last surprise is in store for him, the brilliantly verbal play on "nothing" and the brain-twisting (if we try to reason it out) paradox of the last line. The word "nothing" here is similar to the "mere" in "Academic Discourse"—"Is the function of the poet here mere sound?" Both words indicate the fullness, the absolute presence of the world of utterance created by an individual Stevens poem. "Nonsense" is not quite the word for it, but it is a preferable alternative to treating the poem as if it were a statement about or an attitude toward the real world we presumably share. In poem after poem, Stevens creates outrageous or seductive or plaintive figures of sound, "statements heard in dreams" which appeal to different readers according to the range of their antennae.

One further example must suffice for the moment. "Autumn Refrain," from *Ideas of Order* (1935), begins with naming various sounds no longer to be heard ("The skreak and skritter of evening gone") though now heard in the poem for the first time. The moon and the nightingale are invoked, the moon quickly becoming a "moon of words," the nightingale "the name of a bird" never to be heard. Then the poem appears to turn on itself:

> And yet beneath
> The stillness that comes to me out of this, beneath
> The stillness of everything gone, and being still,
> Being and sitting still, something resides,
> Some skreaking and skrittering residuum,
> And gates these evasions of the nightingale
> Though I have never—shall never hear that bird.

What is it that "resides"? "Something," we are told, "some skreaking and skrittering residuum"—a fancy variation of "shriek" which should grate properly on our ears. Then the final two lines:

> And the stillness is in the key, all of it is,
> The stillness is all in the key of that desolate sound.

The best Randall Jarrell could do by way of identifying his pleasure in "Autumn Refrain" was to call it "that haunting poem no
one seems haunted by"; a good word to characterize the sound, to
name the "key" of this reflexive exercise in melancholy intoning.

One of the most quoted passages from Stevens's prose writings
is the conclusion to "The Noble Rider and the Sound of Words."
Yeats and Pound vied in fixing that epithet ("noble") on each
other's poetry; in his own essay Stevens speaks grandly, if somewhat vaguely, of nobility as a "force," as "out of time" and manifesting itself in particular occasions which are less than itself.
Eventually he calls it "a violence from within that protects us from
a violence without," then identifies it with the imagination in these
closing words:

> It is the imagination pressing back against the pressure of re-
> ality. It seems, in the last analysis, to have something to do
> with our self-preservation; and that, no doubt, is why the
> expression of it, the sound of its words, helps us to live our
> lives.

If this at first sounds slightly like a pep talk on how poetry does
have a moral function, is "equipment for living" in Kenneth
Burke's phrase, I think that when considered in the context of
Stevens's poems a rather different emphasis has to be made. My
own inclination is to take very seriously indeed, even literally—
dangerous as that may be—the insistence on sound—"the sound
of its words." The emphasis then would be less on poetry as
presenting richly complex attitudes toward experience, which attitudes serve to educate and instruct us; rather that we are enabled
to live life better, finding it richer—or finding that a poor or tragic
affair has been momentarily alleviated—because of the sounds of
poems. Not the "sound of sense," not the pleasing and preaching
simultaneously recommended by Pope, but a purer and stranger
satisfying of the ear, and of the mind as it gives itself up to the
desolate or delightful music. To rewrite the last line of "Autumn
Refrain": the nobleness is all in the key of that sound, the mere
sound.

"After all, what is there odd about being a lawyer and being or doing something else at the same time?" Stevens wrote Harvey Breit in 1942, by way of turning down Breit's request for an interview. He had joined the New York office of the Hartford Accident and Indemnity Company back in 1916, moved to Hartford soon after, and was appointed vice-president of the company in 1934. *Harmonium* was published in 1923; his daughter Holly was born the same year, and she tells us in her edition of her father's letters that whatever the causes were—the "failure" of *Harmonium* in commercial terms (Stevens says at one point that he netted $6.70 in profits), the presence of a young child in the house, much time spent in listening to classical music or in gardening, the pressures of his job—Stevens wrote little poetry for eight or so years at a time when (between the ages of forty-four and fifty-two) one might have expected the reverse. His becoming vice-president in 1934 may be considered as the point when his creative energies began to move back into poetry. Holly Stevens suggests that he wanted at all costs to avoid being taken as an "oddity," and thus passed over, by his business colleagues. Years later, in a letter to one of his correspondents about Ceylon, a place he had become strongly interested in imagining, he confided that "I try to draw a definite line between poetry and business," and that he didn't want his Hartford friends to know about his poetry, because "once they know they never think of you as anything but a poet and, after all, one is inevitably much more complicated than that."

One might turn the statement around and consider it from a poetry reader's rather than a Hartford colleague's point of view. Stevens didn't want his poet friends to know anything about insurance and how the money was made, lest they think of him, with sentimental patronization or a tinge of contempt, as an American businessman with a hobby. "One is inevitably much more complicated than that": one doesn't want to be understood as either an aesthete or a robust philistine, though one sees the attractions of both modes of behavior when sufficiently regulated. Why should the left hand know what the right hand was doing? Here we are drawn toward the center of Stevens's immense stubbornness, his insistence on going his own way, caring intensely about only what he cared about. So there is most decidedly no point in pretending that we can appreciate the poems more truly if we dose ourselves up with the life; a life that, through the letters, we get glimpses into only, though they are sometimes rich glimpses.

Hannah Arendt quotes Gilson's remark that if a philosopher should try to write his autobiography, he would find that insofar as he was a philosopher he had no life. This observation takes on special point when Stevens is compared to a poet such as Yeats. The clear connections between Yeats's responses to public and private events in letters or essays, and his responses to them in poems, give us the illusion that both life and work are comprehensible, open for inspection by the rational intellect, no matter how many "irrational" materials they make use of. There is no such security with Stevens; the "definite line between poetry and business" he succeeded in drawing makes both his activities the more inscrutable. Whatever he did at the office of the Hartford Accident and Indemnity Company we imagine to have been thoroughly self-contained, ceasing at 5:00 P.M.; after that, the other life began. And in 1942, an important moment in his poetic career, he wrote in about two months his most ambitious and possibly most successful attempt to demonstrate how poetry can help us to live our lives.

Subject to the literary historian's habit of dividing careers into Early, Middle, and Late, I am tempted to call "Notes Toward a Supreme Fiction" the prime example of Middle Stevens—with *Harmonium* representing the earlier work and the poems from the 1950's, beginning in *Collected Poems* with "The Rock," representing the late. But in fact over half of the collected poems were composed within the last thirteen years of Stevens's life, from 1942 to his death in 1955, and "Notes" is the fully mature expression of a man of sixty-three, not really "middle" anything. With particular respect to this poem but with implications for Stevens's other poems as well, I want to express both my admiration for it, my delight in its rhetoric, its "sound," and also my bafflement at it, my uncertainty that it is a "great poem." But I must do so in what is a dangerously foreshortened way, dealing only with a couple of representative sections.

We are fortunate to have the commentaries of Helen Vendler and Harold Bloom to help in finding our way about in it. Vendler's account is characteristically subtle, comprehensive, and assured; for her the "flawless energy" of "Notes" feels both "liberated and restrained":

> . . . Stevens' willingness to abate the claims of imagination invigorates the verse; the will that had, for so many years, strained toward an aspiring apotheosis is deflected now into an exhilaration of manner and a lightening of mood in all directions. Stevens is freed into equilibrium: released from protesting too much, he can vest himself in easier language and motion.

The triadic stanza which he settled on for this poem, and for succeeding ones like "The Auroras of Autumn" and "An Ordinary Evening in New Haven"—with seven unrhymed tercets to a section and ten sections making up each of its three parts—is perfect for providing him with the room to expand, yet pull himself up after twenty-one lines and modulate into a different key. Vendler also finds the poem memorable for its array of personifications and fables, saying (rather strangely to my ears) that the poem immortalizes not "mythical objects"—as does the earlier long poem "Owl's Clover"—but objects that are "quotidian, recognizable, accessible, or at least naturalized." She then provides a list of the significant figures of "Notes": "the Arabian, the Ephebe, the Mac-Cullough, The Man in the Old Coat, the President, General du Puy, the Planter, Nanzia Nunzio, the Blue Woman, the Lasting Visage, the Captain and Bawda, Canon Aspirin and his Sister, the Angel, The Fat Girl."

Readers familiar with the poem will of course recognize these "figures," or at least most of them, but listing them as Vendler does has rather the opposite effect from convincing me that they represent accessible and recognizable parts of the world. They indicate rather, in summary form, the exotic nature of Stevens's art, in this poem as elsewhere, and the fanciful character—the "belle design of foppish line"—his expression aspires to. Whereas Vendler and Bloom treat these figures as either (in Vendler's case) diverse inventions to be welcomed for their plenitude, or (in Bloom's case) phenomena to be interpreted, I suggest that neither interpretation nor acceptance are adequate responses to the oddities of which "Notes" is full. For this poet of sound and rhetoric, with such a cast of characters as named above by Vendler, not only "resists the intelligence almost successfully"—as Stevens said a poem must do—but teases, overwhelms, wearies, and exhausts us with his fanciful excess. It may be that I am merely confessing to insufficient appetite for certain kinds of poetic extravagance, and my only answer to that charge is to ask whether other readers have felt any of the same discomfort, at least have responded in a more divided way than with either an enthusiastic yea-saying to whatever piece of invention or "figure" the poem brings before them, or an eager plunge into the activity of interpretation.

A comparison of a "fanciful" episode or passage with one which, in Wordsworth's sense, seems more truly imaginative will help distinguish Stevens's highest and finest style from his more idiosyncratic and potentially trivial one. In the second part of "Notes," titled "It Must Change," we confront various sorts of permanences which, like the artificial paradise imagined in stanza VI of "Sunday Morning" ("Is there no change of death in paradise? / Does ripe fruit never fall? Or do the boughs / Hang always heavy in that perfect sky . . ."), do not satisfy the imagination because they do not change. In "Notes" such permanences are represented by the statue of General du Puy which "rested immobile," or by the birds repeating "Ké-ké" ("a single text, granite monotony") or, most wittily, the "President's" ordaining "the bee

to be immortal." In section II Stevens moves from his able mock-
ery of this delusive activity into an elevated lyrical utterance which
shows itself eager to believe that change is good, is life, is the
mother of beauty and fullness:

> Why, then, when in golden fury
> Spring vanishes the scraps of winter, why
> Should there be a question of returning or
> Of death in memory's dream? Is spring a sleep?
>
> This warmth is for lovers at last accomplishing
> Their love, this beginning, not resuming, this
> Booming and booming of the new-come bee.

Here is Stevens's art at its subtlest and noblest, the conceited play
on "bee" being an occasion for something more than clever winks
and nods, the verse rising to celebrate spring and the lovers. It is
poetry which feels extremely witty, also natural and inevitable.

After the section about General du Puy, an instance of how
"Nothing had happened because nothing had changed," Stevens
sets himself in section IV to show something happening, something changing:

> Two things of opposite natures seem to depend
> On one another, as a man depends
> On a woman, day on night, the imagined
>
> On the real. This is the origin of change.
> Winter and spring, cold copulars, embrace
> And forth the particulars of rapture come.
>
> Music falls on the silence like a sense,
> A passion that we feel, not understand.
> Morning and afternoon are clasped together
>
> And North and South are an intrinsic couple
> And sun and rain a plural, like two lovers
> That walk away as one in the greenest body.
>
> In solitude the trumpets of solitude
> Are not of another solitude resounding;
> A little string speaks for a crowd of voices.

The partaker partakes of that which changes him.
The child that touches takes character from the thing,
The body, it touches. The captain and his men

Are one and the sailor and the sea are one.
Follow after, O my companion, my fellow, my self,
Sister and solace, brother and delight.

Aside from the fifth tercet, with its rather obscure reference to the
"little string," this is language and syntax of the greatest dignity
and clarity; and except for the witty play on "copulars," which
feels solemn in import, the diction doesn't call attention to itself.
Like that of the passage quoted above about the coming of spring,
it seems as inevitable as is the gradual building of examples of
"copulars" embracing until, in the last six lines, examples come
thick and fast: from partaker, to child, to the captain and the
sailor. At which point the voice addresses us, and with "O my
companion" invites us into the partaking by a particular rapture
which is the real vindication for this attempt to imagine a "supreme fiction." It is Stevens's most authentic gesture of commu-
nion, akin to the sacramental "Drink this in remembrance of me,"
and celebrating not the blood of our Lord Jesus Christ but rather,
as in "Sunday Morning," "the heavenly fellowship / Of men that
perish and of summer morn." If such a passage can exist only
because it is surrounded and set off by others, less intensely passionate in their directness, then so be it.

But consider now the section from "It Must Change" which
follows: the fable of the planter, which Harold Bloom calls "one
of the triumphs of Notes, the summation of major Stevens," and
with which Helen Vendler begins her discussion of the poem,
singling it out for the "tact" of its "negative praise"—the way it
avoids too-positive enthusiasms and elegiac overstatements.

On a blue island in a sky-wide water
The wild orange trees continued to bloom and to bear,
Long after the planter's death. A few limes remained,

Where his house had fallen, three scraggy trees weighted
With garbled green. These were the planter's turquoise
And his orange blotches, these were his zero green,

A green baked greener in the greenest sun.
These were his beaches, his sea-myrtles in
White sand, his patter of the long sea-slushes.

There was an island beyond him on which rested,
An island to the South, on which rested like
A mountain, a pineapple pungent as Cuban summer.

And là-bas, là-bas, the cool bananas grew,
Hung heavily on the great banana tree,
Which pierces clouds and bends on half the world.

He thought often of the land from which he came,
How that whole country was a melon, pink
If seen rightly and yet a possible red.

An unaffected man in a negative light
Could not have borne his labor nor have died
Sighing that he should leave the banjo's twang.

It is this sort of poetry that, I would maintain, separates the
deepest admirers of Stevens from lesser ones like myself. Always
ready to gloss his poems at the request of inquiring corre-
spondents, Stevens was willing to call the planter a symbol of
change, more specifically "the laborious human who lives in illusions and who, after all the great illusions have left him, still clings
to one that pierces him." He also confessed to a great fondness for
this section. Bloom proceeds to identify the planter with Stevens,
as equally men who could be "pierced"—in the language of the
poem, were not "unaffected"—and he also finds here that Stevens
is "very moved," that his rhetoric persuades us to be "immensely
moved," and that in fact, rather than being a symbol of change,
the planter vindicates the claim of "Le Monocle de Mon Oncle"
that "There is a substance in us that prevails."

It is certainly a Stevens passage par excellence; fabulous, full
of sensuous objects and colors, blue and orange and pink and red,
but especially green: "garbled green" and "zero green" and "a

green baked greener in the greenest sun," with much alliterative transmuting of objects into sound-effects—"garbled green" and "sea-slushes," "pungent pineapples," melons, and above all the cool bananas growing "là-bas, là-bas." It is great fun to read aloud, particularly at the climactic invocation of those bananas. It is charming. But that it is by any stretch of the imagination great poetry, and that Stevens can be regarded with reverence when he composes in such a style with such material—and he does so very frequently in "Notes" and throughout his work—seems to me unthinkable except in the writings of critics who have ceased to think critically and have delivered themselves wholly into the poet's hands, becoming fans rather than discriminators. If this sounds pompous, too much like a high-toned, old, ungrateful critic, I hope to have shown some gratitude; I find the passage, like much of the "Notes," engaging and lively. But I do not believe great poetry can be made out of the color wheel, a few fruits, and the mystical repetition of a French word which can be rolled on the palate and mixed with bananas. It is poetry of the fancy, foppish and extravagant in a not very complicated sense; nor is, to mention the final line, the "banjo's twang" in any way an adequate image to call up the moving elegiac depths which in Bloom's commentary, for example, planter, poet, and reader all occupy together.

So that however "flawless" the "energy" of "Notes" may be (I use Vendler's words), there are reasons for taking the poetry with a grain of salt, for asking whether it ever falls into archness, an all-too-fancy fancifulness, a let's-pretend license to imagine anything, and the more whimsical the better. If it does, and if Stevens's poetry at its best—here and elsewhere—does not, then the distinction should not be obscured or obliterated in the interests of making him the poet of inevitable profundity.

By contrast, Hugh Kenner's account of Stevens in *A Homemade World* must appear to Stevensians as a trivializing and devaluing one, and my own sympathy for it puts these remarks in danger of being similarly misunderstood. At least it should be pointed out that in picking up, as I have done, the cue about "nonsense" most fully developed in Blackmur's early essay, Kenner's and my accounts attempt to emphasize the great stylistic originality and individuality of Stevens's use of language—"The sound of its words"—at the same time as they are unable to take the style with full seriousness as an instrument for illuminating and understanding a real world of people and objects—of the "nature" that in their different ways Hardy and Frost and Yeats and Pound, and eventually Eliot, put us in touch with. Speaking of Mallarmé and other French poets' discovery of Poe, Kenner says wittily, "They thought, so to speak, that they were reading Wallace Stevens," and claims that Stevens, not Poe, deserves the honor of being a constructor of Supreme Fictions independent of existing things: "His word-wizardry is what Poe's was thought to be: a kind of poetry, in the English language, which some very subtle and passionate Frenchmen intuited."

One of the many pleasures in reading Stevens's letters from his late age is to watch the way he constructs elegant supreme fictions, independent of existing things even of the most tempting and elemental sort. Here is a lovely instance of such constructing, beginning with one of his trips to New York to buy wine or food and to look at pictures:

> When I was in New York on Saturday I bought a lot of fruit in the place in 58th Street. One likes to look at fruit as well as to eat it and that is precisely the right spot to find fruit to look at. Then, too, I bought a chocolate cake because it was Saturday and Saturday and cakes are part of the same thing. In any case, last evening Holly and Peter [his grandson] dropped in and as the top of the cake had some sugar on it: a couple of roses, sprays and leaves, we put Peter in a chair and placed the cake in front of him and let him go to it to see what he would do. He had it all over the place. But he liked it and it was a good way to get rid of it because I am afraid that cakes, too, ought merely to be looked at.

This is more than the necessary prudence to be observed in eating habits when the subject is approaching seventy. More positively, the interest is in looking; in looking-on and providing the opportunity for readers to be onlookers also, through the frame of a supreme fiction. The fine last line from a late poem, "Prologues to What Is Possible," speaks of "The way a look or a touch reveals its unexpected magnitudes." More likely, for Stevens, it would be a look rather than a touch; you can only have a vision of "good, fat guzzly fruit" if you refrain from eating it—or so Stevens's way has it. This is the magician's way, that of the user of language who conjures up a scene in poems just as he put the cake in front of his grandson and deployed word-wizardry about it.

Kenner has had the temerity to suggest that we reconsider the seriousness with which we take Stevens's work:

> So many scrupulously arrested gestures, so laborious an honesty, such a pother of fine shades and nuanced distinctions; yet that forty years' work revolves about nothing more profound than bafflement with a speechless externality which poets can no longer pretend is animate. This fact invalidates no Stevens poem, only the terms on which some of the poems ask us to take them.

Surely the main terms on which Stevens's critics have taken him over the past twenty years or so have been extremely solemn ones: philosophical with a modern Continental twist, or Emersonianly Romantic. The last poems in particular have been seen as effecting some final reconciliation between imagination and reality, and it may be that Stevens himself had such an aspiration in regard to them. Yet what makes them—many of them—so splendid, and arguably the best ones he ever wrote, is their preoccupation with (in Kenner's derogatory phrase) "nothing more profound" than how to respond, as a man and poet of seventy years, to the "speechless externality" which is no longer animate.

In the severely limited context of poems considered here, "Sunday Morning" was an early response to speechless externality which proposed an ingenious fiction—"Death is the mother of beauty"—as a way of imaginatively animating a world without God. And so, it is with a personal and terrifying edge that "Madame La Fleurie" welcomes the man to his final home:

Weight him down, O side-stars, with the great weightings of the end.
Seal him there. He looked in a glass of the earth and thought he lived in it.
Now, he brings all that he saw into the earth, to the waiting parent.
His crisp knowledge is devoured by her, beneath a dew.

"Madame La Fleurie" undoes poetry, turns back upon the poet the speech he had so gloriously contrived in so many poems, as in its final four lines:

The thick strings stutter the finial gutturals.
He does not lie there remembering the blue-jay, say the jay.
His grief is that his mother should feed on him, himself and what he saw,
In that distant chamber, a bearded queen, wicked in her dead light.

Bloom reminds us that the "jay" comes in here by way of "The Man with the Blue Guitar," who at the end of that poem would teach us to play "The imagined pine, the imagined jay"; the "gutturals" recall a poem at the very beginning of Harmonium—"The Plot Against the Giant," in which the nymph of poetry would "whisper heavenly labials in a world of gutturals," thereby undoing the giant of reality. But most fearful is the mother, no longer the mother of beauty, and of a different sort than could have been devised in "Sunday Morning" when the vision of "our earthly mothers waiting, sleeplessly" was immediately followed by a ring of supple and turbulent men, chanting their faith in the goodness of mortality. In "Madame La Fleurie" these no longer so supreme fictions are replaced by a darker one which could pass for truth.

The impulse bears a resemblance to Yeats's attempt in his Last Poems to move beyond the metaphors (supreme fictions) or "circus animals" of his early poems which have now deserted him. But in forsaking metaphor in favor of his heart (in "The Circus Animals' Desertion") this incorrigible metaphor-maker can't just call it a "heart"; it becomes an exciting, sinister, rag-and-bone shop of a heart. Likewise in Stevens's poem, the "bearded queen, wicked in her dead light" is at least as aggressive an invention as to "say the jay" or to announce that "Death is the mother of beauty." Stevens confronts this paradoxical energy of the human imagination as it confronts blankness, absence, death, and formulates it most succinctly in "The Plain Sense of Things," where the lesson learned is that "the absence of imagination had itself to be imagined."

A year short of his seventieth birthday, he suddenly confessed in a letter, "What I want more than anything else in music, painting and poetry, in life and in belief is the thrill that I experienced once in all the things that no longer thrill me at all." What is most human about the final "Rock" section of the *Collected Poems* are moments in which the poems become infused with an analogous thrill: the way that, in "To an Old Philosopher in Rome," a poem about Santayana in old age (and about Stevens), the philosopher's room becomes "the threshold of heaven" and a source of happiness:

> The bed, the books, the chair, the moving nuns,
> The candle as it evades the sight, these are
> The source of happiness in the shape of Rome. . . .
>
> A light on the candle tearing against the wick
> To join a hovering excellence,

or the way the "flick" of "Prologues to What Is Possible" becomes, in the concluding list of possibles, a moving response to the pressure of reality:

> A flick which added to what was real and its vocabulary,
> The way some first thing coming into Northern trees
> Adds to them the whole vocabulary of the South,
> The way the earliest single light in the evening sky, in spring,
> Creates a fresh universe out of nothingness by adding itself,
> The way a look or a touch reveals its unexpected magnitudes,

or, in "The World as Meditation," the way Penelope's continuing effort to imagine Ulysses' return, to compose "Two in a deep-founded sheltering, friend and dear friend," finds in the very act of composing that

> It was Ulysses and it was not. Yet they had met,
> Friend and dear friend and a planet's encouragement.
> The barbarous strength within her would never fail.

These poems exhibit the fullest, most ample and leisured response to that "bafflement" Stevens had expressed early on, very beautifully, in "Anatomy of Monotony," a poem which appeared in the revised *Harmonium* and which explored the way human beings are one with the speechless externality—"Our nature is her nature"—yet not one and the same in that we will die and know that we will die. The poem concludes:

> So be it. Yet the spaciousness and light
> In which the body walks and is deceived,
> Falls from that fatal and that barer sky,
> And this the spirit sees and is aggrieved.

The great difference between the last work and *Harmonium* is that Stevens has conceived of so many ways to extend the "So be it" into poems which neither console in facile ways nor divert us through fancy and "nonsense." It is not only Penelope and Ulysses who "meet," but the reader and Stevens, "in a queer assertion of humanity," as a line from "The Rock" has it.

Stevens lived into his seventy-sixth year, and the letters from his seventies are, in their muted, sometimes bleak, but often humorous way, as interesting as the New York ones written fifty years before. He had by now developed ways of coming to terms with nearly everything; such as for example a member of the Yale faculty who had given a Sunday night talk over the radio, in December of 1953, about the religious significance of Christmas: ". . . when I feel sore about Christmas cards and someone gets on the air and talks about the Incarnation and its practical value for all of us, I clap my hands and stamp my feet and say Bravo,

Bravo! Perhaps that only goes to show how queer you become if you remain in New England long enough." He could never live in New England long enough, where ". . . everything is normal beyond belief. My neighbors are returning from cruises. This morning I rode in town with a man burned the darkest brown. Personally I like *not* to go on cruises. There is a specific ease that comes from the office, going to bed and getting up early, which equals the relaxation of cruises. Good-luck and bon voyage! I shall follow you in my mind as you experience Spain anew." Thus he writes to the departing voyager Barbara Church, putting her and himself in their places. It is impossible to overestimate the importance of going to "the office" and its attendant routines in producing the specific ease in which the late poems bloomed; while the privilege of following someone in the mind rather than traveling along with them in reality is essential Stevens.

Knopf published the *Collected Poems* at the end of 1954 when he was seventy-five, to much respectful acclaim and the National Book Award. Stevens allowed as how he "intended to stay 75 for some years after that"; but time would not relent. His wife had the first of many strokes in January of the new year, then in April he went into the hospital for an exploratory operation that revealed an inoperable cancer which he was not told about. Two months later he returned to the office, "coming in at 10.00 and leaving at 1.30 and doing very little in the meantime except seeing people who want to know how I feel." This was in July, the Hartford heat "appalling," the upstairs of his house "like an oven." He wrote to Samuel French Morse that "There is no chance, I think, of any new poems," that most of the time he felt drowsy and limp, and ended his letter with a particularly poignant statement:

> Call me up when you return to Hartford. I have not been to the Canoe Club now for a long time and believe that even a single Martini would be a disaster. The most I might be able to do would be to go and sit on the porch and drink lemonade and I should be glad to do that one of these days because I always loved the porch over there. But I know nothing of the lemonade.

One thinks again of the letter to Witter Bynner from many years before, and it is sad for what has perforce replaced the cool drink, the Panatella, the orchestra playing somewhere nearby, the crowd at a distance. Still, that last straight-faced sentence about the uncertain status of Canoe Club lemonade has the imaginative "flick" which just makes the difference. The next month he was dead.

Near the every end of *Collected Poems* stands one which to my knowledge is neglected by commentators and stands nowhere near the top of most people's list of favorite Stevens poems. It is near the top of mine, however, and is a good poem to close with because of the extremely satisfying way it closes itself yet leaves open the sense of possibility he so warmed to and cherished. It is about subjectivity and objectiveness, about what to do with the mind's "bafflement with a speechless externality which poets can no longer pretend is animate," and about how, it turns out, poets exist to show us the way in which it is animate after all:

> The one moonlight, in the simple-colored night,
> Like a plain poet revolving in his mind
> The sameness of his various universe,
> Shines on the mere objectiveness of things.
>
> It is as if being was to be observed,
> As if, among the possible purposes
> Of what one sees, the purpose that comes first,
> The surface, is the purpose to be seen,
>
> The property of the moon, what it evokes.
> It is to disclose the essential presence, say,
> Of a mountain, expanded and elevated almost
> Into a sense, an object the less; or else
>
> To disclose in the figure waiting on the road
> An object the more, an undetermined form
> Between the slouchings of a gunman and a lover,
> A gesture in the dark, a fear one feels
>
> In the great vistas of night air, that takes this form,
> In the arbors that are as if of Saturn-star.
> So, then, this warm, wide, weatherless quietude
> Is active with a power, an inherent life,

In spite of the mere objectiveness of things,
Like a cloud-cap in the corner of a looking-glass,
A change of color in the plain poet's mind,
Night and silence disturbed by an interior sound,

The one moonlight, the various universe, intended
So much just to be seen—a purpose, empty
Perhaps, absurd perhaps, but at least a purpose,
Certain and ever more fresh. Ah! Certain, for sure . . .

It was not his habit to end poems with ellipses or to use "Ah" in their final line. Their presence here in "Note on Moonlight" is an especially happy indication of the interior sound of his imagination, profound enough to last us for a lifetime.

8

HART CRANE
A Fine Messed-Up Life

With the exception of Robinson's work, which currently provokes little interesting argument (a consequence of his being infrequently read), there is less agreement about the importance and success of Hart Crane's poetry than about that of any other poet considered here. Within the last twenty years Crane has been the subject of a painstakingly detailed and sympathetic biography by John Unterecker and a number of critical studies, the most exhaustive of which is R. W. B. Lewis's full-dress analysis of the poems. Many letters have also been published, particularly ones written by members of the Crane family, as well as the very interesting exchange between Crane and Yvor Winters. Yet one has the feeling that these books have not made much difference in terms of establishing Crane's presence as a great modern lyric poet. Put oversimply, the problem may be that the people who write about him tend toward ecstatic affirmations and approvals, as did his own poetry, particularly *The Bridge*. Crane's admirers tend to welcome, in a famous phrase from a poem ("The Wine Menagerie") about the exciting effects of getting drunk, "New thresholds, new anatomies." Meanwhile his detractors, or at least nonsupporters—

cold and sober—find his work more often than not confused, incoherent, self-indulgent, and rather monotonous in tone.

In his essay "General Aims and Theories," Crane proposed "to go *through* the combined materials of the poem, using our 'real' world somewhat as a springboard, and to give the poem *as a whole* an orbit or predetermined direction of its own." A single example of this effect may be cited, from a poem which most would agree to be one of Crane's very best, the second part of "Voyages," whose second stanza invokes the sea as follows:

> Take this Sea, whose diapason knells
> On scrolls of silver snowy sentences,
> The sceptred terror of whose sessions rends
> As her demeanors motion well or ill,
> All but the pieties of lovers' hands.

What is being said in this passage is not terribly complicated or even particularly interesting, but the "saying" itself is gorgeous, the diapason open as on an organ. Can anyone not be moved by its sheer vocal magnificence? Evidently the answer is yes: as with Dylan Thomas, one may find the volume switched up too high, the alliteration overbearing, the high diction ("knells" and "sceptred" and "demeanors") effecting, as Johnson said about Thomas Gray, a "strutting dignity too tall by walking on tip-toe." In which case Crane's aspiration to use the "real" (in quotation marks) world as a springboard—to go *through* the poem's materials—may feel like a dangerous and misguided aspiration indulged at the expense of the real world.

As far as I know Eliot never referred to Crane, and under his editorship the *Criterion* rejected "The Wine Menagerie" (though it later published a section from *The Bridge*); but the following passage written by him in 1944 (from "Johnson as Critic and Poet") could have had Crane's example in mind:

> The modern inclination is to put up with some degree of incoherence of sense, to be tolerant of poets who do not know themselves exactly what they are trying to say, so long as the

verse sounds well and presents striking and unusual imagery. There is, in fact, a certain merit in melodious raving, which can be a genuine contribution to literature, when it responds effectually to that permanent appetite of humanity for an occasional feast of drums and cymbals. We all want to get drunk now and again, whether we do or not: though an exclusive addiction to some kinds of poetry has dangers analogous to those of a steady reliance upon alcohol.

Yet in "The Wine Menagerie," a poem as a whole obscure to me, the ecstatic promises of redemption, of new thresholds and anatomies glimpsed through wine, are followed by an "Alas," then an unecstatic conclusion to the poem. Crane's poetry usually contains various counterthrusts and checks to uninhibited celebration; it is a good deal more than, and different from, just a feast of drums and cymbals.

But it was not only Eliot who failed to mention Crane by name; indeed of the other eight poets considered here, only Williams had anything to say about him directly, and then only to deplore, in a letter of 1928, his "disguised sentimentality and sloppy feeling" and in one of 1939 to say that though he liked him, "I suppose the thing was that he was searching for something inside, while I was all for a sharp use of the materials." And Crane stands apart from the rest of these modern poets in other ways: they all lived until sixty-five, most of them well beyond; he died a few months short of age thirty-three, a suicide. He was an American Midwesterner, a homosexual, and an alcoholic—attributes few of the others can lay claim to, even if Eliot was born in St. Louis and Robinson's taste for drink was fierce enough to qualify him for the last category. Crane's affiliations with "revivalist" forms of consciousness, whether they operated under the name of Christian Science, Ouspensky, or Arthur Rimbaud, is yet a further signal of his difference.

At the same time—and here I may not be speaking for readers generally—there is a note in Crane's voice as heard in his letters that is absolutely contemporary and with which we can readily identify. As an example of what I mean, take this beginning of a letter to Gorham Munson, written when Crane was twenty-two, living in Cleveland, and brought face to face with a local occasion:

> The "march of events" has brought upon us Cleveland's 125th anniversary with all its fussy & futile inanities and advertisements to make hideous the streets. Blocked, and obliged to wait while the initial "pee-rade" went by today, I spent two hours of painful rumination ending with such disgust at America and everything in it, that I more than ever envy you your egress to foreign parts. No place but America could relish & applaud anything so stupid & drab as that parade—led by the most notable and richest grafter of the place decked out in Colonial rags as the founder of the city. . . . All I can say is—it's a gay old world! If ever I felt alone it has been today. But I must encounter fireworks, bawling "choruses" and more "pee-rades" for 7 more days—as the community believes in celebrations that are productive of business.

It may be merely that as a young man of about Crane's age I had one summer to endure, on a smaller but a more extended scale, the 100th anniversary of the founding of Johnson City, New York, with many "pee-rades" and "celebrations . . . productive of business." But Crane's frustration and contempt, his portrait of the "blocked" poet having to wait while the parade goes by, endlessly on and on to inane purposes, seems attractive and sane, even humorously so, as he warms to the task of excoriating Cleveland and America. Here at least local "materials" are being dealt with very sharply and winningly, in a way William Carlos Williams would surely have approved of.

One of Crane's friends, Samuel Loveman, once referred to the poet's life as a "fine messed-up" one, and the peruser of any of Crane's biographies (of which the first by Philip Horton remains the best) feels something of that quality in the alternation of exhilaration and depression his life so forthrightly exhibits. "As high as we have mounted in delight / In our dejection do we sink as low"—Wordsworth's lines from "Resolution and Independence" seem to have been written as an epitaph for Crane, the American romantic poet; and the events of his brief life have less interest in themselves than in the up-and-down pattern they display. He was born in a small Ohio town, his father the prosperous owner of a maple sugar cannery, later head of the Crane Chocolate Factory, whose life was organized around his business ventures. His mother, Grace Hart Crane, was a put-upon, "sensitive" woman whose relationship with Clarence Crane Hart once memorably characterized by speaking of his own state of mind as "a rather bloody battleground for yours and father's sex life and troubles." Crane's parents eventually divorced and he went to live in his grandmother's house in Cleveland, where in his "tower" room on the third floor he devoured books and music. Between 1916, when he first lived in New York, and 1923, when he settled there more or less for good, Crane alternated between there and Cleveland while holding a number of jobs in advertising and in factory and office work, all of which turned out pretty quickly to be undesirable. In the meantime he was publishing his lyrics in various little magazines, mainly located in New York, where he engaged the support of a number of lively young writers and critical polemicists such as Gorham Munson, Matthew Josephson, Kenneth Burke, and Malcolm Cowley, who also became his friends; as did the young poet and critic Allen Tate, who later claimed that it was with these men, none of them homosexuals, that Crane made his deepest friendships. He told them, or they learned, about his homosexuality; but Crane's sexual relationships were another and separable part of his life, consisting of many transient encounters as well as a longer-term affair with the merchant seaman Emil Opffer, the biographical "source" for some of his best poetry, particularly the "Voyages" sequence.

His relations with his mother revealed their mutually stifling dependence: Grace calls him her "sweetheart" and (in 1917) vows to come to New York and live with him, while Hart excitedly makes arrangements for her to occupy his room, planning himself to live nearby. Philip Horton tells us that when Grace finally arrived in New York, Hart was immediately taken seriously ill with "obscure nervous disorders," whereupon Grace phoned Clarence Crane and asked him to come to town. When Crane's father refused to do this Grace collapsed, leaving Hart to pull himself together and look after her, which he did. Typically depressing incidents like this one (if we harden our hearts they have a farcical effect) make reading the *Family Letters* a painful lesson, if we needed it, in the way families succeed in making their members miserable. Yet the letters between Hart and his father are often affecting. Clarence Crane was undeniably true to a salesmanly vision of life, but when he finally realized that Hart was determined to write poetry tried to accommodate himself to that strange fact. When his son sent him the "River" section of *The Bridge* which contains the passage beginning "Behind / My father's cannery works I used to see / Rail-squatters ranged in nomad raillery," Mr. Crane replied as follows:

> I received your letter the middle of last week, and the enclosure was, I believe, the best I have ever seen of your work. When I say the best it more nearly approached that low standard which I could understand. Something of this nature, in my humble opinion, would sell better than other things I have seen; it does not leave quite so much to the imagination.

This extremely human and modestly sensible response (in fact the passage *doesn't* "leave as much to the imagination" as do Crane's more obliquely aspiring ones) should not be too quickly dismissed; since even admiring readers of difficult passages in his poems have to resort to something as vague as the "logic of imagination"—or as he put it, "new forms of spiritual articulation"—to feel them as holding together.

His main impetus in the early 1920's, for the writing and publishing in magazines of the poems which were to make up his first (and only) collection of lyrics, was T. S. Eliot. "There is no one writing in English who can command so much respect, to my mind, as Eliot. However I take Eliot as a point of departure toward an almost complete reverse of direction. But I would apply as much of his erudition and technique as I can absorb and assemble toward a more positive and . . . ecstatic goal." This letter was written in 1923, and Crane speaks more than once—with particular reference to the three-part poem, "To the Marriage of Faustus and Helen," he was working on—of wanting to "affirm" certain things, and so move byond the brilliant "negations" of the just-published *Waste Land*. His admiration for Eliot was real and deep, but there is something desperately misguided and typically revealing about Crane's aim, as expressed here and elsewhere, to "go *through* him toward a *different goal*." As in the statement quoted earlier from "General Aims and Theories," the aspiration is to move through or beyond Eliot by picking up and yet transforming his style, leaving behind the "negations" but "applying as much of his technique and erudition as I can absorb." But it was Eliot himself who warned, in his preface to the 1928 edition of *The Sacred Wood* (which preface Crane would not have read), that we cannot say where "technique" begins and ends, but that at any rate it is not something you pick up from somebody and "apply" to suit your own ends. Crane's most often-quoted, though not one of his best, letters is one written to Munson in which he reports himself "notoriously drunk," with Ravel's *Bolero* playing away on the Victrola. He tells Munson about the "thrilling experience" he had last winter at the dentist's "When under the influence of aether and *amnesia* my mind spiraled to a kind of seventh heaven of consciousness and egoistic dance among the seven spheres—and something like an objective voice kept saying to me—'You have the higher consciousness—you have the higher consciousness.' " And he goes on, without a hint of irony, to insist that he felt "the two worlds," then implores Munson to believe what a great visionary moment it was. To juxtapose this sensibility, however much inflamed by wine in the instance, with

that of Eliot seems palpably grotesque, especially when we remember that at this time Eliot was mounting (in "The Function of
Criticism") his most devastating attack on what he called "the
inner voice."

Whatever Crane thought he was doing—and the "revivalist,"
"higher consciousness" aspect of his work seems crucial—the
poems he was actually writing, when they are convincing and
original, should not be thought of in the terms he provided. For in
one very important way they complement rather than contradict
or move beyond Eliot, exhibiting something analogous to the
"pessimism" Crane found in the author of *The Waste Land* and
other poems. They reveal a loneliness, an isolation, and a very
moving purity of spirit which make their "affirmative" enthusiasms sound all the more like rattling of chains. In his fine essay on
the poet, Tate claims that far from contradicting or moving
beyond Eliot, Crane's whole career was a vindication of Eliot's
premise "that the individual consciousness had broken down."
But whatever one says about the disintegration of Crane's life, culminating in suicide at thirty-two, his poetry when it is successful—
and often it is so—shows a distinctive individual consciousness
like no other modern poet's.

Allen Tate's essay mentions a letter from Crane to him in 1930,
after *The Bridge* had been published and Tate had reviewed it, in
which Crane admitted that the poem was not perfectly "realized"
and claimed that his soundest work was contained in his earlier
book, *White Buildings* (1926). If the letter referred to is one
Crane wrote to Tate on July 13, 1930, then Tate rather misstates
Crane's point, which is really about how "personal" his poetry is,
how that personal note is probably responsible for the sentimentality Tate found in the "Cape Hatteras" section of the poem with
its invocations of Whitman, and how if he, Crane, writes any

more verse (this seems to be an open question), it will be at least
as personal as the poems in *White Buildings*. Whether there is any
deliberate reference here to Eliot's "impersonal" theory of poetry
one can't know; but since Crane has flaunted the word, it should
be pointed out how different from the usual notion of personal
poetry—in which an "I" lays bare his inner secrets, or dramatizes
himself vigorously within the poem—is Crane's way of writing
"personal" poems.

As a beginning example of that way, consider a curious and unforgettable one which has few of his usual puzzles and obscurities.
"Sunday Morning Apples" is dedicated to his Cleveland friend,
the painter William Sommer, and begins with the calm assurance
that

> The leaves will fall again sometime and fill
> The fleece of nature with those purposes
> That are your rich and faithful strength of line.

It continues quietly to group together, in words, what we presume
Crane's eye to have seen in Sommer's work—its "challenges to
spring," to the nature which it transforms; then the last six lines
address Sommer more intently:

> I have seen the apples there that toss you secrets,—
> Beloved apples of seasonable madness
> That feed your inquiries with aerial wine.
>
> Put them again beside a pitcher with a knife,
> And poise them full and ready for explosion—
> The apples, Bill, the apples!

The "aerial wine" is particularly appropriate since it has been
discreetly and parenthetically confided to us that Sommer lives in
a valley "(called Brandywine)." One might say that here Crane is
gathering the materials for one of the painter's still-lifes; or rather,
seeking to emphasize the tensed, energetic power "ready for explosion" in the painter's and poet's grouping of material: the "sea-

sonable madness" visited upon the artist sensitive to the potentialities in things of nature. The final exclamatory line is itself the explosion—"The apples, Bill, the apples!"—but a very self-contained and controlled one.

But what is particularly interesting about this last line is that it is both a stunning and original way to end a poem, and uncharacterizable as far as assigning any tone of voice to it goes. Reading aloud, one would be bound to get it wrong somehow, giving it too much "intensity" or trying too hard to poise the explosiveness, and end up sounding merely embarrassing. Crane's remarkable ability to write toneless individual lines which are totally memorable has been frequently noticed. The last stanza of "Praise for an Urn" provides a minor instance of his penchant for uttering (the phrase is R. W. B. Lewis's) "utter finalities":

> Scatter these well-meant idioms
> Into the smoky spring that fills
> The suburbs, where they will be lost.
> They are no trophies of the sun.

If one tries to isolate this stanza and say why its use of words seems distinguished, difficulties will be encountered. There is a predominance of "s" sounds, but is that a virtue? There is the dismissive or cynical or unillusioned clarity with which the poet turns on the words of his poem, bidding them farewell and a good dispersal, knowing they are impermanent though "well-meant." But is this in any way a noteworthy attitude? "They are no trophies of the sun" and "The apples, Bill, the apples!" are lines full of promise that do not quite declare themselves, or at least seem to hold back reserves of potential wisdom and passion. Seem to, for that is the illusion they create, as do the sentences in Hemingway's early stories; though unlike Hemingway, Crane practices elegantly cool formulations in a voice which sounds so confidently composed that we are certain it must know exactly what it's doing.

"Repose of Rivers," a much-admired poem from *White Buildings,* is also distinguished for its last line, but its opening is equally impressive:

The willows carried a slow sound,
A sarabande the wind mowed on the mead.
I could never remember
That seething, steady level of the marshes
Till age had brought me to the sea.

As usual with Crane, the originality of the language is a matter of
his way with verbs: the unobvious "carried" in the first line, the
vigorous "mowed" to characterize the wind's work, followed by
what it does to the marshes with iambic regularity—"That seething, steady leveling." But it is ultimately the strange unearthly tone
that carries things and makes the details feel rich and unexpected.
In a more conventional dramatic lyricist, the first stanza would
serve as an initiator of the poem's dialectic; instead Crane proceeds this way:

Flags, weeds. And remembrance of steep alcoves
Where cypresses shared the noon's
Tyranny; they drew me into hades almost.
And mammoth turtles climbing sulphur dreams
Yielded, while sun-silt rippled them
Asunder . . .

The opening two nouns followed by a period offer no certain way
for the reader to "say" them; while "Asunder" (also an extra line,
since most of the other groups are of five) is followed by an ellipsis
impossible to enter into. We may call it a dream, however much
that helps.

In his review of *White Buildings* Yvor Winters admired the
"marvelous appearance and sinking away of the turtles" but provided no reasons for that admiration nor suggested their import to
the whole poem, which continues thus:

How much I would have bartered! the black gorge
And all the singular nestings in the hills
Where beavers learn stitch and tooth.
The pond I entered once and quickly fled—
I remember now its singing willow rim.

> And finally, in that memory all things nurse;
> After the city that I finally passed
> With scalding unguents spread and smoking darts
> The monsoon cut across the delta
> At gulf gates . . . There, beyond the dykes
>
> I heard wind flaking sapphire, like this summer,
> And willows could not hold more steady sound.

Winters also admired the "city," with its scalding unguents and darts, but cites these (and the turtles) to make the point that Crane's virtues are easier to perceive if we isolate lines and passages from the poems.

The reply to this interesting, undeveloped observation is that it is because lines are *already* isolated that one wants to pick them out, quote and repeat them to oneself as if they possessed near-magical powers. I don't of course mean to deny that there are "willows" at the beginning, the middle, and the end of this poem; but that their particular appearances, as a "singing willow rim" or as in the final line, carry a power disproportionate to any developing pattern of meaning they have in the poem. So that Winters's statement might be given an emphasis different than he would have allowed; it is possible, one might say, that Crane's virtues are such as ask to be admired in lines and passages, rather than in whole, sequential poems. Furthermore, that they have a self-sufficient quality about them, like the beavers learning "stitch and tooth" in this poem's third stanza; they feel locked in as it were, candidates for inspection and admiration but not likely to become part of a dialogue with the reader.

Saying this may be doing no more than isolating the symbolist element in Crane's verse. It is surely true that, of our nine poets, he shared with Eliot in his early poems a gift for the unforgettable phrase or line, such as Prufrock's numerous *trouvailles*. But what makes Crane different, at least in his earlier, shorter poems, from the poet he admired and feared above all others, is his tone, in its puzzling but persuasive mixture of qualities. One might with equal justification call it fervid or glacially composed; intense or limpidly relaxed. In the search for oxymorons it is heartening to find that one's critical predecessors had their own difficulties when they tried to describe Crane's tone. Winters speaks of the "curiously heroic tone" heard at the end of "Voyages II," but perhaps "curiously" here means no more than that the critic finds this tone beyond his descriptive capacities (Winters had earlier spoken of the "curiously dewy geometry" of a stanza in "Sunday Morning Apples"). And rightly so, since it is what makes Crane so difficult a poet to hear confidently, in the way we can usually hear dramatic poets like Hardy and Yeats, or ironic ones like Frost or Robinson, or, and with less certainty, rhetorical ones like Stevens. The final stanza of "Voyages VI" presents in brilliantly concentrated measures both the promise and the remoteness Crane's work holds out:

> The imaged Word, it is, that holds
> Hushed willows anchored in its glow.
> It is the unbetrayable reply
> Whose accent no farewell can know.

You cannot betray "it" or make it know farewell; like the other willows in "Repose of Rivers" it—or they—"could not hold more steady sound." Beyond that, just what it asks of one as a reader is undefined, since it doesn't ask, nor demand, nor cajole, flatter, or soothe. Like the "icy and bright dungeons" with which "Voyages VI" begins, the imaged Word is dazzling, austere, and quite a bit beyond us.

The most admired poems from *White Buildings* are the six lyrics making up the "Voyages" sequence. Compared to their composed and quiet atmosphere, Crane's earlier three-part longish poem "For the Marriage of Faustus and Helen" feels—as it was often designed to feel—hectic and jazzed-up, a bit like a stunt man performing for our excitement and applause. "Voyages" by contrast seems unaware of any necessity of pleasing an audience, its preoccupation less that of illustrating a principle or idea than with an impulse (what Eliot once called "the obscure impulse") that needed expression. Written during the period of Crane's most intense and lasting love affair with Emil Opffer, the poem may on that grounds be thought to be somehow more "personal." But as Warner Berthoff demonstrates in his review of R. W. B. Lewis's book on Crane, it is a bad mistake to presume that the poems are "about" a real love affair, and (as Lewis does) that one can move from moments or details in the poems to the "actual" affair. To describe the move from language to life in this way is to make a basic mistake about how Crane used words, and Berthoff's characterization of that way as it is consummately exhibited in "Voyages" is indispensable. He makes the point that for the most part Crane's poems do not have a narrative structure, even though there are moments of narrative in *The Bridge*. Generally the poems cannot be "retold": "Rather they are lyrical and associative; they project a succession of appearances and apparitional events . . . that are positioned and addressed in such a way as to produce an ordered, psychologically reasoned succession of emotional tones." Images, metaphors, idioms, syntax and, I would add, the ring of the voice employing them are all one has to talk about and should be more than enough if, in Berthoff's excellent phrase, the poem is "precisely and beautifully figured"—as he finds "Voyages" to be.

As a testing example we may choose the fifth section, in which, "past midnight," the poem begins to work its materials as if out of the room on Columbia Heights in Brooklyn where Crane and Opffer lived for a time, and where, at the Brooklyn Bridge, "the bay estuaries fleck the hard sky limits":

> —As if too brittle or too clear to touch!
> The cables of our sleep so swiftly filed,
> Already hang, shred ends from remembered stars.
> One frozen trackless smile . . . What words
> Can strangle this deaf moonlight? For we
>
> Are overtaken. Now no cry, no sword
> Can fasten or deflect this tidal wedge,
> Slow tyranny of moonlight, moonlight loved
> And changed . . .

Since, in the language of the last stanza of "Voyages VI," "the imaged Word, it is, that holds / Hushed willows anchored in its glow," words can also strangle the deaf moonlight merely by the saying, the imaging of them. Crane's attempt here is simultaneously to show the inadequacy, the defeat of language when brought up against the tyrannies of nature—moonlight, time, touch, change—and also its absolute dominion, as when the question "What words / Can strangle this deaf moonlight" is given an answer by the deliberate, slow-paced, repetitive assertion ("Now no cry, no sword") and the artful, crucial ellipses after "smile" and "changed" during which the voice drifts off into some inner harbor of its own.

If as R. W. B. Lewis thinks, this poem is about the impending separation of the lovers, "nature" having denied them a permanence, Crane's language is so elegantly apt in finding ways of expressing the separation that all anxiety and nervous movement seem assuaged:

> In all the argosy of your bright hair I dreamed
> Nothing so flagless as this piracy.
>
> > But now
> Draw in your head, alone and too tall here.
> Your eyes already in the slant of drifting foam;
> Your breath sealed by the ghosts I do not know:
> Draw in your head and sleep the long way home.

These concluding lines from "Voyages V" are an excellent example of Crane's uncanny ability to end poems in absolutely conclusive ways, and they are wonderful lines to intone aloud, responding to their incantatory power. But to try to make a sensible "story" out of them is beyond at least this reader's powers, especially since the injunction to "Draw in your head" comes perilously close to the notion of the lover—the other—with his head sticking out into the moonlight, somehow inappropriately elongated. Perhaps, a turtle-like gesture is required? At any rate, Berthoff's advice that we look not for the realistic coherence of story but rather for "a succession of appearances and apparitional events" is helpful in describing the kind of attention generally invited by the "Voyages" sequence.

In "General Aims and Theories" Crane spoke with perceptiveness and accuracy about what he was doing in attempting to realize "the imaged Word" invoked at the end of "Voyages": "It is as though a poem gave the reader as he left it a single, new *word,* never before spoken and impossible to actually enunciate, but self-evident as an active principle in the reader's consciousness henceforward." The statement is perceptive and accurate because its contortions—the "It is as though," the italicized *"word"* (a recurrent habit of Crane's), the denial that it has ever "actually" been spoken before or now, the hopeful assertion of "self-evident" life henceforward in the reader—bring out the purely verbal nature of Crane's operation in this sequence, whether he is instructing the lover to "sleep the long way home," or dazzling us, in the final voyage, by gesturing at where the "imaged Word" is to be found:

> Beyond siroccos harvesting
> The solstice thunders, crept away,
> Like a cliff swinging or a sail
> Flung into April's inmost day— . . .

"Creation's blithe and petalled word" is the continuously appearing subject of these poems: we can understand why it was difficult for the head of the Crane Chocolate Company to understand, no matter how hard he tried, just what his son was up to.

The last six years of Crane's life must be contemplated with a mixture of sadness and boredom, as things repeat themselves but in widening circles of desperation. Quarrels with his friends, particularly with the Tates; the break in 1928 with his mother, whom he never saw again; the drunken cavortings in Paris and in California; the temporary periods of recovery and increased poetic composition—it all begins to seem predictable, then inevitable, and eventually incapable of stirring our sympathies. Or at least incapable of doing so if we forget the ring of Crane's voice in his letters, as in this one written to his mother and grandmother in 1927 from a house in the country in Patterson, New York, where he sometimes lived. He plays the normal, healthy, growing boy: "I have just come in from hoeing my corn and beans. Can't tell you how I revel in having some green things to eat. . . . I eat a great plate of lettuces and radishes twice every day." Then he quotes appreciative reviews of *White Buildings,* and is pleased that Grace and his grandmother like "To Brooklyn Bridge" and "The River," sections from *The Bridge* he had just sent them. I quoted earlier Crane's father's appreciation of the latter section, and it is true that not only "The River" but *The Bridge* as a whole can be more nearly approached by readers who find themselves often baffled and groping while reading the poems in *White Buildings.*

Even Crane's best critics admitted to having some troubles with the earlier volume, as is testified to most amusingly by Allen Tate's remark, in his preface to *White Buildings,* that the only thing difficult about the poems was their "style"—as if with such a difficulty there could be anything easy about them! And indeed not only the more obscure, unparaphrasable ones like "Paraphrase," "Possessions," and "Lachrymae Christi," but the more available and achieved ones—like "Repose of Rivers" and "Voyages"— often seem to be holding something back, as if there were reserves of feeling which have been expressed only obliquely. What makes *The Bridge* easier of access is Crane's relatively dramatic and theatrical mode of operation, such as conceiving the "Ave Maria" section to be understood as spoken by Columbus returning home; or "Indiana" done in the voice of a pioneer woman; or "Cape Hatteras" sung by the rapt ecstatic disciple of Walt Whitman. And though as always with Crane, there are many individual lines and passages whose sense is not clear, one seldom feels that the poet is trying deliberately to be obscure; rather he seems if anything overeager that we should follow along and grasp what he has set out to do.

This latter sense is enforced by the goodly number of prose statements Crane made in an attempt to assist readers with the poem. The longest of them is contained in a 1927 letter to the banker Otto Kahn, who provided financial assistance for the *Bridge* project. At the time Crane had not yet finished the poem, but his description of the various sections was full and confident, and he was able to make a list of nine sections which had already been accepted by prominent literary magazines in three countries, such as the *Criterion,* the *Dial,* and *transition.* Near the end of the letter to Kahn he asks for an advance of "say 800 to 1000 dollars" and adduces the poem's ambitiousness and scope as justifying such a monetary outlay. He is bold to make the largest comparisons: "The Aeneid was not written in two years—nor in four, and in more than one sense I feel justified in comparing the historic and cultural scope of The Bridge to this great work. It is at least a symphony with an epic theme, and a work of considerable profundity and inspiration." Earlier, claiming that what he was handling was "the Myth of America," he had compared it to the Sistine Chapel.

Crane sent Kahn explanatory "notes" on individual sections from *The Bridge* but advised him to read them only after he had read the poem, since (Crane said) the notes weren't necessary for understanding *The Bridge* but would provide commentary on its "architecture." One example is the following about the "Dance" section from "Powhatan's Daughter":

> Here one is on the pure mythical and smoky soil at last! Not only do I describe the conflict between the two races in this dance—I also become identified with the Indian and his world before it is over, which is the only method possible of ever really possessing the Indian and his world as a cultural factor. I think I really succeed in getting under the skin of this glorious and dying animal, in terms of expression, in symbols, which he himself would comprehend.

Put this next to these three quatrains which present a climactic moment in "The Dance," as the poem's "I" effects an identification with the Indian brave, Maquokeeta, at the stake:

> Spears and assemblies: black drums thrusting on—
> O yelling battlements,—I too, was liege
> To rainbows currying each pulsant bone:
> Surpassed the circumstance, danced out the siege!

> And buzzard-circleted, screamed from the stake;
> I could not pick the arrows from my side.
> Wrapped in that fire, I saw more escorts wake—
> Flickering, sprint up the hill groins like a tide.

> I heard the hush of lava wrestling your arms,
> And stag teeth foam about the raven throat;
> Flame cataracts of heaven in seething swarms
> Fled down your anklets to the sunset's moat.

In providing Kahn with this description of the poem's architecture, Crane perhaps imagined that the banker, after encountering twelve lines such as these, might have scratched his head and wondered just what the young man was up to in writing such poetry. But he would be presumed to feel better about it if he were instructed that Crane was identifying with the Indian, was bringing the races together in a moment of apotheosis, was working in the realm of myth. We don't know what Kahn did think, only that he granted Crane the money. But a half-century or so later, such a scaffolding to help prospective readers get a grip on the poem is, like the Grail–Fisher King one contrived for *The Waste Land* by Eliot and exfoliated by critics, a hindrance to reading the poem. Not because imposing such a grid distorts the poem into unrecognizable shapes—there is nothing much wrong with a word like "identification" to describe the relation between poet and Indian expressed in the line "I could not pick the arrows from my side" (though there's not much right about it either). But unless I am mistaken in assuming that my own reluctance is shared by other readers, it is the thematic insistence which is the least attractive and the corniest aspect of *The Bridge:* the idea, say, of "getting under the skin" of a "glorious and dying" Indian; or imagining that in writing, as in the above passage, about "spears and assemblies," arrows and lava and stag teeth, Crane was "describing the conflict between the two races." (One remembers a funny moment from Wyndham Lewis's *Paleface*, where Lewis imagines a Hopi Indian, being stared at darkly by D. H. Lawrence, replying to Lawrence the equivalent of "Chuck it, Archie" in Hopi.) The point is that in trying to persuade Kahn and other readers that there really was a coherence, really *were* important American themes being treated, Crane inflated the poem to a degree where he could compare it to the *Aeneid* or the Sistine Chapel and not see the absurdity in so doing.

Crane was nothing if not unhistorical, and managed to convince himself that he really was writing "a symphony with an epic theme." But as far as I know he never thought much about what difference it made that his expression was typically "difficult," or that he never created a character outside himself in his whole poetic career up to and including *The Bridge.* In a very real sense he had nothing to "say" beyond reiterated appeals for moving onward and upward toward "New thresholds, new anatomies" or, as in the final supplication from "To Brooklyn Bridge"—"Unto us lowliest sometime sweep, descend / And of the curveship lend a myth to God." It may be that I overstate, and it is true that some of the best moments in *The Bridge* occur when Crane speaks in a more muted voice, as in the quiet waverings of "The Harbor Dawn"; or when he becomes reflective and descriptive, as in the passage about his father's cannery works from "The River"; or elegiac, as in the lovely end of "Quaker Hill." And in certain passages, most notably the Mississippi quatrains which conclude "The River," he unleashes his highest, most "noble" rhetoric with marvelous success. As for the connection of the poem's best parts with its larger theme, Allen Tate accurately pointed out in his review that they bear "only the loosest relation to the symbolic demands of the theme" and are primarily lyrical.

At any rate too much discussion of *The Bridge* has centered on whether or not it is "unified," and it is refreshing to read a recent long essay on the poem by Eugene Paul Nassar which finds its unity to lie in no more than being a poem which "says that life is both a blessing and a nightmare and that it is so eternally (as far as one can see) in the cyclic pattern called The Process (figured by the river)." This rather less strainingly affirmative attitude than is revealed by Crane's own remarks about the poem seems to me a sane and interesting one to hold about life, and one which is expressed by the shifting moods of the poem, from ecstatic cry to melancholy or satiric perceptions of how life doesn't live up to the imagination's spacious demands. Admittedly the ecstatic note is dominant, but even within it Crane manages to fuse the blessing-and-nightmare aspects of life by a remarkable expressiveness which (in Jarrell's terms about Frost) makes either optimism or pessimism seem a hopeful evasion.

A great example of such expressiveness occurs at the end of "The River," represented by these two quatrains:

> You will not hear it as the sea; even stone
> Is not more hushed by gravity . . . But slow,
> As loth to take more tribute—sliding prone
> Like one whose eyes were buried long ago

> The River, spreading, flows—and spends your dream.
> What are you, lost within this tideless spell?
> You are your father's father, and the stream—
> A liquid theme that floating niggers swell.

This is a poetry of astutely managed syntax, and its pace is important in making the large question beginning "What are you" as powerful as it is. It is also a poetry of wit, though seldom "humorous," the wit being a matter of trusting to the possibilities of words, such as the many possibilities of "a liquid theme" swelled in various ways by the "floating niggers." At moments like this *The Bridge* feels simply uncharacterizable by any theme it purportedly illustrates, whether the greatness of America (as Tate took the theme to be), the search for a myth, or even (in Nassar's terms) the necessity of having myths. Rather there is a pure concentration of verbal resource that is exciting and life-giving.

At the center of Crane's art in *The Bridge,* this concentration is perhaps the true realization of that more "affirmative and ecstatic goal" which he had set—in opposition to what he detected in *The Waste Land*—as his poetic ambition. Tate, from his religious point of view, reproves Crane for misunderstanding Eliot, and charges *The Bridge* with a "vagueness of purpose" and lack of coherent structure by contrast with Dante's poem, which has a coherent structure. This is a bit like finding a modern novelist inadequate by comparing him with Tolstoy, and it raises the whole question of the appropriateness of finding large-scale works to be "failures." Usually we do not bother to assert that a short lyric is a failure, but wheel the term out only in the case of longer poems; so it might be well to ask ourselves just what sort of unified or coherent long poem could conceivably satisfy us in this century. Williams's *Paterson* is a good deal longer and to my eyes more chaotic than *The Bridge;* Pound's *Cantos* are even longer, and though also dogged by the question of whether or not they cohere, are at least held together by the central presence of Ezra Pound, which presence is a triumph or a disaster (or both) depending on your taste. In its length, Eliot's *Four Quartets* is closer to *The Bridge,* and for all the dissension that exists among readers concerning individual passages and sections of that poem, there is little disagreement about its essential coherence—though that is exactly what proves a stumbling block to unsympathetic, non-Christian readers. Surely Crane's epic is no more conspicuously a "failure" than these other three long poems.

It is certainly very much "Crane's epic." From his correspondence with Yvor Winters we can see how at least by November 1926, before he had finished "The River," he had formulated very fully what he was trying to do. Winters, who at that point had the "Ave Maria" (Columbus) section before him, must have expressed some reservations about the attempt to write a modern epic. Crane replied that

> you are right about modern epics—except—until somebody actually overcomes the limitations. This will have to be done by a new form,—and of course, new forms are never desirable until they are simply forced into being by new materials. Perhaps any modern equivalent of the old epic form should be called by some other name, for certainly, as I see it, the old definition cannot cover the kind of poem I am trying to write except on certain fundamental points. At least both are concerned with material which can be called mythical. . . [Crane's ellipsis] But what is "mythical" in or rather, of the twentieth century is not the Kaiser, the sinking of the Titanic, etc. Rather it is science, travel (in the sense of speed)—psychoanalysis, etc. With, of course, the eternal verities of sea, mountain and river at work.

He went on to say that these mythical factors should not be presented link by link, as in older epic, but in "organic order, out of which might emerge a kind of bridge, the quest of which bridge is nothing less ambitious than the annihilation of time and space, the prime myth of the modern world." And he confessed to worrying about being doomed to a "half-success" which would be worse than failure.

"Language has built towers and bridges, but itself is inevitably as fluid as always," he said on another occasion, quietly bringing out, by a pun, the commitment to metaphor—literally to a carrying-over—that is the poet's commitment. *The Bridge* is a continuous attempt to say one thing in terms of another, and as Frost reminds us (Crane once referred to Frost as "a good, clean artist, however lean"), the largest of such attempts is to say "matter in terms of spirit, or spirit in terms of matter, to make the final unity." Frost also believed that "all metaphor breaks down somewhere," that that was the beauty of it, and that we should fear the metaphor which, so the deluded poet or pedant thinks, never

breaks down, is thought to be fully coherent. In those terms Crane
also knew very well what he was about:

> I left my sleek boat nibbling margin grass . . .
>
> I took the portage climb, then chose
> A further valley-shed; I could not stop.
> Feet nozzled wat'ry webs of upper flows;
> One white veil gusted from the very top.
>
> O Appalachian Spring! I gained the ledge;
> Steep, inaccessible smile that eastward bends
> And northward reaches in that violet wedge
> Of Adirondacks!—wisped of azure wands,
>
> Over how many bluffs, tarns, streams I sped!

The poet is exciting himself with the notion that words can do
anything, can annihilate space and time, can build a bridge or a
tower. But language remains "fluid as always," so there is no
place to stop, and there is no satisfactory way to quote from *The
Bridge* and attempt to isolate a moment from it. If a passage like
this one (which I find extremely attractive) is a good one and a
"high" point in the poem, it does not therefore condemn other
stretches to failure. Even in a passage of excess, like the salute to
Whitman in "Cape Hatteras," one trusts that Crane knows he's
being excessive; that air travel ("O thou Dirigible, enormous
Lounger / Of pendulous auroral beaches"), like Walt, and like alcohol ("What alcohol of space"), represents an exciting and impossible attempt to say matter in terms of spirit and vice versa:

> Thou, there beyond—
> Glacial sierras and the flight of ravens,
> Hermeticilly past condor zones, through zenith havens
> Past where the albatross has offered up
> His last wing-pulse, and downcast as a cup
> That's drained, is shivered back to earth—thy wand
> Has beat a song, O Walt,—there and beyond!

There is no place to stop and no way of putting it that is satisfactory for longer than the moment in which it is put.

In a peculiar sense, one important to emphasize since I think it distinguishes him from the other modern poets, Crane's verse only exists in the act of reading it, making it up as you and he go along, mutually participating in an improvisation. The real "objective" existence of his poems there on the page—as we may presume "Easter 1916" or *Mauberley* or even *The Waste Land* to exist—seems hard to credit; I also think that there are times and moods in which one cannot read him, when the performance simply does not appeal; and the troublesome question arises whether it is the poet's fault or one's own inadequacies. That is perhaps a question not to be answered; when it arises, best to drop the poem and pick it up later on. Nor do I see any way of seriously disputing the claim made by Winters, Tate, and Malcolm Cowley, three of Crane's best friends and most serious critics, artists themselves, that his talent deteriorated after the completion in 1928 of "The River"; even though the excesses of "Cape Hatteras" and the sentimentalities of "Quaker Hill" or "Indiana" may be understood in the context of pressures to finish off the long poem once for all, and though they came at a time when Crane's alcoholic and sexual behavior was landing him in deep psychic and physical trouble. His late, posthumously published "The Broken Tower" has been lately admired, and it undeniably possesses a grandeur of sound and gesture which is impressive:

> Oval encyclicals in canyons heaping
> The impasse high with choir. Banked voices slain!
> Pagodas, campaniles with reveilles outleaping—
> O terraced echoes prostrate on the plain! . . .
>
> And so it was I entered the broken world
> To trace the visionary company of love, its voice
> An instant in the wind (I know not whither hurled)
> But not for long to hold each desperate choice.

Yet after repeated readings there remain obscurities which do not clear up, as well as an uncertainty about the overall movement of the poem; even though when it is read aloud these worries diminish in importance.

Crane's suicide in April 1932, a leap into the Caribbean from a vessel bearing him from Mexico to America, can be seen as an act of ultimate madness or one, as his friend Tate saw it, of courage—the final vindication of his "pantheism," occurring in the most appropriate of ways. The two years which led up to it, read about in Unterecker's massively detailed account, show a depressing sequence of quarrels, brawls, recriminations, dissipations; yet intelligence and humor still dominate his letters. Crane's love affair with Peggy Baird (Malcolm Cowley's former wife, who accompanied Crane on the steamer from which he dove), an interesting complication for the committed homosexual to allow himself to experience, seems to have been going on the rocks in 1932; and both Winters's and Tate's uneasinesses about *The Bridge* must have shaken him. Still, the act remains, like most suicides, both understandable and not understandable. It was at any rate his last improvisation.

In 1961 Robert Lowell, interviewed by the *Paris Review* not long after his *Life Studies* poem "Words for Hart Crane" had been written, delivered himself of these sentiments about that poet:

> . . . I think Crane is the great poet of that generation. He got out more than anybody else. Not only is it the tremendous power there, but he somehow got New York City; he was at the center of things in the way that no other poet was. . . . There was a fullness of experience; and without that, if you just had his mannerisms, and not his rather simple writing—which if done badly would be sentimental merely—or just his obscure writing, the whole thing would be merely verbal. It isn't with Crane. The push of the whole man is there.

By "merely verbal" I take Lowell to mean merely arid, and part of the burden of my account has been to suggest how Crane is the most merely verbal of the modern poets and in a very interesting way. But surely the "push of the whole man" was there for Lowell, and is there for us, partly because of the myth which immediately grew up around Crane after his death. In the same year, Tate said about the "rich symbolism" of his verse that "whatever may be its intrinsic merit, he had the courage to vindicate with death in the end." Coming from a Roman Catholic who knew about original sin, Tate's remarks testify to the myth's power. Years later Winters heroicized it even further in his essay "Hart Crane's *The Bridge:* or What Are We to Think of Professor X?" when he contrasted Crane's ruinous, romantic ideas with the hypothetical English professor's lip-service to them. Winters asserted that whatever his ideas, Crane was an intelligent man and that "it takes a very highly developed intelligence to write great poetry, even a little of it"; and he concluded with this pledge: "So far as I am concerned, I would gladly emulate Odysseus, if I could, and go down to the shadows for another hour's conversation with Crane on the subject of poetry. . . ."

For a final exhibit, there is, once again, Tate's encomium, written twenty years after Crane's suicide and titled "The Poet as Hero," which concludes with a paragraph that cannot be bettered and that—in our own moments of impatience with the poet—jog us into taking yet another look:

> He came to New York at seventeen equipped with an hysterical and disorderly family, almost no formal education, and the cultural inheritance of a middle-western small town; his religious training had been in Christian Science. By the time he was twenty-five, before *The Bridge* had scarcely been conceived, he had written a body of lyric poetry which for originality, distinction, and power, remains the great poetic achievement of his generation. If he is not our twentieth-century poet as hero, I do not know where else to look for him.

One thinks of Yeats's lines from "The Municipal Gallery Revisited" as ones which Crane might have assented to, with reference to Tate and Winters and others—"Think where man's glory both begins and ends / And say my glory was I had such friends." It may be the note on which to leave him.

9

WILLIAM CARLOS WILLIAMS
In the American Grain

A preface to William Carlos Williams presents fewer occasions for puzzlement and uncertainty in the critic since his career, in its main lines, is wholly attractive and admirable, also not *a* career. For everybody knows and respects the fact that Williams was a doctor as well as a poet, and full-time in both occupations. No American myth is more powerful than the goodness of being a small-town doctor, especially one who delivers babies and makes house calls in all sorts of weather, and whose patients can't always afford to pay their bills—this is surely in the American grain. But Williams as a literary artist was also full-time: he wrote not only lyrics, but prose poems and prose, stories and novels and plays. Somehow, at least so the legend has it, he got the American language into his poetry the way nobody else did. User of local materials, he is our answer to his old friend Pound's romance with faraway places with strange-sounding names. Anybody whose address for most of his life was 9 Ridge Road, Rutherford, New Jersey, has a lot going for him in the way of a nostalgia-provoking rootedness we feel guilty about not attaining in our own lives, while doing only a quarter as much as he did.

Williams got so much done because he lived in tension, and instead of being pulled apart by it managed to work within it in the most productive ways. A passage from his autobiographical novel *A Voyage to Pagany* (1928) expresses this tension and its fruits as well as he ever expressed it:

> Some day, my God, let the whole works go. I should never think of the practice of medicine again. Never! And, in all probability this was so. Evans had practiced medicine all his adult life, so far, up to his present fortieth year, in a continuously surly mood at the overbearing necessity for it—wanting always to do something else: To write! Why? Because then only, when he was stealing time for his machine and paper, did he live.

Only *then*, we nod soberly, confirmed once again in the paramount importance of art. But the fine thing about the passage as it goes on is that another kind of life immediately emerges and the voice turns back on itself:

> But he really loved the irregularity of a suburban practice, rushing out into the weather at any hour; in the spring stopping his car at four a.m. to hear the hylas waken, watching the snow figures on the windswept roadways at night in a blizzard, plunging in his car through impromptu lakes of rainwater with lightning flashing all around him and thunder splitting the sky, the new moon coming—and thoughts flinging up words to that accompaniment, words that occasionally would have a bewildering freshness upon them as they rose to his sight. . . .

So Williams wasn't "continuously surly" in the practice of his medicine; or was it that the "irregularity" of his practice gave him stimulus and occasion for making up words, sometimes with "bewildering freshness," to express what he saw? His biographer, Reed Whittemore, devotes a chapter to the importance of "stealing" as a metaphor for where the "life" in Williams's life is to be found—and certainly the above passages bear out this importance. In a moment, the world of things, people, "nature," can be converted to words that will, in Emersonian ways, soar and sing.

This last of our modern poets is also the most extreme in his engagements with life and his aspirations for art. But this extremity has sometimes been understood in too simple and sentimental a way. When in the late 1960's his reputation flowered, while Eliot's (at least so we were told) declined, the popular understanding had it that Williams was the poet who knew life, who experienced real people; the physician who witnessed real births and sufferings and death. Therefore his poetry was correspondingly "real," infused with democratic acceptance of ordinary and imperfect life, whereas Eliot had responded to that life with fastidious recoil. But a truer and surely more interesting way to think about Williams's relation to life and art is to see it dramatically. Insofar as life was composed of strep throat infections, ruptured appendices, apoplectic strokes, thus so far must poetry fling up words with bewildering freshness—so far must it be an expression of nothing more or less than The Imagination. No other modern poet rides this term as hard as Williams rides it, not even Yeats. A poem is a machine made out of words, was another excessive way he had of putting it, and the imagination made the machine. If these metaphors are taken seriously, then, readers would be cautioned not to move confidently from a Williams poem back to life, presuming that it refers to and describes that life in direct, untenuous ways. It is Williams who in response to the philistine's question "What is your poem about?" would most quickly come back with the retort that the poem is its own world, a work of imagination, a machine which must be understood in and for itself. For all his unlikeness to Hart Crane ("We just were on different tracks," he said about Crane), they were agreed that the poem was a new word and a new world.

Again and again in Williams's prose, whether in essays or letters, or within the literary structure of a mixed production like *Spring and All,* he employs the word "escape" with great seriousness and excitement. In *Spring and All,* for example, we come upon the following reflection about Poe:

> a man of great separation—with close identity with life. Poe
> could not have written a word without the violence of expul-
> sive emotion combined with the indriving force of a crudely
> repressive environment. Between the two his imagination was
> forced into being to keep him to that reality, completeness,
> sense of escape which is felt in his work. . . .

For Williams this constitutes Poe's typical Americanness, and it is
something he still found available a century later in Rutherford,
New Jersey when at age sixty-five he wrote the following paragraph to John Crowe Ransom:

> The secret of all writing, all literature, is escape, true
> enough, but *not* in the Freudian sense. It is not, in other
> words, evasion. But it *is* escape—from the herd. Old Ez "im-
> pervious to both patronage and criticism, suddenly rears back
> into the mist and we hear in his place the Voice." Heming-
> way assumes a coak of vulgarity, let us say, to protect a
> Jamesian sensitivity to detail. Just when you think you have a
> good man, he's not there. Plato's exasperation when having
> saluted the sane man, the thinking man, the solid man—sud-
> denly he recognizes that the poet, the unsound man, has
> twisted loose and, by a stroke, brings home the bacon. Is not
> Shakespeare, as hard as scholars (of a certain bent) try to nail
> him to learning, really the escaped man? He is a man who
> from indifference has escaped to the sun itself by the gift of
> words alone. For surely we can't call him an original thinker.

This quite remarkable paragraph has an application to Williams's
own case which is difficult to overlook. Whatever they said about
his art, critics and reviewers have usually patronized Williams's
conceptual powers and have agreed that he succeeded as a sensuous poet of "things" rather than as a trafficker in "ideas." His
own motto from *Paterson*—"No ideas but in things"—was simplified into the cry of a dumb ox, as in the Hemingway grain—let
him write about an old woman munching plums, but leave the
expression of complicated ideas to Eliot or Stevens.

Unless I am mistaken, the sentences to Ransom quoted above
are an interesting example of original thought conveying itself

through apt distinction and example. But they also reveal a "gift of words" by which terms like "vulgarity" and "sensitivity" can exist in the same sentence as "brings home the bacon." It's not that the passage proves something which, by reference to Pound or Hemingway or Shakespeare or other elements in the "real world," we can verify; the proving exists in the telling and showing, in the voice which registers itself as unmistakably Williams's; in the combination of confidence, daring, the risk of sentimentality or hot air (escaping to "the sun itself") taken by the prose. It is human and impure, and it is what makes Williams's best poems as indispensable as they are. Randall Jarrell wanted to think about him as he thought about Whitman: "*Why, he'd say anything,* creditable or discreditable, sayable or unsayable, so long as he believes it." A winning response which one might take one step further by asking what it means, and what it is like, for a reader to believe in a Williams poem.

His parents were not in the American grain, the father born in England and brought up in the West Indies, the mother a native of Puerto Rico. Williams, born in 1883, and his brother Ed, a year younger, grew up in Rutherford and attended public school there except for an interlude in Europe with study in Geneva and Paris, while his father (employed by the Florida Water Company) took a business trip to Argentina. Eventually Williams was sent to Horace Mann School in New York City, which he reached every morning by an impressive commute—walk to the Rutherford station, train to Jersey City, ferry to lower Manhattan, uptown elevated to school. With some haste, and probably at the urging of his parents (Mrs. Williams's brother Carlos was a surgeon), the young Williams entered the University of Pennsylvania Medical School in 1902, graduating in 1906. The most interesting literary fact about his time there is that he became acquainted with Ezra Pound. The letter to his mother in 1904, written after he had met

Pound, is attractive in the defense he makes of this person, evidently detested by many people:

> It is too bad, for he loves to be liked, yet there is some quality in him which makes him too proud to try to please people. I am sure his only fault is an exaggeration of a trait that in itself is good and in every way admirable. He is afraid of being taken in if he trusts his really tender heart to mercies of a cruel crowd and so keeps it hidden and trusts no one. Oh, what a common fault it is—this false pride. True faith is that which dares all and gains love in the daring but there is much truth in his position after all.

Williams certainly found much truth in Pound's attitudes toward poetry. During his years of medical study and his subsequent internships at New York hospitals (about which his *Autobiography* provides classic tales of cockroaches and cadavers) he wrote poems, a long one in the style of Keats, and shorter ones which he eventually published privately in 1909. He had already hazarded some criticisms of Pound's *A Lume Spento* published the previous year; now it was Pound's turn to let Williams know, with respect to the 1909 *Poems,* that Rutherford, New Jersey, was not the center of the artistic universe: "Au contraire, if you were in London and saw the stream of current poetry, I wonder how much of it you would have printed? . . . Individual, original it is not. Great art it is not. . . . Your book would not attract even passing attention here. . . ." When Williams published again—*The Tempers* in 1913, poems which would remain in his collected works—it was with Pound's early publisher Elkin Mathews— while the poems showed that their most important model from ones available in the "stream of current poetry" was none other than Ezra Pound.

Williams began his work as a general practitioner in Rutherford in 1910 in the midst of a three-year engagement to Florence Herman. From the novels he was later to write about his wife's family, we learn that both he and his brother were interested in Florence's sister, Charlotte, and that her decision to marry Ed galvanized Williams into a proposal to Florence. It was accepted, and in 1913 they moved to 9 Ridge Road, to reside there for the rest of Williams's life. Over the next ten years he would contribute his poems increasingly to various little magazines, one of which (*Others*) he helped to edit for a time. This is also the period of his growing acquaintance with figures in the New York art world such as the painters Marsden Hartley and Charles Sheeler (he had met Charles Demuth earlier at the university) and such bohemian poets as Alfred Kreymborg, Maxwell Bodenheim, and Walter Arensberg. The critic Kenneth Burke became his lifelong friend. In 1917 he published a book of poems, *Al Que Quiere!*, in which the distinctive Williams notes are sounded for the first time; this volume, along with the "transitional" poems that followed it, is at the heart of his lyric achievement. In the early 1920's came Williams's most radical experiments, though not his most enduring work: *Kora in Hell* (1920), a series of prose improvisations; *The Great American Novel* (1923), a "travesty"; also in 1923, *Spring and All*—juxtaposed poems and prose containing some of his most anthologized pieces of verse. He was now forty, and we should look more closely at the character of what he had written over the past ten years.

"*Why he'd say anything,* creditable or discreditable, sayable or unsayable, so long as he believes it." Disregarding the question of whether, in the particular poem, Williams "believes" what he says, we may consider the first part of Jarrell's remark as an expression of the pleasing sense of wonder he experienced at certain moments in reading Williams; moments when the utterance, in its freshness and surprise, provoked him to put the equivalent of an exclamation mark in the margin. Such a moment might have occurred—it has occurred for this reader—in one of the best poems from *Al Que Quiere!* ("To Him Who Wants It"), "Danse Russe":

If I when my wife is sleeping
and the baby and Kathleen
are sleeping
and the sun is a flame-white disc
in silken mists
above shining trees,—
if I in my north room
dance naked, grotesquely
before my mirror
waving my shirt round my head
and singing softly to myself:
"I am lonely, lonely.
I was born to be lonely,
I am best so!"
If I admire my arms, my face
my shoulders, flanks, buttocks
against the yellow drawn shades,—

Who shall say I am not
the happy genius of my household?

Though on first glance it may look autobiographical, this is a
poem from which we take such a message only at our peril and
the poem's loss. Even as sensitive an account as that of Reed
Whittemore (who as a writer of a full-scale biography must of
course attempt to trace "themes") threatens to take the freshness
off the poem by using it as evidence of the "stealing" motif in
Williams's life and work. The wife, the baby, Kathleen (a helper)
are still asleep, the shades are still drawn, and the doctor before
going out into the world to perform his tasks indulges himself in a
naked "grotesque" dance before the mirror, chanting of his loneliness and admiring his nakedness. Whittemore says that the dancer
"is stealing the idea of beauty and genius from the world and converting them . . . from a fine figure of an upstanding public . . .
from from a fine figure of an upstanding public man to a 'strange
me'—to a " 'satyric counterpart.' "

Fair enough, except that this "strange me" can be no more convincing than he sounds to us as the poem unravels. It may be

recalled that at about this time Pound—in his *Lustra* volume of
1916—wrote a number of poems in which the poet called upon
his "countrymen" (though not, as in Williams, his "townspeople"), asking them to attend to his own difference from them, his
special strangeness as a poet, exile, truth-teller, and exposer of
social cant. In the main these poems sound loud, flat, and self-
righteous; the voice postures and declaims but does not entertain
us enough. By contrast, the first thing to observe about Williams's
poem is that it is entertaining in the casual assurance of its logic—
if I do this and this and that, who shall say I am not that? But it is
the queerly specified nature of what he does that imparts an air of
wackiness to the whole procedure; he will be performing this rit-
ual in the "north room," he'll be waving his shirt round his head
(like a lasso?), and he'll sing a little song (about how it's best to be
lonely) "softly," so as not to disturb anyone. Maybe the poem is
about sensuousness but it is certainly not sensuous, in any sense
that we might use the term to characterize passages from Stevens
or Crane. In "Danse Russe" the words are counters and mean no
more than they say—the act of admiring oneself is expressed no
further than by a list of anatomical nouns, from arms to buttocks,
naming the objects of admiration; then a dash, a space, and the
final unchallengeable question.

Of course to call the whole thing "Danse Russe"—as if to pretend some relation between this doctor's cavortings and the Rus-
sian Ballet—adds to the strangeness. Isn't Williams the poet trying
to get away with too much? Is he purely and simply amusing himself? Questions of this sort, which might have been asked by
somebody in 1917 upon first reading the poem, seem to me an indication of its originality, of the way a good piece by Williams
overcomes our inhibitions and reservations, and forces us—albeit
in the most offhand way—to believe in it. From time to time, later
in his career, he tried to rationalize what he was doing, as in writing to Pound in 1932 about the "increasingly difficult music" of
modern verse:

Whereas formerly the music which accompanied the words amplified, certified and released them, today the words we write, failing a patent music, have become the music itself, and the understanding of the individual (presumed) is now that which used to be the words.

This blasts out of existence forever all the puerilities of the dum te dum versifiers and puts it up to the reader to be a man—if possible. There are not many things to believe, but the trouble is no one believes them. Modern verse forces belief. It is music to that, in every sense, when if ever and in whoever it does or may exist.

Williams does not become clearer as he proceeds, and indeed finally breaks off, telling Pound he is a little drunk. Years later, in *I Wanted to Write a Poem,* speaking of his early *The Tempers,* he tells how he decided to eschew rhyme and to begin lines with lower-case letters when the carried-over sentence made them appropriate. The short lines employed in "Danse Russe" and many of his other early poems, he said, were "rhythmic units": "The rhythmic pace was the pace of speech, an excited pace because I was excited when I wrote. . . . The lines were short, *not* studied. Very frequently the first draft was the final draft by the time I reached the third book, *Al Que Quiere!*"

"Rhythmic unit" here means about the same thing as Pound's "musical phrase," which good "composition" was supposed to proceed according to. The music of a rhythmic unit must be heard by the reader and judged somehow to be right; but it will not do to pause long over individual lines (as in a poem such as "Danse Russe") and try to prove how "right" they are, and why they should not or could not have been otherwise, even slightly altered. The rhythms are as unobtrusive and unspectacular as the words themselves, both being in the service of evoking a moment, a human observation felt as novel and irresistible—"Who shall say I am not / the happy genius of my household?" It is a question conscious of its own extravagance, of the fact that "genius" has also a less than honorific usage in America, as in "Hey, look at the budding genius." Williams's sense of humor hasn't been remarked on enough; it is not complicatedly ironic, has little of Frost's indirectness and subtlety, is louder and less self-protective, but is nonetheless appealing.

Even when the attitude is not tipped toward the humorous, this open, un-self-protected quality can be essential to the attractiveness of a poetic moment. "January Suite," also from *Al Que Quiere!,* is composed of fifteen short impressions and delivered from the imagination of a doctor on the ferry from Jersey to Manhattan:

> I have discovered that most of
> the beauties of travel are due to
> the strange hours we keep to see them:
>
> the domes of the Church of
> the Paulist Fathers in Weehawken
> against a smoky dawn—the heart stirred—
> are beautiful as Saint Peters
> approached after years of anticipation.

The "poetry" really does not matter; only the fact that no one ever before has paid tribute to the domes of that church in Weehawken, comparing them ("he'd say anything . . . so long as he believes it") to the incomparable. Later the doctor is himself a character in his own poem and also to be contemplated with admiration:

> The young doctor is dancing with happiness
> in the sparkling wind, alone
> at the prow of the ferry! He notices
> the curdy barnacles and broken ice crusts
> left at the slip's base by the low tide
> and thinks of summer and green
> shell-crusted ledges among
>   the emerald eel-grass!

The noticing has to be enough, worthy of exclamations, while criticism intrudes at its peril—what is there to argue about or query? "Who knows the Palisades as I do," begins the next fragment, and the statement creates its own authority by evoking the "little peering houses that brighten / with dawn behind the moody / water-loving giants of Manhattan." A wonderful combination of childlike freshness and sophisticated ease carries us along, secure in the perceptions of this imagination.

Early in Williams's career as a poet we can observe the peculiar way he uses the "local materials" involved in his comment about Hart Crane. There is a sentimental version of this use, which on occasion Williams himself was not above believing, that has him as a man speaking to the men and women around him, poor inarticulate North Jerseyites, ministering to their needs and yearnings by providing them with words for their wordless feelings. "Why do I write today?" he asks in "Apology" from the same volume, and answers that "The beauty of / the terrible faces / of our nonentities / stirs me to it. . . ." But he speaks to these nonentities, when he does, with an odd, almost perverse refusal to deliver the political or social or moral truths that would, it might be presumed, help them understand their situation and their lives. Instead he performs the equivalent of a *danse russe,* behaves more like (in the words of a poem of a few years later) "Light hearted William [who] twirled his November mustaches" than like a sober Wordsworthian or Arnoldian consoler. "Gulls" from *Al Que Quiere!* is a particularly revealing instance of the Williams approach to his "materials," beginning with a direct address to the Jerseyites:

> My townspeople, beyond in the great world
> are many with whom it were far more
> profitable for me to live than here with you,

then telling them that he remains and that therefore they should listen, "For you will not soon have another singer."

What does this singer have to say that he should be listened to so gratefully?

> First I say this: You have seen
> the strange birds, have you not, that sometimes

rest upon our river in winter?
Let them cause you to think well then of the storms
that drive many to shelter. These things
do not happen without reason.

One imagines what the putative factory worker from Passaic
would make of that "saying." And the poem goes on to detail the
circling of an eagle "over one of our principal churches," then the
appearance of three gulls who cross slowly seaward. At which
point the poet addresses his townspeople again:

Oh, I know you have your own hymns, I have heard them—
and because I knew they invoked some great protector
I could not be angry with you, no matter
how much they outraged true music—

You see, it is not necessary for us to leap at each other,
and, as I told you, in the end
the gulls moved seaward very quietly.

So the poem concludes. Of course there is no point in pretending
that a worker from Passaic might read this poem. He is not supposed to read it; it is "for" him only in the sense that it uses him,
converts him into an ideal listener who is struck by the rightness
of Williams's poetic song.

For *song* it is, rather than a "saying" which can be pondered
and somehow acted upon. The "happy genius" of his household
has now turned himself into the genius of the place, of the local
habitation which North Jersey wishes it could look like. It may be
that Wallace Stevens's superficially strange remark, made in a letter of December 19, 1946, about how his friend Williams was
primarily interested in how to *say* things, rather than what was
said, is not (as Hugh Kenner has labeled it) an "extraordinary misunderstanding." If one tries, that is, to abstract some sort of re-
spectable moral or human "content" from "Gulls" and from most
of Williams's other early poems one is left with precious little wisdom or ponderable truth about anything—local or no. It is indeed
their "way of saying," the shape of their gesture, the pattern of

their dance, that make for whatever interest "Gulls" and these other delicate, offhand pieces of inspiration possess—which I judge to be considerable.

My conviction is also that as a poet Williams shows less "development" than any of his contemporaries. This isn't to deny that his work shows changes, some of them—as in the experimental books from the 1920's, and of course in *Paterson* most of all—very loud and deliberate ones. But if the development is measured in terms of delicacy, rightness of gesture, poise of humor, charm and insouciance of tone, then Williams reached his peak in *Al Que Quiere!, Sour Grapes* (1921), and the "transitional" poems which were published in the magazines in those years just after the first World War. The following list, in addition to poems mentioned thus far, I take to be his best lyrics from those years: "The Young Housewife," "Good Night," "Smell," "Spring Strains," "Dedication for a Plot of Ground," "To Mark Anthony in Heaven," "Le Médecin Malgré Lui," "Portrait of a Lady," "To Waken an Old Lady," "Queen Anne's Lace," "The Widow's Lament in Springtime," and "Portrait of the Author." Although some of these poems, "Spring Strains" for example, are "objective" reports on nature, the weather, or the dynamic jostlings of things, most of them exhibit a speaker (often a poet-doctor) who engages us by the play of his tone, the fancifulness and freshness of his gestures, and who often takes a less than solemn perspective on experience. Furthermore, they gain by being read in the context which reading thirty or forty early Williams poems at a sitting (easily done) can provide. By that I mean that the life of a single poem benefits from not being pressed too hard, analyzed for itself, but by being considered rather as one more item contributing to the increasingly familiar relationship we achieve with the poet. By the time one reaches the end of *Sour Grapes* and encounters a little poem called "The Lonely Street" one is at no loss about how to respond, though if the poem were considered by itself alone that response would have been more problematic:

School is over. It is too hot
to walk at ease. At ease
in light frocks they walk the streets
to while the time away.
They have grown tall. They hold
pink flames in their right hands.
In white from head to foot
with sidelong, idle look—
in yellow, floating stuff,
black sash and stockings—
touching their avid mouths
with pink sugar on a stick—
like a carnation each holds in her hand—
they mount the lonely street.

The poem instructs us in the sidelong look, while it speaks directly, refusing to "work" the language or mean more than it says. Yet "idle," "avid," and finally "lonely"—adjectives describing the girls, the street, the scene—work by inviting us to fill in things calmly, sadly, and somehow from our experience: as if we knew all about this phenomenon, and as if the poet trusts that we know, therefore can tell us about it. Even though there is no "I" in the poem, no generalizing or moralizing figure speaking to us, Williams's presence—after a chronological reading of his lyrics—has by this time been fully established, and makes a difference.

"But each must free himself from the bonds of banality as best he can; you or another may turn into a lively field of intelligent activity quite easily, but I, being perhaps more timid or unstable at heart, must free myself by more violent methods." So Williams wrote to Marianne Moore in 1921, referring to his volume of prose "improvisations" *Kora in Hell,* published the previous year. The violent methods referred to were responsible for a number of books in prose and verse, sometimes in both, which Williams produced in the twenty years between the wars and which culminated in *Paterson*. Along with *Kora in Hell*, there is *The Great American Novel* (1923)—"a travesty on what I considered conventional American writing"; *Spring and All* (1923)—"It was written when all the world was going crazy about typographical form and is really a travesty on the idea"; *The Descent of Winter* (1928)—more interspersed poetry and prose; and other prose. Taken together, and with *Paterson* thrown in, they give us Williams the modernist or "objectivist" artist, and it is easy to see why, looked at from a certain point of view, they might be considered a bold advance on the miscellaneous collections of short lyrics he had hitherto produced. In the prologue to *Kora in Hell* Williams quotes part of a letter from Wallace Stevens referring to the "casual character" of the poems in *Al Que Quiere!* and remarks on Stevens's "distaste for miscellany"—this was why (Stevens said) he hadn't himself bothered about publishing a book. So the "violent methods" Williams mentions to Marianne Moore would be designed to remove any notions of a comfortable suburban atmosphere the reader might have begun to intuit from his early poems, as well as removing from the scene the doctor-poet who had not been averse to contemplating himself. In general the new work would disabuse us of notions about an easy continuity between life and art, or of the artist as a describer or conveyor of that life in poems conventional enough that we know they're obviously poems.

The new work will be addressed to the imagination rather. This word occurs again and again in the prose parts of *Spring and All*, in conjunction with other "good" words like "spring" and "new" ("THE WORLD IS NEW"). Work addressed to the imagination will have as its value "an escape from crude symbolism, the annihilation of strained associations, complicated ritualistic forms designed to separate the work from 'reality' "—such as rhyme and meter. If, Williams says, he is accused of divorcing art from life in a self-defeating manner he will reply that "To refine, to clarify, to intensify that eternal moment in which we alone live there is but a single force—the imagination." He asks us to read his book and see for ourselves.

Most recent critics of *Spring and All* have seen what Williams wanted them to see, and understood the book more or less in the terms for understanding it he proposed. James Breslin may be taken as representative of those who admire the capacity of these poems "to bring together violently antagonistic forces and to leave them, suspended and unresolved, in a moment of agonizing tension." Breslin also approves of the way Williams has suppressed the "self" of the earlier poems. In *Spring and All* that self has disappeared, leaving the "objects" to speak for themselves; this is what is "new" about the new world Williams creates, and is his first full displaying of what he was later to call "the poem as a field of action." Webster Schott, editor of the New Directions reprint of *Spring and All* which restored the prose sections (Williams had gone on reprinting the poems, but not the prose), sees it as a "giant step forward," an abandoning for all time of the "imagism and Keatsian classicism" of his previous books of poems. Now, for the first time, Williams—like the grass and leaf beginning to grow by the road to the contagious hospital—"enter[s] the new world naked."

It should be noted that *Spring and All*, like *The Great American Novel* (also published in 1923), appeared only in a limited edition of less than 300 copies for which Williams's friend and man-about-Paris, Robert McAlmon, was responsible. It had no effect on Williams's reputation in the 1920's, and it is the recent admirers who have exalted the book as a "breakthrough," taking its audacities and frivolities (particularly in the prose sections) as the sign of high art. As is evident from my tone, I don't think the book will bear such large terms of praise; nor does it seem to me at all obvious that the move toward "objectivism," the suppression of a personal voice, is a good thing—especially since (I would argue) the pleasure of Williams's poetry is so bound up with the entertaining, charming personality it displays to us. In *Spring and*

All the prose voice too often sounds naïvely intoxicated, drumming up excitement in an idea that neither enlightens nor amuses:

> Yes, the imagination, drunk with the prohibitions, has destroyed and recreated everything afresh in the likeness of that which it was. Now indeed men look about in amazement at each other with a full realization of the meaning of "art."

This is the final paragraph from "Chapter VI" which has been preceded by "Chapter XIII" (printed upside down) and "Chapter 19." In Chapter VI we have already learned that "Through the orderly sequences of unmentionable time EVOLUTION HAS REPEATED ITSELF FROM THE BEGINNING," a profundity which is followed, winningly, by "Good God!"

Some years later, in reviewing *Paterson,* Leslie Fiedler called Williams the Dashiell Hammett of modern poetry, characterized his work as a mixture of realism and sentimentality, and made an interesting application of the phrase "private eye" to him. Williams's sentimentality is much in evidence in *Spring and All* whenever he writes about the Imagination, about "freedom of movement and newness," and about the "new world" the Imagination brings to birth in poems. His partial identification with Poe, that earlier victim of a repressive American environment, is understandable enough (one feels stifled in North Jersey); but Williams tries to convince himself that the Imagination will save him from Poe's fate. Perhaps it did. Certainly he preserved himself magnificently and went on after *Spring and All* to further distinguish himself as a writer—but his insistences on the Imagination, like his later ones on The Poem, are to be indulged rather than admired, while we look someplace else for the fruits of this deliverance. One receives a similar sense from reading D. H. Lawrence's poems—the "Look, We Have Come Through" syndrome which often cries out for the ironic or humorous qualification not given it by the poet.

As for the twenty-seven poems from *Spring and All,* I judge that three deserve to be included in any Williams anthology: "The rose is obsolete"; "The pure products of America go crazy"; and the justly admired "By the road to the contagious hospital." (If "so much depends / upon // a red wheel / barrow" also demands admission, let it in; one should not punish a piece of whimsical originality for the descriptive sentences that have been heaped on it.)

In asking what makes the three poems stand out (one might also want to add "The crowd at the ball-game") I am tempted to refer less to Williams's own terminology of Imagination, the poem-as-machine, or "field of action" (the notion of words interacting in a manner that totally removes them from any real world they have previously been attached to) than to my sense of a personal presence, often there in the earlier poems and still on occasion to be glimpsed. Randall Jarrell ended his classic introduction to the *Selected Poems* (1949) with a statement of what he most cared about in Williams's poems generally: "their generosity and sympathy, their moral and human attractiveness." Jarrell thought that was an "obvious" response to make to Williams's poetry; but insofar as we are instructed to think of the poem as a machine rather than an utterance, this "human attractiveness" is unlikely to be felt.

At any rate I see no reason not to imagine them as—for all their typographical fanciness, their cultivation of "brokenness" and disruption of the pentameter, their silences and white spaces and lack of punctuation—still emanating from the pen and the soul of Dr. Williams who observes that "The crowd at the ball game / is moved uniformly // by a spirit of uselessness / which delights them—" or announces in "The rose is obsolete" that

> The rose carried weight of love
> but love is at an end—of roses
> It is at the edge of the
> petal that love waits
>
> Crisp, worked to defeat
> laboredness—fragile
> plucked, moist, half-raised
> cold, precise, touching
>
> What

or who, in the poem about Elsie which attempts to understand why "The pure products of America / go crazy," speaks of "young slatterns" as

> bathed
> in filth
> from Monday to Saturday
>
> to be tricked out that night
> with gauds
> from imaginations which have no
>
> peasant traditions to give them
> character. . . .

In such lines we may feel the poet has too much fallen prey to an idea, but is certainly not absent from the poem. Even in "By the road to the contagious hospital," what Wallace Stevens once referred to as "the mere objectiveness of things" is suffused with the attentiveness of a human perception:

> By the road to the contagious hospital
> under the surge of the blue
> mottled clouds driven from the
> northeast—a cold wind. Beyond, the
> waste of broad, muddy fields
> brown with dried weeds, standing and fallen
>
> patches of standing water
> the scattering of tall trees
>
> All along the road the reddish
> purplish, forked, upstanding, twiggy
> stuff of bushes and small trees
> with dead, brown leaves under them
> leafless vines—
>
> Lifeless in appearance, sluggish
> dazed spring approaches—

Yvor Winters has spoken astutely about the technique of this poem: "he claims more than he is able to communicate, or more,

perhaps, than he chooses to communicate. At first glance a passage of this sort appears a trifle strained. . . . But in the present
poem the strain is deliberately sought and exactly rendered." And
Winters suggests that this strain creates a feeling of "pathos,
aroused by the small and familiar in austere and unfriendly sur-
roundings. . . ." Doubtless the irregularities of line groupings,
the unpunctuated separating-off of the seventh from the eighth
line, the "nervous meter" (as Winters calls it) are important in the
strained conveying of "pathos." But to believe that Williams's talk
about the Imagination, the "new world," points to some radical
way in which this poem is in advance of more traditional versifiers
seems to me mistaken. Consider the last five lines of a poem Frost
had written, in conventional meters, a few years before:

> How Love burns through the Putting in the Seed
> On through the watching for that early birth
> When, just as the soil tarnishes with weed,
> The sturdy seedling with arched body comes
> Shouldering its way and shedding the earth crumbs.

This birth is every bit as imaginative, every bit as much of a new
world, as anything in "By the road." That Frost ends in a more
elevated or exultant manner than does Williams—"Still, the profound change / has come upon them; rooted they / grip down and
begin to awaken"—doesn't matter for the essential point: that the
best parts of "experimental" Williams occur when he moderates
his practice (whatever his theory loudly proclaims, as in the prose
bits from *Spring and All*) and behaves as if he were a man speaking to men. And as Wordsworth claimed for his own poetry in the
Preface to the *Lyrical Ballads*, "By the road" is written so that
"the feeling therein developed gives importance to the action and
situation," not the reverse.

Writing in 1942 to his son, then a doctor in the navy, Williams
recounted the perils of his own medical practice:

> These last two weeks have been buggers. The principal cause of this has been a strep throat infection that starts without many physical signs other than prostration and high fever. . . . Ran into a lousy case of a ruptured appendix, badly neglected, in a twenty-six-year-old woman, seven months pregnant. Carlisle opened her up day before yesterday. General peritonitis, the appendix rotted off. . . . Delivered a nine pound 13½ oz. kid the other day from a woman who weighed only 93 pounds a year ago. Low forceps. I broke the clavicle getting the shoulders out. Everything's all right though. I've been going nuts.

A year later he wrote to his New Directions publisher, James Laughlin:

> "Paterson," I know, is crying to be written; the time demands it; it has to do just with all the peace movements, the plans for international infiltration into the dry mass of those principles of knowledge and culture which the universities and their cripples have cloistered and made a cult. It is the debasing, the keg-cracking assault upon the cults and the kind of thought that destroyed Pound and made what it has of Eliot. To let it into "the city," culture, the benefits of culture, into the mass as an "act," as a thing.

Juxtaposing these two typical Williams utterances in the light of his much-quoted war cry from *Paterson*—"Say it, no ideas but in things"—reveals the admirable clarity of the first one and the incoherence of the second. It is as if in turning the mind from ruptured appendices and broken clavicles which drive the harried physicians "nuts" to the germinating poem about knowledge and culture debased by "the universities and their cripples," Williams has lost his humor and his sanity. What for example is the "kind of thought" that has "made what it has of Eliot"? (*Little Gidding* had been published the year previously.) What on earth is the "international infiltration" (presumably a good thing) which will uncloisterize knowledge? To let *what* into "the city"? What "culture" into what "mass as an 'act,' as a thing"?

Granted it is unfair to complain about the sentences a man puts down in the attempt to describe a poem he hasn't yet written, and I do it only because the poem which eventually got written a few years later seems to me radically incoherent, even hysterical in a way similar to the letter to Laughlin. I speak as one who tried for many years to think of *Paterson* as a great modernist and a great modern poem, and who has failed in the attempt. Notwithstanding many prejudices and inclinations in favor of Williams's materials and his values—the choice of a city in New Jersey as focus ("Paterson lies in the valley under the Passaic Falls / its spent waters forming the outline of his back"), the vividly American and democratic swagger, the intention of calling things by their right names—the poem has become for me over the years less rather than more readable.

There is no very good way to demonstrate this to someone else, but the surest test I know of *Paterson*'s success is to ask whether we feel a significant discrepancy between the parts we hold continuing affection and admiration for, and other parts which, once the charm of their novelty or their difficulty has worn away, have little left with which to compel us. One of the best passages from *Paterson* is the one beginning "without invention" and proceeding to make a passionate plea for life, growth, variety in "the line":

> without invention
> nothing lies under the witch-hazel
> bush, the alder does not grow from among
> the hummocks margining the all
> but spent channel of the old swale,
> the small foot-prints
> of the mice under the overhanging
> tufts of the bunch-grass will not
> appear: without invention the line
> will never again take on its ancient
> divisions when the word, a supple word,
> lived in it, crumbled now to chalk.

The passage practices what it preaches, magnificently carries the reader along by dint of nothing more than the impulsions of its rhythms. In the first two books of *Paterson* I would single out the following passages as exemplary of such rhythmic life, such imaginative treatment of "the line": in Book I, the opening description of Paterson's lineaments; the passage beginning "Why have I not / but for imagined beauty where there is none / or none available, long since / put myself deliberately in the way of death?" on down through the next two pages—in fact the major part of the first two sections of I. From Book II the opening; the passage beginning "Signs everywhere of birds nesting" and continuing on through two pages; the "without invention" passage; the ones beginning "Sunday in the park" and "The descent beckons"; the passage beginning "That the poem, / the most perfect rock and temple" and the one beginning "On this most voluptuous night of the year / the term of the moon is yellow . . ." Aside from a smattering of such moments in Book III, the rest of the poem seems to me not to contain them, whatever else it does contain.

This may seem a very partial criticism to level at *Paterson:* after all there are all those newspaper accounts of local events, the letters from friends of Dr. Williams, the kaleidoscopic method of juxtaposition generally. And then there is also the possibility that the poem is stirring and important on a thematic level, that it has convincing and serious things to say about the American character, about the pre-eminence of "local materials," about the continuing necessary struggle and the necessary failure of being a poet. I would like to be able to say that these aspects of the poem engage me more with repeated readings—but find the exact opposite occurs. With each attempt at the poem, the prose passages seem less surprising and enlivening, feel more like something to be gotten through; the letters grow more tediously overbearing; the themes—always a dubious source of interest in any poet to my way of reading—sound too familiar, too reiterated:

> Who restricts knowledge? Some say
> it is the decay of the middle class
> making an impossible moat between the high
> and the low where
> the life once flourished. . . .

Occurring in Book I, writing like that is a tough obstacle for any poem to overcome. When in Book III, Williams lets his mother speak in a parenthesis—("What I miss, said your mother, is the poetry, the pure poem of the first parts")—he lets her speak truth, and no talk about his being a realist writer ("If you are going to write realistically of the conception of the filth in the world, it can't be pretty") can get round the fact that the poem goes on for too long and spends itself well before it ends.

This is exactly what Eliot's *Four Quartets* does *not* do, and why as a poem it is so superior to *Paterson*. Williams's best critic remains Jarrell, and no one was more enthusiastic and appreciative of the virtues of *Paterson*, Book I, than he. All the more then did it pain him to report that over the course of its four books the poem grew steadily worse, and that in the "long one-sided war with Eliot" Williams had been waging for most of his life, it was Williams who came off badly, at least when *Paterson* was compared with the *Quartets*. Jarrell put his finger on exactly what is so unsatisfying about Williams's poem: its eccentricity, its idiosyncrasies, its self-indulgence, its lack of organization, and I would add its sometimes bullying air of tough-guy moral superiority. Of course it may be possible to convert all these defects into virtues, to love Williams and the poem for the very things that I find debilitating. But with so many lively and interesting poems to choose from that he had already written, and was to write after the completion of *Paterson*, I don't feel overly guilty about leaving the long poem as mainly a curiosity with some lovely moments in it.

William's later life was marked by a series of physical calamities beginning with a heart attack in 1948, then a cerebral stroke three years later, after which followed several more. He became in the 1950's an unofficial patron to scores of "little magazines," always seeming to have a new poem on hand he was willing to let them print. Some of the most interesting and innovative of younger poets and poetry movements thought of him as their father, particularly Allen Ginsberg, himself born in Paterson, and the Black Mountain School under the leadership of Charles Olson. Williams served a term as poetry consultant at the Library of Congress, gave numbers of poetry readings at colleges and universities even after the strokes had impeded his speech, and continued to turn out fiction and criticism, as well as poetry, at a great rate. Meanwhile he had written in the 1930's and 1940's a handful of splendid poems which belong in any anthology and, taken together, testify to the enlargings and deepenings of his poetic voice: my own list would include "The Yachts" (a justly famous anthology piece), "The Catholic Bells," with its irresistible beginning—"Tho I'm no Catholic—"; "These," the concluding poem in the *Complete Collected Poems* volume of 1938; "Elegy for D. H. Lawrence"; "The Dance" ("In Breughel's great picture, The Kermess"); "Burning the Christmas Greens"; and "To Ford Madox Ford in Heaven," a charming tribute in appropriate tones to the recently dead writer. These poems all seem to me available for appreciation in terms which are in no way dependent on the "objectivist" assumptions about the poem-as-machine, or (as Stevens called it) the poem as a structure of blocks, or (as Kenner calls it) the typewriter-poem, a typographical creation of white spaces and black marks rather than something sung or spoken. This latter sort of poem (of which "The Red Wheelbarrow" is the most famous exhibit) may represent Williams at his most original; but my guess is that it is for other work he will be most remembered, particularly ones like those just listed which continue, with the darker accents of twenty years later, the distinctively personal speech and rhythms Williams had exploited so strikingly in *Al Que Quiere!*

> The year plunges into night
> and the heart plunges
> lower than night

to an empty, windswept place
without sun, stars or moon
but a peculiar light as of thought

that spins a dark fire—
whirling upon itself until,
in the cold, it kindles

to make a man aware of nothing
that he knows, not loneliness
itself—Not a ghost but

would be embraced—emptiness,
despair—(They
whine and whistle) among

the flashes and booms of war;
houses of whose rooms
the cold is greater than can be thought,

the people gone that we loved,
the beds lying empty, the couches
damp, the chairs unused— . . .

These lines from "These" may look upon first inspection to be un-
traditional, experimental in their proceedings; but it doesn't take
long to see that this is a poem about depression, about a season, a
time in history, a part of life that has been and is now no longer.
That is, the poem has a subject which it expresses in a voice that
compels because of its cadences, its rhythms, its images—the way
most good lyrics compel.

I do not think that significantly different terms are necessary to
refer to Williams's "last poems," by which I refer to the ones in
the "variable foot" measure which appeared in *The Desert Music*
(1951) and *Journey to Love* (1955) and were eventually collected
in *Pictures from Breughel and Other Poems* (1962). Reading these
poems soon after they were published was one of my most memorable experiences of "modern" poetry encountered in the present,
rather than in a classroom or anthology, an experience compara-

ble to reading *The Collected Poems of Wallace Stevens* after his death in 1955. There is a lovely letter from Williams to Stevens, written in 1951 after Williams had had his first stroke:

> Dear Wally: I was delighted to hear from you. . . . This is the first time I have used a typewriter again for a letter for a month. It's a major thrill. It's a month today since the damned thing hit—perhaps I shouldn't say "damned," as that might involve repercussions which I can't afford. Let me say the "sweet" thing kicked me in the slats.

Later in the letter, he announces to Stevens, winningly, that "I agree with you we're not old. We may croak at any moment but we're not old." But one read the late poems of Williams—"To Daphne and Virginia," "The Orchestra," "The Yellow Flower," "The Mental Hospital Garden," "The Pink Locust"—and particularly the longer poem in four parts, "Asphodel, That Greeny Flower"—with a consciousness that these were assertions set down by a poet who had looked his own death in the face. For that reason, I at least was unimpressed by the assertion of a younger poet, after *Journey to Love* had been published, that these "variable foot" poems were often distressingly sentimental. To me Williams was beyond such charges.

Looked back at twenty-five years later, the poems still seem fresh in their language and tone, life-enhancing in their sentiments, but are not the sort that invite or demand much criticism. As for the question of their form, Williams believed that in writing the section from *Paterson* II which began

> The descent beckons
> as the ascent beckoned
> Memory is a kind
> of accomplishment
> a sort of renewal
> even
> an initiation . . .

he had discovered something called the Variable Foot, and that he could now make conscious use of this discovery as a way to avoid the shapelessness of free verse. In a letter to Richard Eberhart in 1954 he tried to explain in more detail what he was up to: "not that I ever count when writing but, at best, the lines must be capable of being counted, that is to say, *measured*—(believe it or not), and that one is to count a single beat to each line: Over the whole poem it gives a pattern to the meter that can be felt as a new measure."

Attempts to take these terms seriously seem to me less than persuasive, as far as shaping a usefully critical instrument goes, although Denis Donoghue has made a noble try with respect to the following lines from "To Daphne and Virginia":

> I have two sons,
>   the husbands of these women,
>   who live also
> in a world of love,
>   apart.
>   Shall this odor of box in
>   the heat
> not also touch them
>   fronting a world of women
>   from which they are
> debarred
>   by the very scents which draw them on
>   against easy access?

Donoghue says,

> This is verse at least as well written as distinguished prose. The measure is just sufficiently *there* to enforce discipline and to ensure that the writing (and the consciousness behind it) will be scrupulous, exact. And the pattern, established, allows Williams to lay down the single, final word "apart" and to have its bar filled up with a pause of sorrowful recognition, without rancour. And there is the quite different load placed upon "debarred." Williams is using a measure not to intensify but to control, to test the feeling as it meets the edge of the language.

This elegant appreciation of Williams's "method" and measure fills in the blanks as it were, takes the word / line "apart," and in-

tuits "a pause of sorrowful recognition, without rancour." So that
the "intensification" such a poetry achieves is largely a matter of
poet inviting reader to become active, to create and extend a situation which is not quite there on the page. It seems to me though
that Donoghue is really moved here not by the method, but by his
sympathetic admiration for the presence of Williams as an old
man, a grandfather, close to death and looking as from a way off
on the lives of younger generations. Perhaps such a sympathetic
response is possible only because of the controlled "measure" of
the variable foot line—but I am doubtful. At any rate, there are
moments in these late poems—one of them occurs a few lines later
in "To Daphne and Virginia"—where it seems to me unlikely that
they can be talked about in terms of the line:

> There is, in the hard
> 　　　give and take
> 　　　　　　of a man's life with
> 　　　　　　a woman
> a thing which is not the stress itself
> 　　　but beyond
> 　　　　　　and above
> that,
> 　　　something that wants to rise
> 　　　　　　and shake itself
> free. . . .

Although I can note the movement in "but beyond," in "and
above," in the word "free" standing at the beginning of a new line
and concluding the thought, this passage is, looked at with a
slightly more unconvinced eye, awkward, embarrassing, and to be
tolerated only for its proximity to Williams's more subtle moments. I think that in reading these late poems it is important to
recognize their capability of embarrassing us by their flatness,
their reminder to us that, as always, Williams will "say anything"
as long as he thinks, for the moment, it's true. And not even the
wonders of the variable foot can persuade us that it's perfectly
measured, perfectly "art."

I should argue then that we read these late poems with motives very different than purely aesthetic ones; instead we want Williams to tell us about himself, how it feels to be old, near death, how it is that after so many years of marriage to the same woman, with whatever vicissitudes it involved, he must speak to her one last time, of ultimate things:

> There is something
>   something urgent
> I have to say to you
>   and you alone
>   but it must wait
> while I drink in
>   the joy of your approach,
>   perhaps for the last time.
> And so
>   with fear in my heart
>   I drag it out
> and keep on talking
>   for I dare not stop.

It is the hesitations, the embarrassments, the inarticulateness of the voice which engage us, and about which we may have mixed feelings: admiration for the voice's urgency of sincerity; uncertainty that the poetic "technique" is fully controlling the revelations we wait to hear; some embarrassment at being permitted to overhear. One reads "Asphodel, That Greeny Flower," the poem from which these lines are taken, with a mixture of respect, affection, boredom, and exasperation—with the sense that its imperfections, its unfinished character (he can never quite say it all) are essential to its peculiar power. But perhaps this should be said of any Williams poem.

There were many eulogies to Williams after his death in 1965, an outpouring of testimonies to his irreplaceability as the father-physician to all young American poets. But the two phrases which remain with me were pronounced by his old friend Kenneth Burke, who referred at the close of his tribute to "friendly Wm C. Wms., strong man two-gun Bill," and by Robert Lowell—always at his best on such eulogistic occasions—who wrote about Williams that "he loves America excessively, as if it were *the* truth and *the* subject; his exasperation is also excessive as if there were no other hell. His flowers rustle by the superhighways and pick up all our voice." But Williams had written his own epitaph years before in the poem which begins "I'm persistent as a pink locust" and ends with this unanswerable challenge:

                And so,
                        like this flower,
                                I persist—
                for what there may be in it.
                        I am not,
                                        I know,
                in the galaxy of poets
                        a rose
                                        but *who,* among the rest,
                will deny me
                        my place.

Conclusion

Like that of Johnson's *Rasselas,* this is a conclusion in which nothing is concluded, at least in the line of demonstrated objective truth. Yet in writing *Lives of the Modern Poets* I have confirmed and also grown clearer about my prejudices and inclinations regarding them. Randall Jarrell says finely in his essay about Williams that "The most important thing that criticism can do for a poet, while he is alive, is to establish that atmosphere of interested respect which gets his poems a reasonably careful reading." This seems to me good practice also for poets who, with the single exception of Hardy, have died within the past half-century. In my introduction I tried to recommend myself as possessing a catholic taste, and as unwilling to promote some of these writers at the expense of others. Pretensions to catholicity of taste often go along with honorable disclaimers of this sort, and "ranking" poets is a practice not usually admired; but I will take the opportunity of a conclusion briefly to indulge in it.

Of the first four "older" writers, Yeats and Frost seem to me the absolutely current ones. I say this with all due admiration for Hardy, who turned sixty in 1900, and whose inclusion as a modern poet in this list of seven Americans and an Irishman remains somewhat disconcerting. For all his overlap with other contributors to the annus mirabilis, 1914, his poetic personality is often of another age. And it takes some suspension of disbelief to entertain the notion that Robinson will ever again be read with eager excitement by the younger readers whose tastes will determine just how large he is likely to bulk in the future.

As for the remaining five Americans, Eliot and Stevens are preeminent, Crane and Williams often brilliant, always interesting, but perhaps not "major" poets; while Pound is a unique phenomenon, so much more significant and compelling when we consider his career and writings together than he is when judged solely on the basis of the poems he wrote. And although Williams spent much energy over the years dramatizing his "war" with Eliot, with America versus Europe, it is probably Stevens's work—in its commitment to the imagination and to post-romantic humanism—which represents the largest, most impressive alternative to Eliot's austerity and skepticism.

Yeats, Frost, Eliot, and Stevens, then, are the modern poets whose work presents the largest challenge to us, whose poetic presences are the most continuous and inescapable. It was doubtless evident from the individual prefaces that my favorites among them are Frost and Eliot. When in 1957 Frost prepared to revisit England for what was to be the last time, he wrote as follows to Eliot:

> It would be a great disappointment if my more or less official return to England didn't mean furthering our acquaintance; and I should be less a respector of persons than I am if I didn't hope to give you before I get through with this here world the highest sign of my regard. You and I shot off at different tangents from almost the same pin wheel. We had America in common and we had Ezra in common though you had much more of him than I. If I was ever cross with you it was for leaving America behind too far and Ezra not far enough. But such things look less and less important as we age on. You have been a great poet in my reading.

One understands, from this attractive letter, what Frost meant by gracefully complaining that Eliot had left America "behind too far." But when we read "Portrait of a Lady" and "The Dry Salvages," or the "Landscape" poems—"New Hampshire," "Virginia," "Cape Ann"—or if we try, as one critic has daringly proposed, to think of *The Waste Land* as an "American romance," then we may be reminded of how in a profound sense Eliot never left it behind at all.

In the first chapter of *After Strange Gods,* he describes his return to America in 1931:

> My local feelings were stirred very sadly by my first view of New England, on arriving from Montreal, and journeying all one day through the beautiful desolate country of Vermont. Those hills had once, I suppose, been covered with primaeval forest; the forest was razed to make sheep pastures for the English settlers; now the sheep are gone, and most of the descendents of the settlers; and a new forest appeared blazing with the melancholy glory of October maple and beech and birch scattered among the evergreens; and after this process of scarlet and gold and purple wilderness you descend to the sordor of the half-dead milltowns of southern New Hampshire and Massachusetts. It is not necessarily those lands which are the most fertile or most favoured in climate that seem to me the happiest, but those in which a long struggle of adaptation between man and his environment has brought out the best qualities of both; in which the landscape has been moulded by numerous generations of one race, and in which the landscape in turn has modified the race to its own character. And those New England mountains seemed to me to give evidence of a human success so meagre and transitory as to be more desperate than the desert.

It may seem odd that from among poets in the American grain like Williams who committed himself to New Jersey and Stevens who read about Ceylon while staying on in Hartford, one should put forth Eliot as having a special American claim. Yet the country he and Frost had "in common" is one made, in Eliot's case, all the more sharp and unforgettable by his distinctive mixture of nostalgia and dissatisfaction.

Richard Poirier has spoken of how Frost and Eliot "exhibit different mythologies about the possibilities and function of literature" in this century. I should add that they do so in lifeworks of inexhaustible interest, and because of the depth of their interest they are the most difficult of the modern poets—despite the interpretive puzzles Stevens presents, or Pound's allusive opacities. The difficulty of challenge presented by Frost and Eliot in their individual ways is one which becomes greater, rather than lessens, with repeated readings and re-experiencings. Their critical prose, for all the immense difference in output between them, retains a capacity for freshness and continuous surprise, convincing us that they are great writers (and not so incidentally, great humorists) as well as great poets. And they are the two poets of this century who write about love in ways I find most psychologically, humanly revealing. But taking a hint from Eliot himself, as he prepared to conclude "Tradition and the Individual Talent," this book proposes to halt at the frontier of metaphysics or mysticism, and is satisfied if it has encouraged readers to new engagements with the modern poets.

A Calendar

1899   Harold Hart Crane born, July 21, Garretsville, Ohio.

1901   Stevens enters New York Law School.

1902   Williams enters University of Pennsylvania Medical School; meets Ezra Pound.

1906–10 Eliot takes undergraduate degree at Harvard. Publishes poems in the *Advocate*.

1908   Yeats: *Collected Works*, 8 vols.; meets Pound.
        Pound: *A Lume Spento;* settles in London.

1909   Stevens marries Elsie Viola Moll.
        Williams's first poems privately printed.

1911   Robinson first visits MacDowell Colony in New Hampshire.

1912   Death of Emma Hardy.
        Pound becomes foreign editor of *Poetry*.
        Williams marries Florence Herman.

1913   Frost: *A Boy's Will,* reviewed by Pound in *Poetry*.
        Pound serves as Yeats's secretary.

1914   *Hardy: Satires of Circumstance.*
        Yeats: *Responsibilities,* reviewed by Pound in *Poetry*.
        Frost: *North of Boston,* reviewed by Pound in *Poetry*.
        Eliot settles in London; meets Pound.

1915   Pound marries Dorothy Shakespear; publishes *Cathay*.
        Eliot marries Vivien Haigh-Wood; publishes "Prufrock" in *Poetry*.
        Stevens publishes "Sunday Morning" (shortened form) in *Poetry*.

1916   Robinson: *The Man Against the Sky*.
        Stevens moves to Hartford, Connecticut.
        Crane's first poem published; parents divorced, he moves to New York City.

1917   Yeats marries Georgie Hyde-Lees; purchases the Tower.
        Eliot: *Prufrock and Other Observations*.
        Williams: *Al Que Quiere!*

1917–20 Frost teaching at Amherst College.

1920   Pound: *Hugh Selwyn Mauberley;* moves from London to Paris.
        Eliot: *The Sacred Wood; Poems 1920*.

1921   Robinson: *Collected Poems;* wins Pulitzer Prize.

1922   Eliot: *The Waste Land*.
        Yeats: *The Trembling of the Veil;* becomes member of Irish Senate.

1923   Stevens: *Harmonium*.
        Williams: *Spring and All*.

1924   Yeats receives Nobel Prize for literature.

1925   Pound settles in Italy.

1926   Crane: *White Buildings.*

1927   Eliot joins Church of England.

1928   Death of Hardy, January 11; *Winter Words* published.
       Yeats: *The Tower.*

1930   Frost: *Collected Poems.*
       Crane: *The Bridge.*

1932   Eliot gives Norton Lectures, Harvard.
       Death of Crane, April 26.

1934   Stevens becomes vice-president of Hartford Accident and Indemnity Co.

1935   Death of Robinson, April 6; *King Jasper* published, with introduction by Frost.
       Eliot: *Collected Poems,* including "Burnt Norton."

1936   Frost gives Norton Lectures, Harvard.

1938   Williams: *The Complete Collected Poems.*

1939   Death of Yeats, January 28; *Last Poems* published.

1943   Eliot: *Four Quartets.*

1945   Pound placed under arrest by United States Army. Brought to Washington for trial; committed to St. Elizabeth's Hospital.

1946   Williams: *Paterson,* Book I.

1947   Stevens: *Transport to Summer.*

1948   Eliot awarded Nobel Prize for literature.
       Pound: *Pisan Cantos.*

1949   Pound receives Bollingen Prize for Poetry, provoking much controversy.

1954   Stevens: *Collected Poems;* wins Pulitzer Prize and National Book Award.

1955   Death of Stevens.

1957   Eliot marries Valerie Fletcher.

1958   Pound released from St. Elizabeth's (through efforts of Frost, among others); returns to Italy.

1962   Frost: *In the Clearing.*
       Williams: *Pictures from Breughel and Other Poems.*

1963   Death of Frost, January 29.
       Death of Williams, March 4.

1965   Death of Eliot, January 4; Pound attends funeral service.

1972   Death of Pound, November 1.

Critical Works Cited

Introduction

4   Paul Fussell, *Samuel Johnson and the Life of Writing* (New York: Harcourt Brace, 1971).

4–5   T. S. Eliot, "Johnson as Poet and Critic," in *On Poetry and Poets* (New York: Farrar, Straus, 1957).

5–6   Warner Berthoff, "The Way We Think Now: Protocols for Deprivation," *New Literary History* (Spring 1976).

6–7   F. R. Leavis, "Literary Criticism and Philosophy," in *The Common Pursuit* (London: Chatto and Windus, 1948).

7   Michel Foucault, "What Is an Author?" in *Language, Counter-Memory, Practice,* trans. Donald F. Bouchard and Sherry Simon (Ithaca, N.Y.: Cornell, 1977).

Thomas Hardy

15   Virginia Woolf, *A Writer's Diary* (New York.: Harcourt Brace, 1953).

18   Donald Davie, *Thomas Hardy and British Poetry* (New York: Oxford, 1972).

18   R. P. Blackmur, "The Shorter Poems of Thomas Hardy," in *Language as Gesture* (New York: Harcourt Brace, 1952).

19   Robert Gittings, *Thomas Hardy's Later Years* (Boston: Little, Brown, 1978).

21–22   Ezra Pound, *Guide to Kulchur* (Norfolk, Conn.: New Directions, 1938). See also John Peck, "Hardy and Pound," *Agenda* (Spring–Summer 1972).

26   J. O. Bailey, *The Poery of Thomas Hardy* (Chapel Hill: North Carolina, 1970).

27   John Crowe Ransom, Introduction to *Selected Poems of Thomas Hardy* (New York: Madmillan, 1961).

31   John Middleton Murry, *Aspects of Literature* (London: Collins, 1920).

31   F. R. Leavis, *New Bearings in English Poetry* (London: Chatto and Windus, 1932).

31   Douglas Brown, *Thomas Hardy* (London: Longmans, 1968).

31   Irving Howe, *Thomas Hardy* (New York: Macmillan, 1967).

34   Donald Davie, "Hardy's Virgilian Purples," in *The Poet in the Imaginary Museum* (New York: Persea Books, 1977).

39   Samuel Hynes, *The Pattern of Hardy's Poetry* (Chapel Hill: North Carolina, 1961).

W. B. Yeats

53–54   Denis Donoghue, "The Hard Case of Yeats," *New York Review of Books* (May 26, 1977).

54   F. R. Leavis and Q. D. Leavis, *Lectures in America* (London: Chatto and Windus, 1969).

58   T. S. Eliot, "Yeats," in *On Poetry and Poets* (New York: Farrar Straus, 1957).

58   David Perkins, *A History of Modern Poetry* (Cambridge: Harvard, 1976).

61–62   Douglas Goldring, *South Lodge* (London: Constable, 1943).

67   T. S. Eliot, "A Foreign Mind," *Athenaeum* (July 4, 1919).

68   Frank Kermode, *Romantic Image* (London: Routledge, 1957).

68–69   Yvor Winters, *The Poetry of W. B. Yeats* (Denver: Swallow, 1960).

72–73   On "Easter 1916" see Donald Davie, "Yeats, the Master of a Trade," in *The Poet in the Imaginary Museum.*

78   John Holloway, "Style and World in *The Tower*," in *An Honoured Guest,* ed. Denis Donoghue and J. R. Mulryne (London: Routledge, 1965).

80–81   D. S. Savage, *The Personal Principle* (London: Routledge, 1944).

E. A. Robinson

86   J. V. Cunningham, "Edwin Arlington Robinson: A Brief Biography," in *The Collected Essays of J. V. Cunningham* (Denver: Swallow, 1976).

90   Yvor Winters, *Edwin Arlington Robinson* (Norfolk, Conn.: New Directions, 1946).

90   Yvor Winters, "A Cool Master," in *Uncollected Essays and Reviews of Yvor Winters,* ed. Francis Murphy (Denver: Swallow, 1973).

93   Chard Powers Smith, *Where the Light Falls* (New York: Macmillan, 1965).

100   Warner Berthoff, *The Ferment of Realism* (New York: Free Press, 1965).

100   Irving Howe, "A Grave and Solitary Voice," in *The Critical Point* (New York: Horizon, 1973).

102–3   Conrad Aiken, *A Reviewer's ABC* (New York: Meridian, 1950).

Robert Frost

113   Randall Jarrell, "The Other Frost" and "To the Laodiceans," in *Poetry and the Age* (New York: Knopf, 1953).

113   Lionel Trilling, "Robert Frost: A Cultural Episode," *Partisan Review* (Summer 1959).

127   W. H. Auden, Preface to *Selected Poems of Robert Frost* (London: Cape, 1936).

137   Yvor Winters, "Robert Frost: The Spiritual Drifter as Poet," in *The Function of Criticism* (Denver: Swallow, 1957).

Ezra Pound

145   John Reck, *Ezra Pound: A Close-Up* (New York: McGraw Hill, 1969).

145   Hugh Kenner, *The Poetry of Ezra Pound* (Norfolk, Conn.: New Directions, 1951); *The Pound Era* (Berkeley: California, 1971).

145   Donald Davie, *Ezra Pound: Poet as Sculptor* (New York: Oxford, 1965); *Ezra Pound* (New York: Viking, 1972).

145   Noel Stock, *Reading the Cantos* (London: Routledge, 1967).

146   W. D. Snodgrass, "Four Gentlemen; Two Ladies," *Hudson Review* (Spring 1960).

146   George P. Elliott, "Poet of Many Voices," *The Carleton Miscellany* (Summer 1961).
146   Christine Brooke-Rose, *A ZBC of Ezra Pound* (Berkeley: California, 1971).
154–56 See Wai-lim Yip, *Ezra Pound's Cathay* (Princeton, 1969).
157   R. P. Blackmur, "Masks of Ezra Pound," in *Language as Gesture*.
159   F. R. Leavis, *New Bearings in English Poetry*.
159   John Espey, *Ezra Pound's Mauberley: A Study in Composition* (1955).
160–61 A. L. French, "Olympian Apathein: Pound's *Hugh Selwyn Mauberley* and Modern Poetry," *Essays in Criticism* (1965).
164   Ronald Bush, *The Genesis of Pound's Cantos* (Princeton, 1976).
165–66 C. M. Bowra, "More Cantos from Ezra Pound," *New Statesman and Nation* (September 1949).
169   R. P. Blackmur, "A Burden for Critics," in *The Lion and the Honeycomb* (New York: Harcourt Brace, 1955).

T. S. Eliot

174   Donald Davie, "Mr. Eliot," in *The Poet in the Imaginary Museum*.
176   Lyndall Gordon, *Eliot's Early Years* (New York: Oxford, 1977).
178   Hugh Kenner, *The Invisible Poet* (New York: Macdowell-Obolensky, 1959).
179   Barbara Everett, "In Search of Prufrock," *Critical Quarterly* (Summer 1974).
180   Bernard Bergonzi, *T. S. Eliot* (New York: Macmillan, 1972).
181–82 Wyndham Lewis, "Early London Environment," in *T. S. Eliot: A Symposium* ed. Richard March and Tambimuttu (Chicago: Regnery, 1949).
186   Elisabeth Schneider, *T. S. Eliot: The Pattern in the Carpet* (Berkeley: California, 1975). My own comments on "Gerontion" as well as on *The Waste Land* and *Four Quartets* can be found in *Seeing Through Everything* (London/New York: Faber/Oxford, 1977).
188   See my "Reading *The Waste Land* Today," *Essays in Criticism* (June 1969).

188 Hugh Kenner, "The Urban Apocalypse," in *Eliot in His Time,* ed. A. Walton Litz (Princeton, 1973).

189 Denis Donoghue, "The Word within a Word," in *"The Waste Land" in Different Voices,* ed. A. D. Moody (London: Edwin Arnold, 1974).

195 Donald Davie, "T. S. Eliot: The End of an Era," in *The Poet in the Imaginary Museum.*

200 Donald Hall, *Remembering Poets* (New York: Harper & Row, 1978).

Wallace Stevens

205 Yvor Winters, "Wallace Stevens, or The Hedonist's Progress," in *In Defense of Reason* (London: Routledge, 1959).

205 Randall Jarrell, "Reflections on Wallace Stevens," in *Poetry and the Age.*

205 J. V. Cunningham, "The Styles and Procedures of Wallace Stevens," in *The Collected Essays of J. V. Cunningham.*

210 R. P. Blackmur, "Examples of Wallace Stevens," in *Language as Gesture.*

215 J. Hillis Miller, *Poets of Reality* (Cambridge: Harvard, 1965).

215 Harold Bloom, *Wallace Stevens: The Poems of Our Climate* (Ithaca, N.Y.: Cornell, 1977).

220–21 Helen Vendler, *On Extended Wings* (Cambridge: Harvard, 1969).

225–26 Hugh Kenner, *A Homemade World* (New York: William Morrow, 1975).

Hart Crane

235 John Unterecker, *Voyager: A Life of Hart Crane* (New York: Farrar, Straus, 1969).

235 R. W. B. Lewis, *The Poetry of Hart Crane* (Princeton, 1967).

235 Thomas Parkinson, ed., *Hart Crane and Yvor Winters: Their Literary Correspondence* (Berkeley: California, 1978).

242 Allen Tate, "Hart Crane's Poetry," in *The Man of Letters in the Modern World* (New York: Meridian, 1955).

245 Yvor Winters, "Hart Crane's Poems," in *Uncollected Essays and Reviews of Yvor Winters.*

248 Warner Berthoff, "The Case of Hart Crane," in *Fictions and Events* (New York: Dutton, 1971).

255   Eugene Paul Nassar, "Hart Crane's *The Bridge* and Its Critics," in *The Rape of Cinderella* (Bloomington: Indiana, 1970).

259   On "The Broken Tower" see Marius Bewley, "Hart Crane's Last Poem," in *Masks and Mirrors* (New York: Atheneum, 1970).

William Carlos Williams

267   Randall Jarrell, "An Introduction to *The Selected Poems of William Carlos Williams,*" in *Poetry and the Age.*

270   Reed Whittemore, *William Carlos Williams: Poet from Jersey* (Boston: Houghton Mifflin, 1975).

275   Hugh Kenner, *A Homemade World.*

279   James E. Breslin, *William Carlos Williams: An American Artist* (New York: Oxford, 1970).

280   Leslie Fiedler, "Some Uses and Failures of Feeling," *Partisan Review* (August 1948).

282–83   Yvor Winters, *In Defense of Reason* (Denver: Swallow, 1947).

291   Denis Donoghue, "For a Redeeming Language," in *The Ordinary Universe* (New York: Macmillan, 1968).

293–94   The eulogies by Burke and Lowell are included in J. Hillis Miller, ed., *William Carlos Williams: A Collection of Critical Essays* (Englewood Cliffs, N.J.: Prentice-Hall, 1966).

Index

Page numbers in italics refer to extended discussions of individual poems.